Badge, Tie and Gun

Life and Death Journeys of a Miami Detective
By
Ramesh Nyberg

While every precaution has been taken in the preparation of this book, the publisher assumes no responsibility for errors or omissions, or for damages resulting from the use of the information contained herein.

BADGE, TIE, AND GUN: LIFE AND DEATH JOURNEYS OF A MIAMI DETECTIVE

First edition. February 1, 2024.

Copyright © 2024 Ramesh Nyberg.

ISBN: 979-8224044030

Written by Ramesh Nyberg.

For my parents, Rasamma and Rolfe

Acknowledgements

To say that this book has been a labor of love would be narcissistic, and in truth, the reverse is more accurate; at times it was more a "love of labor." I had to like what I was doing, and be able to see the finish line, which I often could not. That's due to the sporadic nature of the writing process. I didn't sit down and blitz-write this memoir. It was compiled, written, re-written, edited and re-edited over a period of eight years.

I could spend pages upon pages thanking the people who helped me along the way, but instead I'll sum it up easily: Mom and Dad (for whom this work is dedicated), for correctly predicting that my writing would rise up in my life one day. My dad loved to read. It was what he did when he wasn't sailing or building a boat. He would always tell me of the great books he read and re-read. Mom rarely had the energy or time to read. She was so deeply involved with education and helping others succeed that she used to come home exhausted. Still, she put me in the car when she went to peoples' homes to teach piano lessons. Later, she came home and burned the midnight oil to attain her PH.D.

I thank the thousands of police officers with whom I worked in my twenty-seven-year career. I'm indebted as well to my children, Erik, Greg, and Linnea, who many times missed out on me because of my police career, my writing, or both. My wife, Mandira, who I married years after I retired, patiently listened to the tip-tapping of my laptop computer as I went through the process of bringing this project to finality. My career finished before we met; she knows of it only from the many stories I have told her. The same goes for her wonderful children, Puja, Rahul, and Kiran, who have come to be my own, though they all encouraged me in ways they may not even know. I love you guys.

Without question, I must bring the spotlight to a person who imbued in me a love of words—my fourth-grade teacher Irma Pollans, better known as Terri Star. She made me and my classmates memorize poems (which I remember word for word to this day) and read us countless stories that had us on the edge of our seats at South Miami Elementary School. It was at that particular time that I began to write.

Two of my closest friends encouraged me and provided feedback, and still do so to this day with the novels I'm working on. One is Jon O'Neill, former *Miami Herald* reporter and film producer. The other, Bill Schwartz, is my colleague from North Miami PD, fishing buddy, confidant, and a stage actor extraordinaire. The friendships of these two men never faded after retirement, they only deepened, and I am forever grateful for their love and support.

Many others, such as David Shanks, Dave Rivers, John LeClaire, Jerry Crawford, and my wonderful partner, the late Greg Smith, have been part of this tale, which is ongoing. There are others, and if I have not mentioned you, forgive me—you know who you are. Maybe that's why a memoir that includes growing up is so hard to finish: we should never stop "growing up", so the story is never really over.

PROLOGUE

The federal inmate sitting across from us seemed indifferent about being out of the prison facility for the evening.

Then again, Mort Koppler always had that look, that same look, no matter where he was or what he was doing. It was a shrug of a countenance; half pragmatism, half resignation: *I'm a lawyer. I did some stuff. I shouldn't be here, but I am. I've got a hit out on me...Ah, prison, shmishon. Pass the salt.* Mort wore the look of a man walking through the desert, thinking that he just might not make it, but to stop walking made no sense. There is the vague possibility of an oasis, somewhere. His wife, Rosie, always looked the same too, though a complete contrast to her husband—cheery, effervescent, and ever-positive. They were a pair.

My partner, Greg Smith, and I sat across from the Kopplers as the waiter took our orders. If we look like a relaxed group of friends enjoying a night out, then we were great actors indeed. We were at Victoria Station, a popular restaurant on NW 36th street, just across from Miami International Airport. Victoria Station, housed in a beautifully renovated train car, drew crowds for their prime rib, among other dishes. The place was busy that night, clinking and bustling with conversation, laughter, and briskly moving staff. I looked around at the relaxed faces. Why wouldn't they be happy? Didn't everyone bring their favorite federal inmate here on his birthday?

I didn't show it, I hope, and neither did Greg, but this was gut-wrenching. A group of very dangerous smugglers had figured—correctly—-that Mort was informing on them, and they put a hit out on him. Mort used to work with Ben Kramer's gang, a ruthless organization that brought mountains of cocaine into the country during the early and mid-1980's. Kramer had little time for people who refused to do business with him (let alone informers) and he ordered the murder of speedboat tycoon Donald Aronow, creator of the *Donzi*. That's why we were here. I glanced at all the passing waiters and wondered which one would suddenly pull a MAC-10 from under his apron and spray the table with lead. I had my 9mm in my ankle holster, and I wanted to take it out and put it in my lap, under my napkin.

This was what you did with witnesses who decided to cooperate with you. Most of the time, the witness was someone from "the 'hood," and you could get by with taking them to Burger King and eating it in the car on the way to the State Attorney's Office for the briefing. But Greg had decided that with Mort, we needed to take it to another level. Mort was doing some world-class ratting here, and Burger King would not do. Besides that, it was Mort's 64th birthday, so Victoria Station (with Rosie along) was going to be the plan. The officials at the federal prison would be furious if they knew where we were. We had lots of leeway with state facilities, but with the feds, you had to jump through a bunch of hoops to get on the list to take an inmate out of a facility. You needed a good reason too, and most of the time it had better be a visit to the U.S. Attorney's Office for a debriefing, or something of that nature. Victoria Station was not on the list. I never believed that rules were made to be broken, but they sure as hell did need to be bent and twisted from time to time, when you needed to keep a witness like Mort feeling warm and comfy with you. We were just hoping he didn't burp back at the prison and smell like glazed carrots.

Rosie announced a surprise, and I hoped it was the only one of the evening.

"I've got something for you gentlemen," she said with a gentle smile, "for being so good to us." She brought out a tie for each of us. Technically, we couldn't accept gifts from anyone, especially a cooperating witness in a murder case, but we thanked Rosie and accepted the ties, knowing they would soon go on a property receipt and be impounded as found property. A strange looking waiter caught my attention just then, and I remembered that I wasn't being paranoid. Ben Kramer had money stashed everywhere (Mort had helped him launder much of it) and still wielded plenty of influence, enough to have arranged for an outrageous prison escape involving a helicopter, which landed inside Miami Correctional Center to ferry him to freedom. Spectacular as that was, it failed, but it put everyone on notice as to how far-reaching the Ben Kramer organization was. It wasn't beyond anyone's imagination that he could place a hitman in a waiter's uniform at a popular restaurant. That got me thinking that this witness schmoozing had gone way too fucking far.

I had been shot at in the ghetto more than once and survived the 1980 race riots. I wasn't about to go out before even sampling the horseradish sauce. I took the 9mm out of the holster and slid it under my napkin.

Chapter One
Badge, Tie, and Gun

<u>The First Badge</u>

I never saw the car coming.

Nine years old, kicking a soda can down the street, I usually rode my bike to and from school. But we had been running late for school and Dad had dropped me off that morning. Nine-year-old kids walked home back then, rather than get picked up by parents.

After about thirty yards or so of kicking the can, something made me pick it up and throw it across the street. Sheer boredom, tired of kicking it, who knows? I wound up and side-armed the half-crushed can towards the other side of the road, and a black car came screeching to a halt as the can went skidding under the front fender. The driver's window slid down, and a man in a jacket, short dark hair, and sunglasses looked at me, expressionless.

"Get in the car," he said with a slight toss of his head.

I stood there, transfixed. I was in the third grade. They told us in school not to "take rides from strangers." So I told him as much.

"My dad told me never to take rides from strangers."

The man nodded, and his demeanor seemed to soften slightly. "Good. I'm glad he told you that. I'm a police officer." He showed me a black wallet with a badge inside.

"Why did you throw the can at my car?"

"I didn't," I told him. "I didn't mean to throw it at your car. I was just...throwing it." He stared again, unconvinced. "Well, let's go. I'm going to take you to your house because I want to talk to your parents."

I got in and looked around the car. So—there are policemen without uniforms, I thought.

The policeman sat in our living room with my mother and father, who listened carefully as he explained.

"He was kicking this can, just like a kid will typically do, and then he suddenly picked it up and threw it at my car."

My parents were calm, and later, after the policeman with regular clothes left, Mom and Dad seemed to accept my version. Accusations, I learned that day, have different sides.

We had no policemen in the family, though my Swedish grandfather would have argued that sternly. He had been in the Swedish Royal Guard, a sort of national police who I think were more ornamental than anything else. I knew he had been in the Swedish Royal Guard because he would tell me (and show me), every time we went to their apartment.

"Come here, Ramesh," he would say with his Swedish accent. He would bring out a folder with two photos. On the left was a young man an ornate uniform with a Napoleon-style campaign hat, on the right was the same young man, in the white uniform and cap of a U.S. Navy serviceman.

"You know, I was in the Swedish Royal Guard," he would say, pointing to each picture with a shaky finger as he spoke, "and the American Navy."

"Wow grandpa," I said, each time.

That was my earliest memory of being shown a uniform. Grandpa Carl Gustav Nyberg was fiercely proud of his two endeavors as a uniformed man, and he was always impressed with the bearing of authority. Twelve years later, when I visited him at an adult living facility, I told him I was a police officer. He was eighty-nine then.

"Do you...wear a uniform?" he asked. .

"Yes, every day."

He raised his eyebrows, impressed. "Ohh," he sang softly.

It had been a grueling twenty-two weeks, but it was ending now.

"We have learned how to save life," I said to the gathering of friends, families, and law enforcement luminaries, sectioned off to the left of my podium, "and we have learned how to take it." I concluded the speech a with the quote about "evil triumphs when good men do nothing," and how the men and women of Basic Law Enforcement Class #41 were very good, and we were going to do whatever we could to fulfill our oath.

It was December 14th, 1979, and since June, thirty-two fellow recruits and I had run, studied, practiced, puked, agonized, grappled, and trained for this day. After all the tests were graded, I ended up as number one academic recruit, and the class voted for me to give the graduation speech. I was fucking terrified. I didn't know how terrified I would be until the rehearsal, when I almost blacked out. The goddamn *rehearsal*, and I'm blacking out. I made it through the real deal on two feet, and the next step was getting out and really doing the job. Vivian, my wife at the time, pinned the Opa-Locka Police Department badge on my uniform, and off I went, into a cyclorama of the unexpected that would last almost three decades.

The First Tie

The oldest picture I have of myself shows me in the arms of my dad, with both of my parents smiling at me. It's black and white, and I'm no more than two. Dad is wearing a tie, the one and only time I have ever seen him with one on. You don't need a tie when you're a boat builder and a sculptor.

I wore my first tie in 1966 when I got my first job, at eight years old. I was a pageboy at an insurance company called Southeastern Surplus Lines, on Ponce De Leon Boulevard in Coral Gables. My godfather, Allan Pither, was the CEO of the place, and my parents thought it might be a good idea one summer for me to experience what it means to work for someone and show up on time at a job—all the things my tie-less father had refused to do.

I loved being the page boy at Southeastern Surplus Lines, and it taught me a lot about responsibility. On the rare occasions when Mom or Dad would drop me off late, Al would dock my pay (usually a penalty of some seventy-five cents or so, which he would document with an official inter-office memo). Though he did it half in fun, he really did subtract the miniscule amount from my pay. This first brush with administrative discipline taught me a lot about what it means to be on time, and how important it is that others know you to be reliable. When I wasn't delivering coffee, memos or mail to various people in the two-story office, I sat in the front with Helen Phelan, the switchboard operator. She worked the phones with the old-style plug-and-wire switchboard, exactly like the character Lily Tomlin used to play on Laugh-In. We joked and talked and I kept her company when the phones were quiet.

"I'm hungry," I would say when lunch time was approaching.

"I'm Helen," she would always say.

The memos I delivered were voice-recorded on a memo machine that saved the audio on a wide blue tape, the cutting-edge technology of the day. The blue tape was clipped to the typewritten copy and I ran those up or down the stairs to the different offices some twenty times a day.

On the last day of my job, the office gave me a going-away party, complete with a cake and a type-written letter from Allan Pither, thanking me for my employment and wishing me well, as if I were a high-level exec heading off to another company. That was Al. While cutting the cake, my black clip-on tie fell into the frosting. Helen was there to wipe it off and tuck it into my shirt pocket. She told me to always be careful with a tie when leaning over something like a cake.

Here's how you do it when you work a body: You open the middle button of your shirt and tuck your tie inside, then button it back up, so that when you are documenting and searching the body, it doesn't fall into anything nasty, like blood, brain matter, or decomposing body fluids. You roll up your sleeves on the inside for the same reason. You take everything out of your shirt pockets and put them in your pants, and you put on your latex gloves. That's how we did it. No one walked around with masks or biohazard suits on, like you see on the bullshit TV shows.

At one scene, the naked body of a male stabbing victim lay on the kitchen floor. A new medical examiner doctor doing his internship with the M.E. office was on the scene, and he leaned over the body to take a photo. His sunglasses fell out of his shirt pocket and landed right on top of the victim's genitals. As we smirked, he washed the glasses off in the kitchen sink. Art Nanni, an Italian cop with a sandpaper voice, gruffed, "You can wash 'em all you want, Doc, but you'll never forget where they were." We all got a great laugh.

You take out what's in your shirt pocket, Doc. And you tuck your tie in.

<u>The First Gun</u>

My first real gun almost got me arrested. Before that, I had many fake ones. All the boys in my neighborhood played "army." We would use sticks or branches, or just hold our invisible weapons in our hands as we stalked each other in backyards and hedges, hiding, creeping, gunning at each other and making the gunfire reports with our voices. My parents thought I was a little too much into it, but I was really a peaceful kid. I never got into fights, and when I did, I became adept at talking my way out of them. You learn to do that when you are the youngest kid on the block.

I did have an unusual obsession with the Civil War, and this came from nowhere that anyone could discern. My father was not any kind of historian or military expert. There wasn't one book about the subject in our household, until I started—at the age of nine—to bring them home from the school library. I read everything I could get my hands on—Stonewall Jackson's life, Vicksburg, the Monitor and Merrimack battles, and a baffling obsession with Gettysburg. The first two police departments I worked for had dark blue uniforms. Dark blue, like the uniforms of the victorious North. Somewhere, somehow, something in me was sated. The most riveting thing I have ever read about military subjects is Colonel Joshua Chamberlain's "The Passing of the Armies", in particular his depiction of the defense of Little Round Top, one of the most remarkable stories of resilience and heroism anywhere. I still have not visited Gettysburg. I don't know if the avoidance has been intentional or not.

The first real gun in my life was a silver Smith and Wesson model 15, .38 caliber. I bought it when I was 19, after the switch in my head was flipped, and it was suddenly law enforcement I wanted to pursue, not music, which I had been majoring in for two years at Miami-Dade College.

The nucleus of that decision formed one night at the apartment of my good friend John Marcus, a fellow music major and an exemplary bass player. We were studying for a music theory exam, and I heard a scratchy voice coming from a radio in his room. It was a police scanner, he explained. He liked to listen to the police calls and transmissions and had learned many of the signals and codes just from the context of the metallic chatter. I found it interesting, and we took a break from our studying—a talent I was way too good at it—-and listened for a few minutes with John explaining some of the codes. Just then, something almost mystical happened: Red flashing lights, coming through John's bedroom window. A Metro policeman had pulled over a car on the other side of

Kendall Drive. From John's window we could see him clearly. Just as I wondered whether we would hear him or not, I saw him pick up the microphone in his car and speak, and his voice came loud and clear over John's radio. I was mesmerized. The codes, the brevity of the radio communication, the procedure...it was enthralling.

From that night on, I wanted to learn more. I signed up for a "civilian observer" ride in Metro's South District. It only sunk the hook deeper into my skin. I rode again, a few weeks later, and then a third time, with the City of Miami Police a couple of months later.

A couple of weeks after that last ride, I changed my major from music to criminal justice. After I bought the Smith and Wesson, John Marcus and I would go to a spot on the edge of the Everglades with a box of empty cans and bottles and plink away to our heart's content. John introduced me to his friend Harry Rivenbark, a withdrawn redheaded country boy who wouldn't say much until you started talking about guns, fishing, or hunting. Harry had a bunch of guns, and he joined us—as did another mutual friend, Garry Rindfuss—on many a summer day out there. The place was about the last paved road in western Dade County off Grossman Farm Road, past Chekika Hammock State Preserve. There had been a building there, but shooters had blasted the crap out of it to the point where there was nothing less than a pile of rubble and four nubs of concrete where the wall corners had been. When you stepped out the car, you walked on a carpet of empty casings of every caliber imaginable. Beyond to the west was nothing but sawgrass and oolite rock. We would shoot for a couple of hours, then drive back to my place and barbecue, drink Jack Daniels, and play poker. Another guy I met, Chuck Markman, joined us once or twice. Those were about the most easygoing summers of my life. I liked Harry, and the four of us had some great terrific times together.

On Chuck's eighteenth birthday, he and I were downing Miller talls at his apartment, off SW 144th street. It was just past midnight when I had an idea.

"Let's go shooting," I suggested.

"What??" He laughed. "Drive all the way out to the Everglades now and shoot in the dark?"

"Hell no. Close by. Here. You know, the construction site around the corner."

I was referring to a large area of land at the southwest corner of 136th street and U.S. 1, where construction was in its early stages to start the foundation for a shopping center. It would later be the highly popular "Falls" shopping mall, a semi-outdoor place with lovely waterfalls and lush landscaping, high end retail spots like Bloomingdale's and Macy's, TGIF and Williams & Sonoma. But in 1977, it was a huge stretch of rock and dirt mounds.

Chuck shrugged and laughed. "Ok, let's go."

It was perfect. I had purchased a box of "snake shot"—basically tiny pellets inside a .38 caliber cartridge; much like a miniature shotgun shell with a range of just a few feet. The mounds of dug-up dirt were perfect berms to absorb the snake shot, an ideal arrangement to set up our empty Miller tall boys. The fact that there were residences just a quarter mile away didn't deter us; the snake shot would fall harmlessly after ten or fifteen feet anyway. The plan was to empty a couple more of the Miller talls while we were there, and that certainly boosted our bravado.

We were there in a minute, maybe less, and we set up the cans on the waist-high dirt mounds. I squeezed off the first round.

Boom! We marveled at how the report echoed, and just as quickly realized it was echoing off the walls of the condo buildings we could see faintly outlined in the distance.

"Wow, that's loud," I remarked.

"Yeah, it is," Chuck agreed.

We shot two or three more rounds, and then decided that maybe going shooting at one in the morning in this spot might not be a wise choice. So we left, and drove back to Chuck's place. Once there, I realized that my holster was missing.

"I don't know," Chuck said, "Maybe it's back at the dig site." We left my pistol at his house and drove my mother's Toyota station wagon back to our makeshift shooting range. We looked all over the place to see if the holster had fallen out, only to find it had fallen between the seats. I backed the Toyota out and suddenly one of the rear wheels got stuck in hole, wedged in by a large rock. I tried to back and fill, to no avail. We got out and assessed the situation, then put our beer muscles to work trying to push the car off the rock enough to give the tire some traction. No dice.

Two Metro police cars came rolling down 136 street just then, climbed the curb, and entered the construction site, heading for us.

We were here to meet a couple of girls, we decided was the adequate story; they never showed.

"Is there any shit in this car I need to know about?" One of the officers asked.

"No sir."

They separated us, and grilled us about what we were doing there, and why the Miller tall cans were set up on the dirt berms.

"We got a call that someone was shooting out here," another officer said. "Were you shooting?"

No, we told them. We heard it too. Sounded like fireworks. We were just leaving after we realized the girls stood us up when we got stuck.

They searched the car, tossing the back of the Toyota thoroughly, and there was no way in hell they missed the holster and the box of .38 snake shot rounds, but they never said a word about it. It was drugs they wanted to find.

"Alright," the first officer announced, "get the hell out of here and don't let us catch you back here again."

We ended up jacking the car up enough to free the tire from the rock and got the hell out of there—as instructed—sans arrest record.

I did go back there, many times, and I occasionally still do—to shop at the beautiful Falls Mall. When I'm there, I can't help but try to picture exactly where in the mall the two idiots with the gun and the beer cans would have been standing when that first round went off.

Gordon Ransom was a gruff, demanding firearms instructor. Every one of us in Basic Law Enforcement (BLE) Class# 41 feared him. He growled, even when he said, "Good morning." A former Marine Corps drill instructor, Ransom quizzed us daily on sight alignment, trigger pull, and the nomenclature of our .38 caliber revolvers. He made us run. Then he barked more questions at us. If you didn't know the answer, you might cause the entire platoon—our class of 33 academy recruits—to run again or do push-ups. He wanted us to push hard, give "One *hundred and ten* percent!", and internalize everything he taught us during our two weeks at the range. He told us stories of officers who had gotten hurt or killed for not being totally focused and aware. "Always know the status of your weapon!" He would bark, at least a couple of times a day. Another favorite of Ransom's: "Learn from other people's mistakes. You'll never live long enough to make 'em all yourself."

God help you if you said or did something stupid, because he would give you a verbal shredding that could be heard two ranges away, over the gunfire.

I liked the firearms training. It was a break from the regular classroom and defensive tactics stuff we had been doing daily. We reported directly to the range and we didn't have to report to our regular academy location for uniform inspection. We could get right to the good stuff.

One morning, before the daily inspection of our revolvers, Ransom asked us for a definition of "time." No one made a sound.

"Time," he snarled, "is what keeps everything from happening at once." Then, he went through the seconds it takes to remove a revolver from a holster, fire all six rounds, reload, and fire again, and how it all had to be done with smooth efficiency and fortuitous use of time.

Shotgun training was a favorite of mine at the range. I had never fired a shotgun before, but after the first hour, I was hooked—the Remington 870 and I became fast friends. Pull the trigger once, and send a spread of twelve .38 caliber-size projectiles at your target? Hard to beat. Our last day of shotgun training, I was on the second relay, and the first line of recruits was up there, qualifying. Edgar Foss, a nice guy with the IQ of a platypus, had a question for Ransom, who stood about fifteen feet behind him. Foss turned around, smiling, and swung the 870 with him, finger on the trigger, and the barrel trained directly at Ransom's midsection.

"Sir...?" Foss said, "I have a question..."

We all saw it, and we all froze, waiting for Ransom's reaction. We were sure he would unleash the wrath of the gods on him. But we never heard him speak so softly.

"Mr. Foss..." Ransom almost whispered.

"Yessir?"

"Slowly," Ransom said calmly, "put the shotgun *down* on the deck, and let go of it."

Foss frowned. "Yessir." He did as he was told.

Then, Ransom exploded, "You stupid son of a bitch! You nearly killed me! One flinch of your finger and I would have been filled with double-ought buck, you goddam idiot!! Only then did Foss understand his grave—and nearly fatal—error.

It had been a tense moment, but when it was over, we reenacted it at our weekly BLE 41 "Beer Committee" meetings on Friday nights. None of us ever repeated Foss's dumbass move. We had learned from Edgar's carelessness, since we had accepted that we would never live long enough to make every mistake ourselves.

Chapter Two

Opa-Locka

The robberies on the "Front"—the city of Opa-Locka's six-block stretch of drugs and violence—were brutal because they often involved outside buyers, stupid enough to venture into the hellish neighborhood to buy their coke, heroin, and Quaaludes. One night, a white guy was robbed and beaten with a tire jack so badly he was nearly killed. When I got to the scene, he was sitting on in the middle of Ali-Baba Avenue, thick rivulets of blood coursing down his face from the jagged head wounds.

"Oh god!" he wailed, "someone help me!"

A couple of the locals whispered in my ear: it was a guy named "Bay-Bay," a robber with a violent streak who liked to punish people after he relieved them of their money. Robbery was a way of life on The Front. With all the drugs being sold, it was way too tempting for local robbers to resist pouncing on the cash-carrying buyers.

This robbery seemed a little different. "Bay-Bay", it seemed, had some sort of axe to grind, and it seemed plausible that he would strike again.

One of our detectives caught me in the hallway. "Hey, that robbery you had on the Front? Good work getting the subject's nickname. We identified 'Bay-Bay.' His name is Jonathan Wilcox." He gave me a picture of Wilcox. "We got p.c. for him, so if you see him, pick him up."

Word was out that our detective bureau was doing some pretty good work over on The Front. They had successfully penetrated the heroin coming into town and were identifying the major dealers over there. The Front reminded me of junior high science class when we looked at a drop of pond water under a microscope, all manner of organisms constantly hustling, oozing and flagellating around and across the boulevard in their own method of survival. The pond denizens seemed to have picked up the pace now, scurrying or creeping, amoeba-like through the alleys and sidewalks with new purpose now that the pressure was on. Robberies were down, dope busts were up. The police weren't laying back anymore.

Afternoon shift—4pm to midnight—was the busiest, and that's all I worked during the eleven months I worked there. Some nights these calls went past midnight before you could wrap them up. We weren't *solving* any problems, we were just settling things down so that we could leave without the parties killing each other, and without us getting hurt. In uniform patrol the idea was to calm things down and get out of there without any blood and dirt on your uniform.

I was riding along 22nd avenue with Winston Lampkin, a big Guyanese fellow, when we spotted "Bay-Bay." Winston had been on for about four years. In his thick (tick) island accent, he would identify himself to the dispatcher as 1803—"etteen-oh-*tree.*"

Bay-Bay was walking along the sidewalk by himself. I fully expected him to take off running when we stopped, but instead he just stood there. When we put up him against the wall and started to cuff him, he turned around and tried to shove Winston out of the way. The next thing I knew, we were rolling around on the sidewalk with him, then over the sidewalk into the gutter. I was afraid we might get hit by a car coming north on the avenue. There was a lot of grunting going on, but in a minute or so we had him cuffed and in the backseat.

"Shit," Winston said, grinning, "good thing my gun didn't go down the gutter." With that, he reached down by the storm drain and picked up his revolver, which had come out during the fight. "Did you see dat muddafucka trying to get my gun?"

Fuck, *no*, I had not, and I was pissed off. Why didn't Winston yell something to me?

Winston, you dumb shit, dat muddafucka could have scooped your gun out of the gutter and killed *both* of us.

****

I leaned over and peered closely at the corpse. *Really* closely, because I wanted to show everyone that all 6'3, 165 pounds of my skinny rookie ass was immune to the brain matter. The chubby dead victim lay face down in the muck, which surrounded his head in soupy clumps. The other reason was that other than visiting the morgue in the academy, it was my first dead body out in the field, and I was transfixed. I had been on the road just two months, after graduating as the number one academic recruit in my police academy class out of thirty-three trainees. I would soon discover just how useless that award was out here.

Tiny black curly hairs stuck out of the mess, and a ragged hole near the top of his head was sticky with blood. Suicide? The way he was kneeling on the floor, with the gun resting on the carpet beneath him, I thought it was. The crime scene photographer stood above me as I leaned down, examining the stillness of the heavyset black man. Just minutes before we got there, he had been moving, breathing, agonizing perhaps about his decision.

"Brain matter?" I asked, pointing to the goop just inches from my face.

"Naw," the photographer said, chomping on gum. "That's puke. It happens sometimes when people shoot themselves. Move over so I can get this shot, will ya?"

I backed off—no, *recoiled*—and made a mental note to identify any muck I encountered prior to getting too close.

Just a few minutes before, I had raced to the scene, blood pumping. The call had gone out as a "3-30"—shooting with injuries—and often those turned out to be fatalities. In my rookie zeal, I had screeched to a stop in front of the apartment building, leapt out, and rushed to the scene. My sergeant had already arrived.

"Whadda we got?" I asked him in one breath.

"A dead male," he said tonelessly. The young sergeant was clearly adept at not jumping to conclusions. He glanced out the window. "Go out and turn your overheads off. No need to attract more people in the parking lot." When I went outside to the car, I realized with immense dread that I had locked the keys in the patrol car, engine running, red and blue lights still flashing dutifully. My first 3-30, and the keys were locked in the fucking car. What now? I went back inside the apartment.

"Um, sarge," I said to him. "I locked my keys in the car."

He looked at me, then looked away, around the scene, taking it all in. "Well," he said with no tone or expression, "get them the fuck out of there before the locals do."

"Right," said the number one academic recruit.

I went next door and borrowed a coat hanger—*what? The po-lice want a HANGER??*—and went to work on the driver's lock, cussing myself for being so stupid. I felt eyes on me. I glanced to my side and saw three little black boys, no more than seven or eight, standing side by side, staring at me in silence as I struggled with the coat hanger. They knew full well what a coat hanger inside a car door was used for. Why would a police officer, they must have wondered, need to steal a police car?

Opa-Locka was basically a large ghetto of about fifteen thousand residents, crammed into Dade County's northern reaches, flanked by an unincorporated area called Carol City (present day "Miami Gardens") to the north. In 1980, it had the highest homicide rate of any municipality in the United States. For a young cop stepping out of the police academy in December of 1979, there was no better training ground. You didn't have to go looking for anything; it would likely fall in your lap. Stop three cars for traffic, and one of them will either have a wanted driver, drugs stashed somewhere, or a gun under the front seat. Once, I actually hit a trifecta and got all three.

I was a lean and eager 21-year-old when I graduated Basic Law Enforcement (BLE) Class #41. To join the academy you had to have a department sponsor you—in other words, you got hired first, and they put you through the program, paying you while you trained. The County had a hiring freeze for a couple of years before I went in and I applied everywhere I could: eight police departments in all. Opa-Locka was the first to thaw, while the much larger departments like the City of Miami and Metro-Dade (county) all struggled with budget monsters and waited for their lumbering bureaucratic governments to give them the green light. "Can you pay your way through the academy?" the Opa-Locka background investigator asked me on the phone. No, I told him. That would about three thousand dollars and I didn't have it.

"Ok," he said, "We'll pay your way. Welcome aboard." It was May 1979 and I was going to start my training the very next month.

I was ecstatic.

Reuben Morris Greenberg was an average size man, with an average looking face, and an average brown complexion. And that ended the list of things that were average about Reuben Greenberg. Greenberg was black, and Jewish. He became the first black—and the first Jew—to be Chief of Police for the City of Opa-Locka. Greenberg made sure to interview every new officer just hired, and I would be no exception. Corruption wasn't a problem in Opa-Locka, it was *routine*. It started at the top and trickled down from City Hall down to several officers on the department. Ruben Greenberg, however, would have no part of it. There was a quiet energy about the man, an intensity in his eyes that told you police work was way more than a job for him.

"Let's say," he said halfway through the interview, "you went on a burglar alarm call at one a.m. You and your partner get there and find the window of a hardware store shattered. You look over and your partner is taking tools out of the store and putting them in the trunk. He tells you no one will miss them—it's a burglary, and the burglars probably took them. What do you do?"

Easy, I thought. "I...would go to my supervisor. Tell him what happened."

Greenberg nodded. "But it turns out there is some sort of close connection between your partner and the supervisor. He tells you to forget it."

"I would, umm..go right up to the Chief. To you, sir."

He nodded again. "It looks like a pretty big conspiracy. The Chief tells you to keep your mouth shut."

I felt stuck. "I..uh..." I shrugged. "I'm not sure."

He stared at me. "What about the State Attorney's Office? Couldn't you go to them, report the whole thing so they can start investigating?"

"Yes," I said, realizing that there is always an outlet. "Of course I would go there." "Nyberg," the Chief said, "if another officer ever asks you to do something illegal, you tell him, 'Fuck you and the horse you rode in on,' and you report it."

I nodded. "Yessir."

"There's no such thing as cops 'gone bad,'" he said. "You're either a criminal, or you're a cop. You make your choice. You can't be both, and I'm not having any criminals on my police department."

Ruben Greenberg said that to me, and he lived it.

The streets of Opa-Locka were constantly alive. My first day on my own—without a training officer shadowing me—was laced with the exhilaration every new officer feels when they are in that patrol car all by themselves. Driving down the street in a police car is an experience one cannot truly appreciate unless you've done it. Everyone's eyes are on you, with either expectation, fear, or gratitude. Sometimes it's just a quiet acknowledgement. The older denizens of the ghetto will nod their appreciation that you are there, but every so often, if you slow down and look hard at someone, they might run. The savvy ones will yell down the street, or do something to distract you, while they furtively drop whatever they were selling onto the sidewalk or in a nearby trash can.

One seller we used to watch would lean against a light post, drinking from a carton of milk. Only there was no milk in it. If you got out of your car, he would calmly "drain" the carton, drop it in the trash bin, and walk away. The carton was full of nickel bags of cocaine.

Steve Zimmerman was hip to all the tricks of the trade, especially the ever-active strip of Ali-Baba Avenue east of 22nd Avenue we called, "The Front." He knew this dude's little milk carton game and explained it to me as watched from down the street. Steve was one of the best cops I ever worked with, and I was lucky to have him break me in. We worked The Front every day. Every cop in Opa-Locka tried to swing through there at least a few times on their shift, and there was a good chance you would get a call there anyway. The Front was five blocks crammed with every species of drug dealer, robber, whore, and swindler imaginable, sauntering or scurrying in and out of dirty gambling dens and storefronts (with alternate "businesses" in the back), and it was a place where you constantly had to be on top of your game. A marked police car drew every eye from every shabby storefront, and *your* eyes had to be on the move the whole time. A hundred felonies were taking place all over, all practiced and disguised, or at least ready with an escape route when the police showed up. Dealers with fake milk cartons...whores who took their johns behind the market, hiked up their skirts, and leaned against the wall for ten bucks...burglars trading stolen jewelry for a packet of heroin...robbers ready to pounce on cash-carrying buyers...the denizens of this pond always kept life interesting. You never knew who was armed, who was holding, who was getting ready to do something.

"Sometimes, you're going to come out here, and you're gonna shit," Zimmerman told me my first week with him. "Just don't let them smell it."

The robber came out of the bushes, and I was on my bike..

"Go get some butter," had Mom told me. "Here's five dollars."

The U-Totem convenience store was on the next block, less than a five-minute bike ride. It was 1967, and 62nd avenue separated the black neighborhood from ours. I was nine years old. We lived on 62nd court, barely a half block to the west, and everyone from both sides of the neighborhood used the U-Totem, which sat on the corner of 62nd Avenue and 64th street. With the bag of butter clutched in my hand as I held the handlebars, I pedaled home, and the kid, probably fourteen or fifteen, was suddenly next to me, grabbing my handlebars and slowing the bike to a stop.

"Stop," he told me. "Give me all your money or I'll kill ya," he said, holding up an immense fist. I wasn't going anywhere, so I yanked the four dollars out of my pocket.

"This is all I got," I said. I wasn't all that scared. I knew, somehow, that he wouldn't kill me, but the damage that massive fist would do wasn't worth four dollars.

He took the money, then did an assessment of me, to make sure I wasn't well-connected enough to orchestrate some kind of revenge.

"Do you know Larry Smith?" No, I told him.

"A guy they call Doc?" No. He went through a list of several other people—presumably dudes with fists larger than his—and then trotted off.

"Thanks," he said over his shoulder.

Thanks?

I pedaled home, enthralled with the fact that I was a crime victim.

"I got robbed!" I said to the moonless night sky as I rode. I almost giggled at the thought. It was some sort of rite of passage, a step up into the adult world. I was bigger than before, more worldly somehow. When I got home, Mom was anxiety-ridden by the news.

I sat in the parking lot of Lum's, filling out a report of a battery case I had just been to. The intersection of NW 135 Street and 27th avenue was the town's biggest intersection, 135th connected Opa-Locka to Hialeah and Miami Lakes to the West, and North Miami to the east. 27th avenue was a major artery that ran all the way from the county line north of us, south through all the northwest section's black neighborhoods, across the river into Little Havana, and eventually all the way into the posh, narrow streets of Coconut Grove.

The radio crackled with a B.O.L.O. ("Be On the LookOut") for a white over tan Oldsmobile Cutlass with two black males in it. They had just used a sawed-off shotgun to rob the clerk at a Farm Stores in Miami Lakes, just a mile or so to the west of us, and it made sense that if they were coming this way, it would be on 135th street. The subjects were described as "very young" black males. When I glanced up from my report, there facing me at a red light was a white over tan Olds Cutlass with two black males in it. The driver's head—which barely cleared the dashboard—was on a 180-degree swivel back and forth, nervously sweeping the expanse of 27th avenue.

I picked my mike and started telling the dispatcher I had a vehicle fitting the description, and at that very moment the driver looked directly at me. Even from across the street I could see his eyes widen when he saw me looking at him and talking into the mike. He gunned the Cutlass through the red light and made a wild right turn, overcompensating and bumping up onto the sidewalk next to an empty field. I turned on my overheads and scooted across the street, dodging traffic, and by the time I reached the field, he and his buddy had thrown open the doors and were high-tailing it on foot through the weed-choked field. These were teenage black boys, and I normally would have had little chance to catch up to them, with my shiny Corfam uniform shoes on. The advantage I had here, though, was that the driver was short, and the grass in this overgrown field came nearly to his hips. With my height and longer stride, I was clearing the grass a lot better than he was, and about fifty yards into the thickly overgrown field, I reverted to my high school football days, lunged for his waist, and tackled him. Dwayne Burks, 14-year-old robber extraordinaire, went tumbling with into the tall weeds with me on his back. The other kid got away, but our detectives caught up with him later.

On the back seat of the Cutlass (which he had stolen from his aunt's house) was a sawed-off shotgun and the *entire cash register* from the Farm Stores.

Back at the station, my lieutenant clapped me on the back. "Nice catch, Nyberg. Next time, calm down on the air. You were yelling into the mike." He laughed. "You'll learn."

I filled out the arrest affidavit and went back to where Dwayne Burks was sitting in the holding area. The robber who had just a half hour before pointed a loaded shotgun at a Farm Stores clerk, was now resting his head on the table, and sucking his thumb.

They say you get your most valuable field experience in your first three years in uniform. In Opa-Locka, you got three years of experience in one year.

Things could go from marginal to very shitty in no time flat in this town. I was dispatched one afternoon to a theft of a bike at a large apartment complex. There isn't a call more benign than a theft that has already occurred. You get the info, you write it all down, you assure the victim you'll be on the lookout for the bike, and you're done, off to the next call. When I got there, the complainant was telling me how his son's bike had been taken from the front porch. I stood in the open doorway as we spoke. A small crowd gathered on the second-floor balcony facing us, and a few people came out of the apartment next door to see why the cops were there.

In seconds, someone from the next-door apartment started arguing with the dad. It looked like maybe the neighbors might know something about the bike.

"Wait a minute," I told the neighbor. "Let me finish up here, and I'll talk to you."

But it was too late. Another person from next door tried to get in the complainant's door, yelling, "you *muthafuckah*!!" at someone.

Just as I tried to get the neighbor out, the dad came barreling out of the kitchen with a large salad fork, screaming, "I'll kill yo' black ass, bitch!" The real story of the bike might be unfolding, albeit with sharp objects doing the talking.

Suddenly, I was wedged in the doorway with these two maniacs shrieking death and destruction at each other. I pushed my head out of the doorway and lifted my hand-held radio to call for a backup, and an electric blender—minus the pitcher—came sailing down from the second-floor balcony, missing my face by a mere inch, if not less. It crashed onto the walkway a couple of feet away.

I looked up and saw a wild-eyed woman with a large afro swinging a large potted plant in a macramé hanger, like a knight twirling a mace. This woman had *nothing* to do with the theft of the bike. I'm not sure if she even knew why I was there. If she was *not* the person who hurled the blender, then I had two assailants. Either way, she was getting ready to launch the potted plant my way.

Family members had pulled the fork-wielding dad and the crazy neighbor away from each other, and I broke free of the doorway. I yanked out my revolver and pointed at the plant lady and yelled out one of the silliest things a police officer has ever said to anyone: "*Drop the plant*!"

She glared at me, dropped her medieval weapon, and fled around the corner. When I re-holstered, two county officers, my backups, came trotting up.

"What's going on? You ok?"

"It's just Opa-Locka," I told them. They smiled knowingly. Everyone was told to go inside or go to jail, and in minutes, the place was quiet. We got out of there with our asses intact. That, every cop learns in Opa-Locka, is the major goal on every call.

The town of Opa-Locka was full of crazy people. I'm not sure to this day whether crazy people gravitated there, or whether living there made them crazy. One of the most celebrated of these whacky people was this old lady named Susie Howard. Susie was completely batshit and she used to call the police several times a week. Sometimes it was to complain about her boyfriend taking "rooster pills" and "bouncin' me all over the bed," and other times it was to say she was dying, which she never was. Sometimes she was nasty, sometimes funny, but once you got to know here, she was relatively easy to deal with. My first call to her house was one of my funniest memories of my rookie year. She said someone was in her yard trying to kill her, but it was all her wild imagination. We were someone for her to talk to.

"You one of dem new polices, ain't you?" She said, staring up at me. "I ain't never seen you."

"Yes, ma'am, I am."

She studied me up and down for a moment and seemed confused by my dark skin and straight hair.

"What you is, anyway?"

I was starting to tell her I was part Indian, when she cut me off.

"You a Haitian, ain't you?"

"No, I'm not Haitian—"

"Yes, you is—-you a muthafuckin' Haitian!"

I just smiled. "Susie, I've got to go. Other calls to handle."

Susie ignored me and asked, "What yo' name is?"

"Nyberg."

"What?" She cupped her ear. Her hearing wasn't great, or her brain just didn't absorb things as well as most people, or both.

"*Ny-berg*," I repeated.

She reared back, frowning.

"Night-bird?! What you doin' flyin' around in the *daytime??*"

Everyone on the squad got a big kick out of the story, and of course now I had a new nickname. Cops nicknamed each other all the time, so being called "Nightbird" by fellow squad members was a sign of affection, or at least, acceptance.

Besides a healthy per capita of unstable people, Opa-Locka was well-known for throwing things at police officers. There's little doubt that in past decades, the city's cops weren't the most professional, and apparently their nasty reputation carried on to us. Like the bike-theft-turned-riot incident, where I was nearly conked with a blender, people were always throwing things at us. In the space of ten months in that little town, I would have more objects hurled in my direction than I would in my life, before or since, combined.

In Opa-Locka, stopping a young male on a moped carried about a sixty percent chance that the driver was going to flee. Most mopeds we encountered were stolen, so when activated my red-and-blues one afternoon to stop the teenager turning onto Alexandria from 135th, I took the mike off the holder and put it in my lap in case I needed to tell the dispatcher that a chase was on. This kid was at most fifteen, but when he saw my lights behind him he surprisingly pulled over into the parking lot of an apartment building on Alexandria Drive. Alexandria was a tumultuous stretch of tenement buildings which always had some shit going on. He stood patiently while I sat in the cruiser and ran his driver's license. Suddenly the car shook with an explosive sound that almost made me shit my pants. A chunk of brick bounced off my car door and tumbled onto the pavement.

"Fuck!" my partner yelled. He was all of nineteen, a reserve officer.

Another rock sailed over the car and landed to the right of us.

"Let's get out of here," he implored me.

"No," I told him. "Get out and rack one in the shotgun."

He did as he was told, just as a bottle crashed on the pavement a few feet in front of the moped, which was now laying on its side, with the kid *underneath* it in a fetal position.

The *kaa-chunkk* of the Remington 870's slide echoed off the building's walls as I got out and scanned for faces, but I only heard footsteps. The brick culprit was gone. 12-guage shotguns had that effect on people.

"*Maaan*" the kid cried from underneath the moped, "could you *please* just let me go??"

The moped wasn't hot, and we were on our way. I don't know who was happier, us or the kid. He got a ticket for not having a tag on the bike, but at least he didn't get brick in the head.

The boy next door was named Eddie. He was about three years older than me and had a southern accent, like his parents. He always called his father "sir." They were a popular family, because they were the only ones in the neighborhood with a pool. During summer they invited all the kids on the block and there would be fifteen or twenty of us splashing around on those intensely hot days while all the parents sat around the edge of the pool in lawn chairs, sipping beers, wearing sunglasses, and chatting.

Eddie had just turned twelve and we talked at the edge of the road between our houses.

"Look at this," he said proudly. He dug several bullets out of his pocket. I had never seen bullets, or real guns of any kind that I could remember. "My Dad got me a .22 for my birthday. He's going to take me out huntin.'"

I was flabbergasted. I didn't know a person so young could have a gun, much less shoot one. I wondered what it was like to hold a real one. A real gun, at twelve, I thought. Imagine that. .

The most dangerous call in police work is not a bank robbery in progress. When you get a call like that, your blood and adrenaline are pumping, and while you are on your way there you are planning your arrival, where you'll park, how you'll position your car, thinking about your back-up, and whether he'll get there first. In other words, you're amped up, you're preparing...you're *ready.* In police work, the most dangerous is the "disturbance" call, which is usually husband-wife, boyfriend-girlfriend. We get hundreds of those a week, so they tend to feel routine. But what makes them dangerous is the unknown. The formula is a time-honored one. Separate the parties, calm them down, assure them that you are going to listen to them. Most of the time, you get one of them to leave for the night to cool off, and we all go home happy.

It was another one of the dozens of calls to Alexandria Drive we got every week: Boyfriend-girlfriend, the dispatcher told me, the girlfriend says the boyfriend is getting violent.

The door was already partially open when we got there. We could hear them yelling and could see the guy pushing her up against the wall. He was a big dude, about 6'4, maybe 230-240 pounds and muscular, like he worked out a lot.

"Hey man," I said, "Let's let go of the lady so you and I can talk."

My partner and I got them separated but in the same room, so we could both keep tabs on each other. They were both jabbing their fingers at each other, yelling threats and vile names as we tried to get them quiet. I glanced around the room every so often to check for weapons laying around, but I didn't see any.

Then something caught my eye.

There were trophies everywhere, on every tabletop and shelf, maybe six or eight in all. Basic officer safety says that you have to keep your eyes on the person's hands—that's what will hurt you—but I kept glancing back at the trophies and then realized that they had his name on them. They were *karate* trophies. This dude was a triple-black belt of some kind. Calming him down was now a major necessity.

With both of them still squawking at each other and trading insults, I felt a tug on my trousers. I looked down and saw a beautiful little four-year-old girl. As if offering me a plate of food, she held in her hands a shiny .357 magnum revolver. Her tiny hands barely cradled the weapon; the barrel and grips stuck out of either side.

"Here's the gun," she said helpfully.

When I drove home that night, I couldn't get it out of my head. The police had obviously been there enough times so that she knew they would ask if there were any weapons in the house. So while all the adults were in chaos, she quietly went under the bed, where she knew it was kept, and did her good deed. For many nights after that, when I went to sleep, I wondered where that little girl was, and whether the bed her mother was sleeping in had a gun under it.

Today, I've still not forgotten her face.

The stretch of 22nd avenue from NW 136th street up to 151st was a dimly stretch of grimy tenements, a lot like Alexandria Drive. The call was another 3-30: shooting with injuries. When I got there, someone gave us the .22 rifle. The shooter was lost somewhere in a growing crowd. I quickly locked it in the trunk and hurried up the stairs to meet my backup and the victim. The guy was about forty, and from what we heard he apparently owed the shooter some money from a dice game. He took six rounds in the back and was laying on the second-floor walkway, moaning. Fire-Rescue paramedics were right behind us. and they quickly knelt on the narrow second floor walkway, getting vitals and setting up an IV. Everyone in the building was out of their apartments watching, and a crowd of at least fifty people quickly gathered downstairs in front of the building, looking up at us, watching. The paramedics asked me to hold the IV bottle while they worked on him and contacted the hospital. Devorah Weintraub, the only female officer on our squad, knelt next to me to help.

The people downstairs were yelling but we couldn't hear what they were saying. Suddenly a beer bottle went sailing just over my head and crashed against the wall behind us, sending shards of glass all around us, and on the moaning victim. Someone threw a can, and then a couple of rocks came our way. We squatted low with the paramedics, who were getting ready to transport the guy, but were afraid to move. I got on the radio and requested a 3-15, which means we needed emergency backup.

Devvie yelled down at the crowd, "Hey we're trying to save this guy's life, goddammit!" Her voice was drowned out by the mob, which was getting louder every minute. It was chaos.

Then a shot rang out and dust jumped off the wall behind us. "They're fucking *shooting* at us!" Weintraub screamed.

I could hear the sirens of our backups. Please get here *now*, I thought.

Our backups came racing up to the building, and the crowd scurried off in different directions. We got the victim down to the Fire-Rescue truck, which now had its headlights smashed out. The guy lived.

Miraculously, so did we.

My drive home was about twenty minutes, and it took another hour after that to concentrate on anything else. I found myself feeling detached from my friends now. When they told me about things, I kept comparing it in my head to what I was experiencing—which wasn't fair—-but nothing they talked about seemed dramatic, or even important. I was the same person I had always been, but I was looking at the world through a different lens now. I had trouble looking at my surroundings, my neighborhood—indeed, the people in my life—without being constantly aware of my cop-ness. I had married just three weeks before the police academy started, to a Cuban girl named Vivian. We both knew as much about life as I knew about police work at the time. It all lay ahead of us. She worked full time as an LPN at a hospital northeast of Opa-Locka. We partied occasionally with friends on our off time and spent time with my parents, having dinner, playing board games, having fun. But my time off was disappearing, and so was my interest in anything beyond what had happened on my shift the night before. I took on an off-duty job at the Winn Dixie supermarket on one of my days off. $12,000 a year went just enough for us to afford our old, one-bedroom apartment in Hialeah. Then, the department was so short-handed they offered an extra day for anyone who wanted to come in and work. For a while, I was working seven days a week.

At twenty-two years old, police work was my life, and it was becoming my identity.

And the horse you rode in on...

I put the handcuffs on the woman as carefully as I could, but when people were struggling, it was going to hurt. She had just shoplifted about a hundred dollars' worth of groceries, and the supermarket manager said they were pressing charges, because it wasn't the first time for this woman. I walked her out to the police car while she pulled, tussled and called me every name she could think of. As I opened the back door and started guiding her in, she pushed against me, screaming to high heaven. I looked over and there was Reuben Greenberg, standing by his car in full uniform. He made a habit to get out of the station and show up on his officers' calls. Most Opa-Locka residents knew him by sight. Damn, I thought to myself. The one time the Chief rolls up on one of my calls, I have a berserk shoplifter trying to make me look like an abusive cop. Out of the corner of my eye, I saw the Chief glance over at me. The maniacal woman saw him too.

"Hey!" The woman shrieked, "Help me! This goddamn cop is treating me like I'm *a common criminal*!"

Greenberg walked up and looked at the squirming, snarling woman. "That's exactly what you are, lady," Greenberg said. "Now get in the car like you were told and stop giving my officer a hard time."

Greenberg, in his quest to bring Sir Robert Peele's principles to Opa-Locka, was not a dictator. He was a leader. Among other things, he required us to log our "foot patrol" times on our worksheets and mark down the names of the business owners we contacted.

"Go into bars, restaurants, and businesses. Ask the people who work there how things are going and if there are any problems they are having that we can help with. We need to get out of our cars and show our faces more."

It actually worked. The older citizens of Opa-Locka loved Greenberg. We were starting to get more assistance from them. They were turning in wanted subjects and speaking up more often. That's what happens when people start trusting their police. The heroin investigation our detectives were involved in was lapping at the door of an Opa-Locka City Commissioner. Some of the dealers were singing, and all fingers were pointing to the same person at City Hall. Two months later, Reuben Greenberg was out on his ear.

We were getting a new Chief of Police. We were in disbelief, but the veterans there just shook their heads cynically.

"They don't want things to change around here," Steve Zimmerman muttered.

Greenberg's departure was swift and uneventful. The powers-that-be were soon championing the arrival of Robert Ingram, a former Sergeant from the City of Miami Police. His administrative experience was limited. He had been a sergeant in Miami PD's juvenile division. In every way, he and Greenberg couldn't have been further apart. Ingram lacked not just the educational and career credentials Greenberg possessed, he lacked the fire and commitment our former Chief had. Where Greenberg sought to transform a limping, corrupt city into something respectable, Opa-Locka got a "yes" man in Ingram.

One thing Ingram did have, though, was the ability to make fast friends on the department. Within a month of him taking over, there were promotions. In police work, promotions are guided by civil service rules, and are supposed to be announced. Eligible officers are supposed to be given an opportunity to test or compete in some way for a higher rank. Before Ingram, we had a chain of command that went: officers, sergeants, two lieutenants, Chief. Within a month of Ingram's new appointment to Chief, we came to work and found three officers were wearing corporal's chevrons on their sleeves. *Corporal?* We didn't have corporal rank until that day. Ingram had created a new rank and promoted people without announcing it to anyone. Two others were promoted to sergeant, and one sergeant was promoted to lieutenant, overnight.

Things were going *Animal Farm* around me all of a sudden. I missed Greenberg and the level of excellence he had demanded from us. He was now in Charleston, South Carolina, turning around a shabby, brutal, police department in one of the great reform stories of American law enforcement. The city of

Charleston became one of the South's safest and most livable cities anywhere. Greenberg would get national acclaim, be featured on *Sixty Minutes*, and appear in documentaries about policing for his transformation of Charleston. I couldn't think of anyone who deserved it more. Lucky Charleston, and poor damn Opa-Locka, which had slowly started to see a ghetto-less future on the horizon. I didn't have much time to contemplate the new regime, though. The shit was about to hit the fan like never before.

McDuffie

On December 17th, 1979, a black insurance salesman with a suspended driver's license raced through the streets on his motorcycle, driving like a madman. When a county officer tried to stop him, Arthur McDuffie decided to outrace him. The chase was on, and McDuffie pushed the bike harder, up to 100mph at some points. By the time the stop was made, several cops were on the scene and McDuffie tried to fight his way out of the situation. He fought like a banshee and the adrenaline-charged sheriff's deputies, fresh from a chase, responded in kind, at one point using their heavy "Kel-lite" flashlights to whack McDuffie into submission. When it was over, Arthur McDuffie was in a coma. He died four days later. Then the cops made a horrible decision. Rather than just tell the truth, they stupidly decided to make the incident look like a traffic accident. They gouged the street with a tire iron, damaged McDuffie's bike to make it look like a crash, and wrote it up as a tragic accident resulting from a high-speed chase. They scooped up evidence of the violent encounter and tossed it onto a nearby roof and they lied to investigators.

But you don't fool Doc Davis.

Joseph Davis was the medical examiner's medical examiner. Few, if any, pathologists in the country knew death as he did and his reputation—worldwide—was impeccable. Born in Scarsdale, NY in 1924, Davis opened the first Medical Examiner's Office in

Miami in 1956 and was soon widely renowned for his expertise, insight, and achievements in the world of death investigation.

When he performed the autopsy on Arthur McDuffie, Davis knew without question that the head injuries were not sustained in any car accident. The blunt trauma injuries to McDuffie's head, he determined, were not the result of him falling to the pavement. Rather, they were the result of being beaten with a heavy object with such force that it "cracked his skull like an egg shell," as Davis wrote in the post-mortem report. Cause of death: Massive blunt trauma to the head. Manner of death: Homicide.

The news of Davis's findings sent ripples through the community. Metro Police was already getting slapped silly in the *Miami Herald* on police brutality stories. Tensions—genuine and heavily fanned by the news media—had been growing in the black community. A wrong house raid during a 1979 search warrant, in which an innocent black homeowner named Nathaniel LaFleur was beaten, didn't help matters. Now this.

One of the officers finally broke and told the State Attorney's Office the real story. There was no accident. We beat him, and we covered it up. Manslaughter charges were levied against the officers involved. Too many people in the Miami area knew details of the case and emotions were running high. The defense motion for a change of venue was granted, and the trial was moved to Tampa. The jury—*all white*—acquitted the officers. The court delayed the release of the news, but on May 17th, 1980, the story broke, and in black neighborhoods all over Dade County, people poured into the streets.

I got ready for work that day completely oblivious to the jury's decision. What was on my mind that day was the Mariel Boatlift. The infamous agreement President Jimmy Carter made with Fidel Castro to accept Cuba's "political prisoners" was well underway, and in Opa-Locka we were feeling the brunt of it. Opa-Locka

Airport, a municipal airfield created for military traffic during WWII, was the processing center for thousands of the refugees. On top of the regular menu of madness, we had to work security checkpoints there that weekend.

The prevailing belief about Mariel was that Cuba would ship many of its "political prisoners"—those who had done nothing more than protest or criticize the regime—to American shores. What the naïve Carter didn't expect was for Castro to scoop up the worst denizens of Cuba's slums off the streets and shove them onto boats at the port of Mariel. As Fidel himself put it, "I have flushed the toilets of Cuba onto the United States." While there were certainly non-violent political prisoners in those crowded boats, Havana's rapists, robbers, drug dealers, and other undesirables also jammed hundreds of vessels to the gunwales. We found out in many future interviews of *Marielitos* that the Havana police approached them and gave them a choice: go to jail, or hop on a boat to Miami. Cuban jails—most of them already knew—were hellish places of pain and suffering. A trip to the United States had no downside whatsoever.

It was that bizarre political scenario of Mariel that occupied my mind on that May 17th as I got in my 1978 Toyota Corolla and headed to the police station. As I drove, I noticed two large columns of smoke reaching high above the city. It looked like somewhere north of downtown. Huh, I thought, imagine that—two large fires, so near each other. What a coincidence. I could have turned on the radio and found out a lot more, but I opted for *Steely Dan* on my Pioneer cassette player instead. In 1980, without Twitter and texting and the lightning-fast news flashes of today, information traveled slowly. If you didn't have your TV or radio on, you would miss a lot.

At roll call, our sergeant calmly said, "Oh, you guys should know that the verdict came back 'not guilty' on the McDuffie case. They're having some trouble down in Liberty City, some rock throwing, stuff like that. Keep your riot helmets handy and be careful." If it was nothing more than rock throwing, we were all pretty used to that.

I wondered, could those fires I had seen been from the "trouble" the Sarge said they were having? Liberty City was mostly county and some City of Miami jurisdiction; a mere ten-minute car ride down either 22nd or 27th avenue from Opa-Locka. It was essentially a larger Opa-Locka, or one could say that the entire stretch of Dade County's northwest section was one huge contiguous black community.

At 4pm, when I loaded my cruiser and hit the road, I didn't see anything going on. A couple of hours later, just around sundown, I got a call to a traffic accident on 22nd avenue and 144 street. As I sat in the car filling out some paperwork on the drivers, I heard honking. I looked down 22nd avenue, and a line of cars with their headlights on was coming northbound. Funny, I thought, people in most funeral processions don't honk. Then I noticed that the drivers all had their fists out the window. Clearly, this was not a not a funeral.

The next twelve hours went from real busy to chaotic, then to abject anarchy. By nine o'clock that night, several buildings were on fire just in our town alone, debris was all over the streets, and bonfires raged in the middle of all the major intersections around town. Everywhere we went, people were showering us with rocks, bottles, anything they could find on the ground. Every grocery store and convenience store in the city was looted many times over. We chased some people at first, but after a while we learned it was wiser to just get the fuck away. The rioting was rampant, and we were losing the streets.

The radio never stopped. After a few hours, you could hear the frustration and fatigue in the dispatcher's voice as she sent out call after call of "rocks and bottles," "juveniles setting fires," "subjects looting a store," "shots fired," "subjects with machetes and bats marching." After a while, the dispatcher stopped assigning the calls to individual units, the way it is normally done. She would just give out the address, and say, "Subjects setting fire in the street…" and leave it unassigned. Whoever was nearby would go. Five, six, seven units—from both Opa-Locka and the County—were arriving at every call.

At Alexandria Drive and 135th street, a group of fifteen or twenty people were looting the U-Totem convenience store on the north side of street. The dispatcher announced looting there a dozen or more times that night and in one of the alerts, there was information that someone was trying to set fire to the place. On the south side of 135th and Alexandria was a four-story apartment building, the same one where I had met the little girl with the gun. We had been chasing looters out of the U-Totem. By ten that night there was a trail of merchandise going across the street from the store to Alexandria. The windows of the store were all smashed in, and cans and packages of food were strewn all over the place. Those of us who had tear gas grenades were tossing them inside the looted stores just to keep people out.

When I heard the possible arson call go out, I rolled up on the east side of the store and several people scooted across 135th. One guy stayed—a large dude carrying a gas can and walking towards the store, seemingly oblivious to me. I got out, racked the 870, and leveled it at him.

He froze when he heard the shotgun being racked. "Oh, this is not happening…." he said.

"Yes, it is," I called out to him. "Put down the gas can and get on your knees." I got him handcuffed, and Steve Zimmerman and two other units showed up. One of our officers had a prisoner in the back already, and they yelled to me, "Hey, put him in here, we're going to the station anyway. We'll take him. You can come by and do the A-form later."

I took them up on their offer, and we looked over to see three women and a guy taking a bunch of food out of the store and loading it into their trunk. We ran over and they took off, packages falling out of their trunk as they sped away west on 135th street. Right then, shots rang out and I saw the dust jumping up just a few feet away. Shit—they were *shooting* at us now. One of us yelled, "They're shooting, let's go! Get outta here!"

We couldn't see the shooter, but the most likely spot was one of the balconies from that Alexandria Drive apartment building. I jumped in my car and started pulling out as more shots rang out, and I heard Steve get on the radio and say, "1821, I'm hit." I looked back, and saw our sergeant, Jim Brogan, putting Steve in the back of his car. At least Steve was moving around on his own.

Brogan announced, "I've got 1821 in my car, and I'm en route to Parkway." I saw him squeal tires out onto 135th street and disappear like a fighter jet down State Road 9, which would have him at Parkway ER in about two minutes.

I didn't have time to contemplate Steve's wound. Another officer was calling for a 3-15, and we streaked off to his location. A couple hours later, it was shift change, but we weren't going home. The lieutenant called a meeting at the station while the midnight shift came on and took the streets. I wondered how Steve was doing. We were going to be working a few hours more, and the entire department—all the departments in Dade County, in fact—were on "alpha-bravo," which meant twelve-hour shifts. If you were alpha shift, you worked 7a-7p, and bravo worked 7-p-7a, with no days off until further notice. When I looked around the room, I saw Steve Zimmerman sitting near the back, a bandage around his right arm. The bullet had grazed his forearm deeply, and lucky there was no major damage. When the bullet struck, his arm was right over his forehead. He had instinctively shielded himself when the round struck his arm. Inches lower, and he would have taken one in the forehead. Brogan told him to go home and rest, but Steve refused.

"We need everybody out here," he said quietly.

It wasn't until this meeting that we heard some of the details from the beginning of this mess. Earlier that afternoon after hearing the verdict, a large angry crowd marched on the Metro Justice Building on NW 14th St. It turned bad quickly. Bricks and bottles were thrown, and some cars were overturned and or had their windows smashed. Metro-Dade's police headquarters building sat right behind the Justice Building with the Dade County Jail in between. HQ had literally been under siege as hundreds of rioters tried to get in and burn the place down. The rioting spread northward into Liberty City, Opa-Locka and throughout the rest of the northern neighborhoods. The fires I had seen on my way to work *were* in the heart of Liberty City, and one of them was Norton Tire Company, on the corner of 54th street, and northwest 27th avenue. Norton Tire was the biggest employer of black citizens in Dade County. Rioters torched it, and it burned to the ground. The company never returned.

Seventeen murders occurred that night, and several of them were unknowing white motorists, driving through Liberty City on their way home from work as they had done every day. Crowds of rioters blocked the streets, dragged the motorists from the cars, and beat them to death. The northwest section of Dade County, some fifty square miles, was a war zone.

The rioters from Alexandria Drive tried twice more to burn down the sacked and tear-gassed U-Totem later that night, and each time we chased them off. During their last effort, about twenty police cars with forty or so officers, arrived. We parked in the middle of 135th street, and without any planned design, marched towards the crowd, racking our shotguns. It was a formidable sight and an even more hair-raising sound. The looters and would-be arsonists high-tailed it for home never came back.

They called our afternoon shift back in to go home at about 4am, and I gunned it down 22nd avenue, now deserted. Just as I passed the tenements at 142nd street, I heard the crack of a small caliber weapon, and I'm sure it was meant for me. There was no one else around. I sunk low in my seat and put the pedal to the floor. The first long day of riots was over for us. The midnight shift was still out there, mopping up the occasional looting, brick throwing, and scattered incidents of mayhem. The rioters had tired themselves out, for the time being. The county commissioner had ordered a 9pm curfew. Anyone on the streets after that time without a legitimate purpose would be arrested.

It took me three beers and a couple of cigarettes to slow my mind and my body down to where I could sleep. Finally, after talking to Vivian about all the shit that I had been through the last twelve hours, my body started shutting down, and I slept.

We were on alpha-bravo for the next eleven days. The next day, May 18th. there was still rock-and-bottling of our police cars and random looting incidents, though not as widespread as the previous day. The shooting and burning incidents had tapered down considerably. Things were slowly returning to normal. At the order of the Governor, the National Guard had been called to Liberty City to help the exhausted county officers secure the streets. Dade County jail was jammed with hundreds of arrestees from Saturday's rioting. In addition to Steve, another County officer had been shot, but like Steve, his wound wasn't life-threatening either. The guys on our detective bureau were busy trying to identify the sniper on Alexandria Drive who had shot Steve as they fired on us at the U-Totem.

Every police department in Dade County was on alpha-bravo, including the Florida Highway Patrol. Even Broward County sent people down to help, so by Sunday afternoon there were police cars everywhere. It was comforting, compared to the chaos of the night before, when we saw more rioters than cops. By Monday night, we had taken the streets back, and though there we were still getting peppered with rocks and bottles every so often, the fires, looting, and random shootings were only sporadic. We were still arresting the occasional curfew violator by Monday, and we could feel the town was returning to normal. You couldn't drive a quarter mile in any direction without seeing another police car, and by Tuesday, it wasn't unusual for *us* to pump a fist out the window when we saw one of our own.

It was at that moment that we all began to realize something rather amazing: Since that Saturday night when the riots broke, Chief Robert Ingram was nowhere to be found. I figured he had been in the station the whole time, directing the show. The truth, we discovered to our astonishment, was that he had stayed *home*. In a critical time, when his police department needed leadership, he had hidden under a rock. Greenberg, I was sure, would have had been out there with us with *his* riot helmet on.

Ingram showed up Monday and wanted to ride around the city to see what was going on. Glances darted across the roll call room when we all heard the news. Now? Now he decides to show his face? Amazingly, he chose to ride with *me* for a couple of hours. There wasn't much going on. We chased off some juveniles from a burned-out building and arrested one curfew violator. It was quieter in Opa-Locka now than it was in *normal* times. I suppose Ingram wanted to say that he was "out on the streets during the riots." One thing he did accomplish was to write a commendation for Steve, for continuing to work after receiving a "grievous" injury.

I would always needle Steve about how "grievous" his wounds were, and we shared a few good jokes on that.

"Trust me," Steve said, "my asshole was more grievous than my arm that night."

In police work you had better keep your sense of humor. If you don't, you'll drown in despair. It's too easy to let your vision of the world—and your opinion of people in general—get skewed by your experiences. In Joseph Wambaugh's *The Choirboys,* a group of cops are talking about a colleague who is in the hospital after being shot.

"It's too bad he ran into such an asshole," the youngest patrolman says.

The old grizzled veteran turns away, head down, and says, "They're *all* assholes,

rookie."

Perspective. It's what a lot of police officers lose if they don't have an outlet, a hobby, or the ability to laugh at things. Policing might be a job, but it is unlike any other. It takes unsuspecting young men and women and makes them deal face to face with one "grievous" situation after another. In the academy they teach you how to shoot, how to drive, how to fight, and how to arrest. They don't teach you how to take your uniform off and function in the world outside your patrol zone. For many of us, our sense of humor just wasn't enough to stem the tide of discontent which now seemed to be oozing into every corner of the department. The agency Reuben Greenberg had breathed life into was reverting. The Front, which Greenberg had started to clean up, was back to being a combat zone again.

We had a strange, secretive cop on our department that I'll call "Red." He was into something. You could tell by the people he would be talking to while he was on duty. He spent a lot of time on the Front, going into a restaurant and talking to a certain guy in there, always by himself, never with a partner. He seemed to know everyone in that shady, dangerous stretch of the Front. I actually saw him there *off* duty, wearing a hat, a toothpick sticking out of his mouth, jiving and joking with the locals. He looked like a pimp. There were rumors that he was dealing drugs or at least taking protection money. He let a guy in a stolen car walk one night, and that was mild compared to some of the shit I was hearing about him.

Steve Zimmerman bristled quietly whenever anyone talked about the oily Red. "The guy's dirty as hell. I don't know why he hasn't gotten fired or arrested yet."

We all knew that the only person who might have been able to get that done was now in Charleston, South Carolina.

Day by day, the timid and toothless Ingram was losing ground with the troops, and his absence from the tumultuous McDuffie riots hadn't helped. I wasn't the only one who had seen the writing on the wall. Devorah Weintraub put in her papers and got a job with the Coral Gables Police Department along with another officer, Jeff Wander. My buddy and mentor Steve Zimmerman left to go work with the County. These were fine cops, some of the best I would ever work with, and their departure was a loud statement that the surrounding pastures were greener indeed. I started looking, and I didn't have to look far. The City of North Miami, which bordered us on the east, was hiring. North Miami was a much quieter community, and their pay was significantly better. They started officers at $15,300, a solid $2800 per year better than Opa-Locka was paying me to get to get pelted with rocks, bottles, and blenders. I applied and met with their recruiting officer. When North Miami opened their door to me, I put in my resignation.

Ingram called me into his office and shut the door.

"I'm sorry you want to leave," he said. "I'd like you to reconsider." He pushed a piece of paper between us and wrote on it.

"You're making $12,500 now. I'll make you a Corporal, and you'll get a raise to $13,200. Sound good?" Oh. I could be one of those Corporals.

I took the pen from my uniform shirt and wrote $15,300 next to his number. "Chief, this is what North Miami is going to pay me."

"Oh," he said, raising his eyebrows. "Yeah, that's pretty good." He leaned back in his chair. "So, tell me. What problems do you see in the department? Anything that needs improvement?"

I hesitated. "Chief, I don't know if you want me to go into all that."

"No, really, I'd like to know. Tell me what you think could be changed."

"Well Chief, it's...you."

He raised his eyebrows again.

I decided to press on. Hell, what was he going to do, fire me? "I don't think you're doing a very good job managing the department. I'm sorry, I have nothing against you personally. I just don't think things are running as well since you got here."

He nodded calmly. "I'll admit, I did get in over my head when I took this job."

Though he was an incompetent police chief, I had to salute him for at least being honest enough to admit it. Some guys would have hustled me out the door and set fire to that bridge. Ingram shook my hand and wished me good luck, and I did the same.

That Friday, I turned in my badge and uniform. By the time I left, nine officers—a *quarter* of the entire department in the space of three months—had headed out the door.

Chapter Three

A Tale of Two Cities

September 1980

North Miami was Opa-Locka's neighbor to the east, sharing a common border along NW 17th avenue and 135th street. North Miami's "west side"—from 17th avenue to 7th avenue—was much like Opa-Locka's single-family residential area: predominantly black with some West Indian families and Hispanics mixed in. That was where the similarities ended. The middle of the mostly rectangular city was long-time white Anglo residents, the east side heavily Jewish and decidedly more affluent. Along Biscayne Boulevard—which connected the wealthy from Broward all the way down to Miami Beach—south Florida's elite snorted coke off tabletops at popular restaurants like Tin Lizzie' and nursed their hangovers at Pumpernick's and the Ham and Eggery in North Miami Beach. The "east side" was characterized by lavish homes, stylish waterfront condos, and regal yachts moored in the many canals of Sans Souci and Keystone Point. People in the city's middle sector actually smiled and waved when a police car drove by, and it took a little getting used to for me.

South Miami Elementary School didn't have a school newspaper. But every week, after our 3rd grade classes played one another in softball—spirited games, mind you—I handed my teacher a sports article, complete with catchy Miami Herald-like headline and a complete rundown on the game. I remember Mrs. Kruglick looking at it, kind of confused, and saying, "Well this is...nice...very good. But Ramesh, we don't have a school newspaper."

I know, I told her with a happy shrug. I write them anyway.

Mrs. Kruglick assigned us to write a poem, and I wrote one called "The Dark, Dark Night." It went something like, "I like the silence of the dark, dark night...", and went on to describe the peace it gave me. I can't remember the rest of it, nor do I recall what inspired the poem. I do remember Marnell Bradley, though. She was our school's principal, a stout, bespectacled woman with a strong voice and a keen eye for anything going awry in the school. One day, I got called into her office. What had I done? I started inventorying all the stuff that had happened in class, on the play field...I was a bit of cut up and received a few reprimands for talking to my "neighbors" in class. Would something like that justify a visit to Mrs. Bradley's office? I wondered nervously as I padded down the hallway.

When I was ushered inside, Marnell Bradley smiled at me and said, "Do you like Mountain Dew?" I did, so she went to the vending machine just outside her office and got me one.

Then, she took out a piece of paper, and said, "Your teacher just showed me your poem." She read the first line, then looked up at me and smiled. "This is a very good poem!"

I thanked her, relieved that I wasn't in some sort of trouble. She asked me some questions about what prompted me to write the poem, and so on. There was enough conversation for me to finish the Mountain Dew.

"You write very well," she said. "I hope you will keep writing. I look forward to seeing more of your poems."

Years later, my parents wept when they found out I wanted to go into law enforcement. We were going to send you to journalism school! You're going to waste your writing talents? I was too enamored with the idea of police work to worry about it. I would have plenty of time to write, I thought to myself.

"Why did you stop them?" Sergeant Geller asked.

I thought for a moment and glanced at the boys, who sat handcuffed in the back of my police car. I had seen them driving slowly up NW 7th avenue, a popular stretch of highway for armed robbers. You could knock off a convenience store and quickly get south to Liberty City or north to a spaghetti-like complex of expressways called the Golden Glades interchange. From there, Opa-Locka or Broward County were easy options. This crew was tooling slowly north on the avenue and slowed even more as they eyed the gas station at the corner of NW 135th street and 7th, unaware that I was behind them. One of them reached down under the seat just before I decided to flip on the blue lights of my cruiser.

"They had 29 written all over them," I said to the Sarge. Twenty-nine was the radio signal for robbery.

The sergeant smiled. "Yeah. I know that and you know that. The question is, how do you express that in your report? You have to justify the stop. You've got to make sure that the elements are all in there, that whoever is reading it would have wanted to stop them for the same reason. Get it?"

Ah, Sarge you're talking about *writing*. He didn't know me yet. In the police academy, when I would get "gigged" for lint on my wool pants at morning inspection, I would breathe a sigh of relief when our Training Advisor would bark at me, "Lint on your pants, Nyberg. Write me an essay on the importance of proper appearance. I want it in my office tomorrow morning."

Oh, sir, not an *essay*. Don't throw me in the briar patch.

The flashing blue overhead lights danced off the sergeant's badge, the gas pumps, and the brown faces in the back seat. Then I started talking, but what I was doing was writing—out loud:

"They exhibited unusual behavior, driving slower than the speed limit, slowing down at each business, almost stopping in the right lane at the gas station, making furtive moves under the seat. All this occurred in an area where armed robberies have occurred frequently. I felt alarmed for the community. Numerous armed robberies had been taking place along this area of NW 7th Avenue. I believed that their behavior indicated that an armed robbery was going to take place."

The Sarge stared at me for a moment, then nodded. "Ok, sounds good. Get that all in your report. We just don't want to lose that gun," he said, referring to the .38 caliber revolver I found under the driver's seat.

I wrote an arrest form that impressed the Sarge, and the case stuck. I thought I knew how to write reports then. After all, I had been a police officer now for a whopping twelve months. The old-timers in North Miami, guys with sixteen or seventeen years in patrol, would call you "rookie" until you had at least two years on the road. They were an interesting bunch, a far more odd and eclectic collection of personalities than we had in Opa-Locka. Or maybe it was just that things were always so rollickingly busy and crazy in Opa-Locka that we never had a whole lot of time to get to know each other.

One of our guys, Butch, was convinced he was the reincarnated spirit of Elvis Presley. Another, Steven Bauer, was a hot-wired ball of energy, full of pranks and laughter. Police officers always razzed and tormented each other—it was how we kept each other sane and honest—but Steve took it to another level. If you found a voodoo doll in the back seat of your police car, or firecrackers rigged under your chair, Bauer was the likely suspect. With the mischievous glint in his eyes and handsome smile, it was impossible not to like him. Of all the characters I would meet in my career, however, Phil Sublette had to be one of the most unique.

Forty-four years old when I met him, Phil had a slightly bowlegged gait and tinted glasses that always sat crooked on his face. Strands of black hair hung loosely on his forehead and a plastic cigarette filter was always clenched in his mouth. He called everyone—man or woman—"babe", and his old school presence commanded your attention. He always took the rookies aside to tutor them.

"Never call a rich man by his last name, and always call a poor man Mr. Smith," he would say. "When you're giving someone a sobriety test, after they do the heel-to-toe walk, don't just tell 'em to turn around. Bark it—*turn around!* They get startled, see. They stumble." He winks and chuckles a bit at that one.

His DUI strategies had more tricks. "Put a few coins on the pavement and ask them to pick 'em up. After they do, ask 'em how much money was there. Most people don't count it." His face crinkled up with a soft smile. Then he turns serious, his countenance black as coal.

"And you do *whatever* you have to do to go home at night, babe. You watch your ass out there. You feel yourself getting sleepy on a slow midnight shift, then goddammit you come into the station and go downstairs and lay down on one of the couches. Get fifteen minutes rest. I don't give a shit. I just don't wanna see you wrapped around a tree."

Phil was great at talking to citizens, but he had no time for people getting verbally abusive. He told one guy who called the station to snarl about one of the officers, "Well if you can't listen and be civil, then *fuck it*, ok?" *Slam* went the phone.

Two months into my North Miami tenure, one of our officers was killed. Carl Mertes, a veteran of about eight years, stopped a car on Biscayne and 135th on night and the car turned out to be stolen. The driver jumped out during the traffic stop and ran into the nearby wooded area on the west side of Biscayne. Carl took off after him and tried to find the man in the thick—and very dark—woods. When the dispatcher lost contact with Carl, a search was on, and a K-9 officer found Carl's body.

The entire department—there were only ninety officers, and everyone knew each other—plummeted into a state of mourning. I had met Carl only a couple of times, and he was a quiet, nice guy. It was disorienting, just arriving there and facing a tragedy like that. I was still a bit of an outsider, but it was North Miami's first line-of-duty death, so we were all experiencing that for the first time. Gordon Ransom's words reverberated back to me: "Learn from other people's mistakes; you'll never live long enough to make them all yourself."

Geller bit back his tears at the end of roll call. "Watch yourselves out there, ok?" he said with a shaky voice. And with that, we all had to get back to work—back to handling drunken marital disputes, car accidents, suspicious incidents—and stopping cars.

Our house had roaches. Dozens of them. Palmetto bugs, people in south Florida call them. Big, fast, and ugly, they could take flight if they needed to, and that was when they were the most terrifying. They are the reason exterminators do a huge business in Florida. But we couldn't afford an exterminator. Well, we could have, but then Dad couldn't have afforded two bottles of Cutty Sark a week.

One night when I was about eight, I got up in the middle of the night to go to the toilet, and when I switched on the light, at least a dozen of the hellish creatures started scurrying in all directions. I yelled so loud my mom came out of her bedroom. The two of us grabbed shoes and started fighting back. We were the humans; it was our bathroom, not theirs. A couple of minutes later, Mom and I stood there, triumphant—I did the body count, and we had killed eight of them.

Dad still never got an exterminator.

"Woman screaming." That's a call every police officer gets as often as once a week. Bill Schwartz and I rolled up on the apartment complex in North Miami's east side about the same. Bill and I had met at the physical agility test when we had both first applied for the job. Bill was different than most cops I knew—thoughtful, sensitive, and quietly humorous. He had a background in theater and had done some TV commercials before landing in law enforcement.

"An actor," he told me that day. "That's what I really wanted to be. But here I am." His words reminded me of Harry Chapin and the song, "Taxi".

After the dispatcher assigned me the "woman screaming" call, Bill and I were greeted at the door of a townhouse by a young couple who were calm but extremely anxious about the man's sister.

"I apologize," he told us, grimacing, "but my sister is on LSD, and we can't seem to help her at all. She thinks she's being attacked. By bugs." He looked embarrassed, and gestured to the patio. We went out to see a heavyset woman in her late twenties, slouched back in one of those large, round Oriental chairs. With her eyes wild with fear, she swatted at empty space and made small whimpering noises, as if despairing in her futility.

"The bugs!" She cried. "They're everywhere!"

There wasn't a palmetto bug or any other insect to be seen.

Bill and I looked at each other, and a silent plan materialized between us. There were several legal and procedural remedies at our disposal. We could have easily taken her in under the "Baker Act" for involuntary psychiatric examination. The law allowed for this if the person posed a threat to themselves or anyone else nearby. We made a silent choice to observe first. Baker-Acting her meant taking one of us off the road for at least a couple of hours.

Without exchanging a word, we started killing the bugs.

"Got one," I announced, as I slapped my hand against a nearby table.

Bill swung his clipboard in the air and smacked it against his open hand. "Got 'em!" he snarled with an air of solidarity. We kept up the charade, clapping at the insect-less space on that townhouse patio while the woman's head swiveled back and forth as if she were at Wimbledon with huge stakes on the winner. We smacked and smashed and clapped with our hands and clipboards for a good minute or more. Until Bill announced. "They're dead. All of them."

"One more, Bill," I cautioned, pointing, "by your leg!"

He frowned with intensity and nailed the invisible creature with one vicious swat. We shared a brief glance, acknowledging that we should end it.

"There," I told the woman, "we got them." She looked at me. I knelt next to her and put my hand on hers. "You're safe now, they're dead."

"No more bugs," Bill assured her.

Her wide eyes went to me, then Bill, and she began to cry softly. "Thank you," she said shakily. "Thank you so much."

I looked over at the couple, who had been standing by the sliding glass doors. They looked utterly dumbfounded.

"Thanks, officers," the sister-in-law said, "Thanks for everything. We..." she ran out of words, and we headed for the door, anxious to get out of there before the next hallucination started.

"No need to thank us," Bill said, "you two take care of her now."

When we got out to our cars, I looked at Bill and said, "Did what I think just happened really happen?" Bill laughed and shook his head at the wonder of the whole thing.

"Yeah," he said, "I think it did. It really did."

And it was off to the next call, whatever that would be, though we both knew that nothing else that night could top the Bug Lady.

One warm evening, an unassuming 66-year-old man named Philip Glanzer went to the Publix supermarket at NE 6th Avenue and 128th street to bring groceries to take home to his ailing wife. When he walked back out to his car with the bags, he was accosted by three robbers. Wordlessly, they shot and killed him, though he couldn't have given them a fight if he wanted to. As his life drained from him on the pavement, they took his wallet, and left.

I glanced at his form under the yellow blanket while I filled out the remainder of my police report. The Metro Homicide guys, in their ties and button-down shirts, were working: talking on the radio, getting descriptions from witnesses, taking pictures, and carefully documenting the scene. I watched them with interest. A young blonde detective named Remmen thanked me for securing the scene so quickly and jotting down the names of nearby shoppers who heard the shots. As I watched him, I suddenly realized the dramatic difference between my job and theirs. I'll leave and go to another call in a little while. They'll be busting their asses to find Glanzer's killers—all night, it if takes that long—possibly well into tomorrow. I certainly would. Hell, I *wanted* to.

That's when it hit me like a crack of summer thunder. That's the ultimate challenge in this profession, isn't it?—solving the murder of a human being. I surveyed the scene and looked over at Remmen, who was talking to a witness. Yep, that's it. Homicide.

I want to do *that.*

Chapter Four

Brown Gown

The problem was that the City of North Miami Police Department didn't have homicide detectives. Hence the presence of Detective Remmen and his Metro-Dade Homicide colleagues, working the Phillip Glanzer murder. This was typical of most of the small municipalities in the county. Most didn't have enough homicides to justify getting detectives trained to do it, so Metro handled it, the same way they handled other major crimes like arson and sexual battery. Metro had the trained personnel; the crime lab and other resources North Miami did not have. If I wanted to work Homicide, it looked like I would have to make yet another agency change and go to the County.

I didn't want to be one of those journeymen, bouncing from department to department. But there wasn't much of a future in North Miami now that I had been bitten by the homicide bug. In North Miami PD, you either worked uniform or the Detective Bureau, relegated to handling burglaries, thefts, and frauds for the rest of your career. Going from a ninety-man department to a sprawling Sheriff's Office of more than three thousand sworn officers would be a change for sure. But Metro not only had Homicide; they had special units like Aviation, Marine Patrol, K-9s, Sexual Battery, Robbery, Narcotics, and seven different regional districts to work out of. Maybe I could get assigned one of the south end districts, and not have to drive across the county to go to work from now on.

The decision was made. I would go from the pond to the ocean, and it would be my last change of jobs. I applied to the County, got accepted, and in August of 1982, I said goodbye to the North Miami Police Department. I attended a two-week orientation class for officers transferring from other agencies—called a "lateral" class—and got assigned to South District down in Cutler Ridge.

Even though I had three years' experience under my belt, I couldn't just go to Homicide without earning my stripes on the road. Just as I had done at Opa-Locka and North Miami, I had to do my obligatory "probationary" period. My dark blue uniform from North Miami was no more, and I now donned the dark brown trousers and tan uniform shirt of Metro-Dade—"the Brown Gown", as it had been dubbed by its road officers a couple of decades before.

I had to have a training officer to break me in and make sure I was ready to handle calls on my own, and that was fine. Uniform work in the County was almost exactly the same procedurally, so wasn't much breaking in to do. There were some minor administrative details, and I didn't mind learning them from someone. The last thing you want when you're new is to earn more nicknames for the wrong reasons.

Glenn Crosby was my senior officer. Glenn had about six years on the job, and we got along well. Quiet, calm, and intuitive, Glenn was an excellent cop, and we had good chemistry as a two-man unit. Getting along with your partner is essential. You learn each other's habits and quirks intimately and depend on one another quite literally for your survival. I liked Glenn. Even better, the rest of the squad were real good people and solid, experienced cops. Still, I looked forward to riding alone, and even more, getting to the point where I could put in for Homicide. For now, I would "ride the Brown Gown" for however long that took.

Metro-Dade had gone through a couple of name changes. By charter, the agency was the County Sheriff's Office and we were all Sheriff's Deputies. Our badges read "Police Officer" on top, and in the middle, where the Florida seal was, it read, "Deputy Sheriff." Dade County no longer had elected sheriffs, like the rest of the state. In an attempt to be more cosmopolitan and less redneck-sounding (so the unofficial theory went) they decided to call themselves a "police department" rather than a sheriff's office. Rather than have an elected Sheriff, the County opted to have an appointed "Director". We went from being the Dade County Sheriff's Office, to the Public Safety Department, to Metro-Dade, and by the time I retired, some genius County Manager named Alex Penelas decided we should be called "Miami-Dade", so visitors would know that the City of Miami was our geographic neighbor. All this did was confuse the holy hell out of people—residents included.

My time training with Glenn Crosby was brief. After a month, Glenn went to our Sergeant, Mickey Brelsford.

"He doesn't need to be riding with anybody," Glenn told Mickey. "He knows what he's doing. You can cut him loose anytime." Mickey gave it his stamp of approval, and I was back on my own again.

Within a few months of riding a one-man unit, I did some asking around to find out how to apply for an assignment transfer to Homicide. I got an interview a couple of months later. There were five Homicide supervisors in the room, and it was intimidating as hell. They sat in a semi-circle around me, launching questions, glancing at each other, nodding, and taking notes as I answered. I had studied what they told me to be ready for: search and seizure, the Florida Homicide statute, warrant procedures, and some other legal policies. They asked about personal things too. Can you work long hours? Is your wife ready to put up with late nights, overtime work? Homicide is demanding on family life, and so on. Then, one sergeant leaned forward and clasped his hands together.

"You know, we're pretty hard on each other around here."

With four years of police work under my belt, I was used to the chiding and good-spirited harassment cops put each other through.

"Oh, I can handle that, sir," I assured him.

"No," he said, smiling at the other supervisors in the room. "I mean, in Homicide, we're probably a bit rougher on each other than any other place, because of the nature of the job."

I nodded, and he went on. "What if someone called you a 'camel jockey'?" The others listened intently for my reply.

"Sir," I said with a straight face, "My people ride *elephants*, not camels, so I'd correct him and tell him I'm an *elephant* jockey."

The room exploded in laughter, and one of the sergeants smiled and said, "Good answer."

Despite what I thought was a good showing, I didn't get in, and it was primarily because the opening they thought they were going to have didn't happen. Wait, they told me. We might call you back again. A couple of months later I attended the annual Police Memorial ceremony at Tropical Park and ran into Homicide Sgt. David Rivers, who had been on my interview panel.

"You did well, Nyberg," he told me. "Unfortunately we just don't have an opening. But you should definitely keep trying."

Then he smiled. "No one forgot your elephant comment. As far as we were concerned, you were *in* at that point."

In the meantime, I worked the long stretch of South District, which spanned from 152nd street all the way down to the County line, where the upper Keys begin and the state of Florida's lower peninsula begins to dissolve into the salt water of Florida Bay. It was an immense county—thirty-two miles north to south and nearly forty-five miles wide, from Biscayne Bay west to the Collier County line in the Everglades. That's an area larger than the state of Rhode Island. In South District, you could be in the far reaches of southwestern Metro-Dade County taking a report of a theft of a pig from a farm, and half an hour later be rolling up on a burglary at a million-dollar mansion off of Old Cutler Road, some thirty-five miles away. In between, we had the very tough little neighborhoods of West Perrine and Goulds, both inner city environments plagued with poverty and drugs. Both places reminded me of Opa-Locka. The variety of South District made it a fun place to work, and the fact that I had grown up there didn't hurt.

The department had just started its Field Training Officer program. Before this, rookies were assigned to random veteran cops for on-the-job training, as I had been with Glenn. The new FTO program was more structured: to be accepted you had to go through an interview, a three-day class and a screening process, and then you're certified, with a 5% pay stipend for the certification. It wasn't much, but having the FTO pin was a nice feather in one's cap, especially if you wanted to get to some place like Homicide. The rookies coming out of the academy had three phases of one month each, and they rode with a different FTO for each phase. Each FTO had to write an evaluation and pass the officer to go on to the next phase.

I put in for the program and got certified. They assigned me Phase 3 officers, so my job was to make sure their training was complete and they were ready to go out on their own. The entire squad was FTOs and their PPOs (probationary police officers), headed up by a Field Training Supervisor. Our squad sergeant was Gary Wilcox, and we got along great.

When we were on the midnight shift, it could get pretty quiet around three to four a.m., and I didn't like wasting time just driving around. We would patrol a neighborhood, and then I would stop and put my rookies through scenarios, so they could practice. Mike Byrd, one of my phase three guys, was a super nice fellow with a great attitude towards learning. But things were going slow, and he was just not getting a lot of it. He overthought things and needed more practice with procedures. One slow night we parked in front of a closed convenience store at 2:30am.

"Okay, you just rolled up on an armed robbery that just occurred," I told him. "I'm the victim. Let's roleplay it."

I took a "10" with the dispatcher, which meant we were out of service, so she wouldn't dispatch without checking with us first. I turned up the car radio, so we could hear her, and put our hand-held radios on point-to-point, which means only the two of us could hear our transmissions.

Mike started slowly interviewing me, getting my name, address, and all the pertinent data, and then started asking detailed questions about how the robbery went down. Three minutes later, I stopped him.

"Mike, this is a robbery that *just occurred*. What's the first thing you want to do after checking that no one is injured?"

"Uhhh...interview the victim, like we're doing?"

"How about getting a description of the subject out on the air as soon as possible?"

"Yeah," he said, rolling his eyes at his omission. "The BOLO. Yeah. Shit. Sorry."

"Okay," I said. "That has to be second nature when you go to a call like this. Everyone in the district is going to know you just arrived on a robbery that just occurred. The dispatcher and everyone else will be waiting for the BOLO. You interviewed me for three minutes, and the subject could be miles away by now. Let's try it again."

We practiced like that every night, until Mike got pretty good at putting out BOLOs. One night, Wilcox heard me taking a "10" and asked for my location. He must have been getting curious about the tens that were being taken every time it got quiet. Moments later, he rolled up on us.

"What are you guys doing?"

I explained the scenarios Mike and I were doing to improve some weaknesses when things got quiet. I was hoping he wouldn't be pissed off.

"This is great!" Wilcox said. "I like it."

Before too long, Wilcox had me brief the entire squad on what I was doing with Mike, and he ordered the rest of the FTOs to put their PPOs through similar training "scenarios." We even got the squad together one night and did some larger situations like setting up perimeters, doing arrest techniques and searches, utilizing multiple people as witnesses and suspects. Wilcox clapped me on the shoulder one night as we headed out of roll call.

"Let's see if it's slow tonight, we'll get the squad together and do scenarios." He ended up writing me a commendation for it.

By the end of his riding assignment with me, I still didn't feel like Mike was ready. As much as I liked the guy—and he was hard not to like—I failed him; that is, sent him back to repeat his second phase. He had a great attitude towards the whole thing, and never once got bitter or angry about it. In fact, later when Mike was on his own—after completing his third riding assignment with another FTO—he thanked me.

"You had the courage to flunk me and make sure I was ready to do the job. Not many FTOs would do that."

I wasn't done with nicknames. We had *zero* Indian police officers in the County, so I was somewhat of an anomaly. One afternoon I got a call about a highly unstable man in the back yard of a residence, yelling and screaming. He was wild looking—like he had just crawled out of the wilderness—with intense, bugging eyes and a huge shock of red hair that stuck out in multiple directions. He was in the back yard of the residence, with both arms around a tree by a fence line separating two houses.

The reporter of the incident struggled for words. "He's, uh...channeling, or something," an embarrassed family member told us. "He thinks that ancient spirits are speaking to him through the tree."

Two other officers approached him slowly as I spoke with the man's kin. I watched as the guy suddenly bellowed gibberish, as if talking in tongues, his foot tapping wildly on the ground while he embraced the tree. He looked at the officers but had no reaction except to continue belting out the messages of the spirits whose messages made his entire body quake and shiver. I thought of Bill Schwartz and the bug lady momentarily, and then approached him. He saw me and suddenly froze, staring at me intently.

With his voice full of awe, he said, "*It's a man from another land!*"

Karin Pedersen, a wiry redhead herself, found this hysterical—as did I—but the remark gave me an inroad, and I was able to talk him away from the tree and to a place where he could "communicate with the spirits safely."

"I'll even take you there," I assured him.

"Ok," he said, obviously content to go anywhere with the "man from another land."

After a year of FTO work, I got another interview at Homicide. The District gave me a break from training and moved me to a regular patrol squad. I walked in to introduce myself to the Sergeant of the squad, a blonde, bespectacled fellow who looked vaguely familiar. I didn't recognize him at first, even when he said his name: Jack Remmen, the homicide detective I had encountered on the murder scene of Philip Glanzer in North Miami. He had obviously taken the sergeant's exam, and I was now working for him.

I loved climbing trees.

We had a ficus tree in our front yard in South Miami, on 62nd court and I spent most of my free time as a I kid climbing it or sometimes just sitting up there for a couple of hours. Most of the time I climbed barefoot, enjoying the feel of the thin ficus bark on the soles of my feet. It was easier to get leverage too. What I most enjoyed was the fact that I could see cars and people going by and they never noticed me, just ten feet above. We had an umbrella tree too, and while that was not as leggy as the ficus, I could still get up in that one, and see the roof of my house.

I spent so much time in trees as a kid that when my Dad would come looking for me, he would first look up.

I had a good time working for Remmen. I found him to be a really smart, solid, and fair guy. One day, he announced he was leaving South District. I was disappointed.

"Back to Homicide, buddy. This time as a sergeant. I'll keep you posted about your application once I get settled."

I was happy for him, and now I knew somebody there. After Remmen left, an interesting opportunity came up. Jimmy Brown, a lieutenant in South District, wanted to put together a squad focused solely on midnight criminal activity. Some of the business districts were getting torn up with burglaries and auto thefts, and the uniform guys in those areas were missing them. He wanted a group of plainclothes guys to work it, do surveillances, and catch them. He interviewed me, and before long I was coming to work in jeans and t-shirts with the rest of our squad. David Shanks was our supervisor, and Dave and I became fast friends.

We came in every night around 11pm and checked the reports to see where the burglars and robberies were happening, and then meet with the rest of the squad to set up our operations. Dave taught me that getting up on rooftops was a very effective way to watch an area, so we would generally have two to three guys placed on business rooftops, strategically spread out so we could cover a big area and overlap each other's range of view, with one or two guys on the ground in chase cars.

Sometimes we would drive up on an area and I would point out a business that looked like it would have a good vantage point.

"Well maybe, but you can't get on top of that building. Look at it."

Can't get on the roof? Really, I thought. Dave didn't know about my childhood and my love of tree-climbing. I would have Dave drop me off and usually I would find a pipe, electrical housing, or some fixtures to get a foothold on, and with my long arms and legs I would be on the roof in a matter of a couple of minutes. Getting on a new roof was a challenge from which I would never back down. Dave was wildly amused by this.

"Spiderman!" he exclaimed with a laugh. And behold, I had yet *another* nickname.

The Winn-Dixie supermarket was a great roof. It was easy to get up on, and the Winn Dixie logo was emblazoned on a fixture that provided a wall to hide behind. I spent many an hour up there, and our surveillances paid off handsomely. We caught burglars on a weekly basis, and most we got before they committed the deed. We would see them snooping around, looking up and down the streets (never *up*, however), and we would whisper to each other on point-to-point radios, and guide the guys on the ground in. The arrest would usually be for "Loitering and Prowling," Florida's crime prevention law, the elements of which amounted to being in an unusual place and acting in a way that arouses suspicion. If the subject could not "dispel the officer's alarm" with a reasonable explanation, then you had a good L&P. One night, we had all the elements of a great L&P, guy in his late twenties, walking around and checking doors and windows across the street from the Winn-Dixie. Finally, we stopped him, and the records dispatcher came back with his criminal history: he was wanted for First Degree Murder. I hoped the news of his arrest—and my involvement—made its way to the ears of the supervisors in Homicide.

We had some great characters on the squad, besides David. One of them was Milton Sims. Milt was "Li'l Abner" in the flesh, a large, strong, country-boy with an *aw shucks* persona. One day he and I were driving down U.S.1 on our way to one of our operations, and he spotted a man of about 45 years limping along the side of the road.

"Hey," Milt said to me, pointing at the guy, "stop the car. I know him. I shot him in Central District a couple of years ago."

"You're shitting me," I said, smirking at him. Police officers don't shoot people very often. Most cops go through an entire career never firing their weapon. Both parties in a shooting incident would remember one another well. I pulled over to the side, and Milt got out and went up to the guy.

"Hey there," he drawled, smiling at the guy, "Remember me? I shot you!"

The man stared at Milt for a second and then smiled back, "Ohhh yeah! How you doin?" and shook Milt's outstretched hand. I sat in the car, shaking my head. You really cannot make this stuff up, I thought.

One night, while I was watching from the top of the Winn Dixie, Milt was on the Perrine Liquor store roof a block away.

"Hey guys," he transmitted, "I'm hearing some scraping sound. Something metallic maybe. Can you guys hear it?"

I couldn't, but one of the other guys could after a few seconds.

"Holy shit," Milton said, "you guys won't believe what I'm looking at."

It was three young guys walking across U.S. 1, from the West Perrine neighborhood, *dragging* a pick axe. He described it to us and before long, the subjects were on the sidewalk, headed north towards me, but they had picked up the axe and weren't making any noise now. I still couldn't see them, but Milt said they were going behind the Golden Rule Seafood store, which was across the highway from Milt's position and a block south of me. I decided to climb down, as we would probably need more people to move in on this one. As I made it down to the back of the store, I heard a loud *whack* echoing throughout the otherwise quiet business district. Another *whack,* followed by several more, and I jogged towards the Golden Rule.

"They're trying to chop a hole in the back of the place," another one of our guys said.

Milt, Dave, and I arrived about the same time, and we watched for almost a minute as one of the geniuses swung the axe. The hole they had made was about a foot in diameter, and there was no place for them to go.

"Let's take these idiots down," Dave whispered with a grin.

I drew my handgun and yelled, "Hey! Hello there..." Dave and Milt had their guns and badges out, and the team of burglars turned around completely stunned.

"Drop the axe," Dave told them. "Hands on the wall." We called uniform, and they came and loaded them up.

"Man," one of the burglars lamented, "how did you find us?"

We looked at each other and cracked up while we cuffed them.

We had many more comical scenes like that play out during our surveillance operations. Dave got some magnetic letters and other props from the County surplus and dressed up a plainclothes car to look like a taxi. We were doing a surveillance on a robbery, and the subject took off running after trying to take down an all-night convenience store. Dave came wheeling into the area, and the guy ran over to him, waving him down. Dave slowed and opened the door, and the robber jumped in.

"Get me outta here, man," the guy said breathlessly, "the cops are after me!"

One day I got a call from a homicide detective named Julio Torres.

"Do you have a brother-in-law named Jose Luis Rodriguez?" he asked me.

Yes, I told Torres. Jose was Vivian's younger brother. A very intelligent but strange and antisocial guy, Jose had drifted around from job to job and lived with his mother. He got very interested in Eastern philosophy, and then took off for India. My god, Homicide was calling. Was he dead? Was there an accident?

"Any idea where he is?"

Clearly, he wasn't dead. "Last I heard, he had gone to India for vacation."

"India. Ok, well, I hate to tell you this, but he's the number one suspect in one my cases."

I was thunderstruck. "Murder case?"

"Yeah. First degree," Torres added. "I heard you put in for the unit. If you get up here, I'll sit down with you and show you the case file. He and his cousin from *Mariel* did some armed robberies, too. A couple of jewelry stores. We got Jose on video pointing a semi-auto handgun at the salesman."

Torres was confident that Jose was his guy, but for weeks it was hard to reckon with. Then I started to take inventory of some of the things he had said—coupled with his narcissistic personality—and it started to make sense. The previous Christmas, he gave me and Vivian watches and jewelry. It never dawned on me that the stuff could have been taken in an armed robbery. I had a long talk with Vivian that night about her brother and she was distraught, but not in denial. She had seen the signs, but as a sister just didn't want to think the worst.

Our surveillance squad, which we nicknamed M-CAT (Midnight Crime Apprehension Team) eventually disbanded. Dave Shanks got a transfer to VIN (Vice, Intelligence and

Narcotics), another member got married and didn't want to work midnights anymore, and so the District Commander–who was leaning towards dissolving us anyway due to budgetary constraints—decided the District could survive without M-CAT.

Back in the Brown Gown, where more bodies were needed anyway. Fine with me. I would continue in uniform until something opened up in Homicide, whenever that would be.

The U-Totem store sat on the corner of SW 64th street and 62nd avenue, barely a minute's bike ride from my house. Or I could hop my back fence, walk across the gravel alley way behind the buildings, and be there in thirty seconds. It was a home away from home, of sorts. A place where I could bring twelve empty soda pop bottles and get two cents each for them—with an extra penny to buy a pack of football cards. My collection grew—I had every NFL great there was in the 1960's—-and I eventually had to use a second shoebox to house them all. The bubble gum in the card packs was awful, a brittle pink rectangle that I usually tossed in the garbage on the way out, eager to see who was in the new pack. On this one day I wanted a piece of gum. On the counter there was a large, uncapped jar full of Bazooka Joe single bubble gum pieces. They were a penny each. I suddenly felt daring. I wanted to see if I could get one without the clerk noticing. Would he miss just one? When he went to the back to tend to something in the cooler, I nabbed one.

At home, I felt so guilty I couldn't even look my parents in the eye. In my room was a cigar box with loose change, so I grabbed a penny, hopped the fence, and went back. The clerk looked like a guy in his thirties, tall with curly, sandy colored hair. I handed him the penny.

"What's this for? You want a piece of gum?"

I shook my head. "I already took it when I was here yesterday. I didn't pay for it though. I'm sorry."

The clerk stared at me. "Ok," he said quietly. "Don't do that again."

"I won't."

On a typically steamy August evening, I sat across from a 7-11 store in West Perrine, scratching out a report. The sergeant had told us to spend more time near and around convenience stores. They had been getting hit pretty hard in this area of the district with armed robberies, and it was probably the same group of guys. Within a few minutes, I saw a tall guy wearing a trench coat walk up to the front of the store slowly. He turned and looked west, then east, then inside, peering at the clerk.

Shit.

I took the mike off the clip holder asked the dispatcher for routine backup. Who the hell wears a trench coat in muggy, eighty-five-degree weather? This guy was about to do something, and I could feel the adrenaline begin its familiar rush in my limbs.

He went into the store and started walking back and forth. I noticed then that there was a little kid in there, about seven or eight, walking the aisles too, and he kept looking at Trench Coat. I could see only the kids head, as it bobbed around the store. The bobbing head would stop, stare at Mr. Trench Coat, then at the clerk. Did this kid see a gun on the subject, or what was going on? I was just about to get a backup when the kid came out of the store, walking parallel though the parking lot. My cruiser was in the dark and he never noticed me. I needed to find out what this kid saw in there, so I wheeled my green-and-white across 184th street, into the lot, and swung open the door.

"Hey kid," I called to him, "come here."

The boy stopped, frozen, and stared at me. Then he burst into sobs.

What the hell is this? I thought. The kid started walking towards my car—still sobbing—while pulling pieces of candy from his shirt, his underwear, his pants pockets, his socks, from any place that could hide gum and candy. I watched in amazement, as more candy than I thought any 8-year-old could secrete was jettisoned in all directions as he made his way to the car. By the time he made it to me, he left in his wake a trail of gum, bars, jujubes and who knows what else, some thirty yards long in the parking lot. The kid collapsed onto my leg, wailing uncontrollably, pleading, "Please don't call my mama...*please!*"

Good grief. I looked at the hapless, sobbing kid, whose nose and eyes were now dripping all over my pants. I was stunned. I looked at him, whining loudly in my lap, and then over at the serpentine trail of candy from my car to the walkway.

"Ok, ok, calm down," I told the kid, trying to peer into the store to see what Trench Coat was up to. My backup rolled up just as the tall guy came out. The clerk was fine; I could see him busy behind the counter. The suspect turned out to be unarmed—just a local weirdo who liked to wear trench coats during summer. We patted him down, wrote an FI card, and let him go. Nothing had happened.

Except of course, the discovery of the Great Perrine Candy Heist.

I spent another few months in uniform and then got another call from Homicide. This one was from Jack Remmen.

"Good news, buddy," Jack said. "You're comin' to Homicide, and you're workin' for me."

Chapter Five

GOYAKOD

On January 28th, 1985, four days after my twenty-seventh birthday, I walked into the Metro-Dade Police Department's Headquarters building, a dilapidated four-story building on NW 14th street next door to the Dade County Jail, and took the elevator to the second floor. I was finally here. I was finally a homicide detective.

The office was an open bay area with three clusters of desks pushed together. Senior detectives had a desk. Junior guys, like me, sat wherever there was spare seat, and we shared the phones. The sergeants' and lieutenants' offices were around the perimeter of the detectives' area. You could see everyone with one sweeping glance, unless they were sequestered away in one of the sergeant's offices, dictating a report. Under the yellowed fluorescent lighting, detectives worked every kind of death case imaginable. And some none of us could have imagined.

Above the entrance was affixed a carved wooden sign that read simply, GOYAKOD. It was an acronym we all lived by: *Get Off Your Ass and Knock On Doors.*

A new detective didn't take long in understanding GOYAKOD. If you were sitting at your desk, it had better be to make appointments with witnesses, study for an upcoming deposition or court appearance, or talk to a prosecutor, M.E. doctor, or lab analyst. Yes, we took a moment or two to exchange the well-worn jabs and insults. "Down time" was a mythical concept in Homicide. The answers to your unsolved cases were not going to be found within the walls of that building.

"Roll call!" the admin lieutenant would bark at seven am sharp. At that point all the conversation and bullshitting ceased and the LT would read whatever memos and directives had come down from the third floor (command staff). After that, he would go the previous days' cases.

"Sergeant Wesolowski, your team got one yesterday?" he might say, nodding to the lead detective, who would then briefly outline the case for everyone. Irv Nehr, our admin lieutenant, would conduct the rest of roll call that way. At the end, he would pick someone in the room, who would call out "Break!" and roll call was over. Nehr would continue with the *Miami Herald's* local section, reading excerpts from crime or political stories, smirking, joking, and making commentary as if he were hosting a late night show. Some of us would be half-listening, smiling and adding commentary of our own, but for the most part, it was *Goyakod*.

John King was my mentor in Homicide. King was senior man on our five-man squad, and Remmen assigned him to break me in. John had been in Homicide a good fifteen or so years at that time and he knew the ropes well. His *sotto voce* New England accent was often so faint it was sometimes hard to hear him. Stringy dark hair dangled along the top of his glasses. One afternoon, he loped in and waved his hand in the direction of the door.

"Suicide," he mumbled. "Let's go. This one's yours."

The FNG (the fuckin' new guy) on a homicide squad got all the non-homicides in the beginning: natural deaths, suicides and accidentals, to get broken in to the way things were done. If you were the FNG, you helped when the squad got a homicide, too, doing basically whatever the lead detective told you. I had worked with John on a couple of natural deaths and had been on a few scenes, but this was the first that I would be assigned to.

Stephen Jenkins' Toyota was parked in a field on a dirt road, surrounded by the brush and debris of a nearby seedy neighborhood. His body, slumped in the passenger seat, was cool and reeked of exhaust fumes. A plastic hose was taped carefully against the rear passenger door window with duct tape and routed down to the exhaust pipe of the vehicle, where it was tightly secured again. I learned that day that the 34-year-old's cherry red complexion was a typical marker of a carbon monoxide victim. On the passenger seat was a note to his wife, a small bottle of vodka, and a cassette tape that had come to the end who of what were probably his favorite songs. I wondered which song—his or the tape's—ended first.

His wallet was there, too, and John and I headed for the house. "What do you say to people?" I asked him.

John shook his head. "There's no easy way to do it. You just tell them, try to be as respectful as you can. Just do the best you can, you'll be fine."

By the time we finished the fifteen-minute ride to Jenkins' house, my heart was in my throat, and I was hoping there was no one home. Ah, but we had to do this eventually. I wondered about how she would react, and I steeled myself practicing some phrases in my head. We pulled onto the swale, and when we opened the car doors, the front door of the house opened a moment later. A brown-haired woman of about thirty-five, nicely dressed, stared hard at John, then me.

"He's dead," she said, "isn't he?"

Now what?

John and I exchanged a glance, and John shrugged slightly.

"Yes, Ma'am, he is," I heard myself say.

She nodded, turned, and waved us in. "I knew it. Come on in."

No other next-of-kin notification in my next twenty-one years went quite that smoothly. Stephen Jenkins' wife had struggled with his mental illness and several suicide attempts for most of their marriage. After our conversation I could see that his death was not only expected, it had come as a relief.

At the autopsy, the medical examiner sliced open his body and Jenkins' blood was a brilliant red, not the darker shade you usually see during a post-mortem exam. That, the doctor explained—just as John had said on the scene—is classic carbon monoxide poisoning.

Everything about my first-ever assignment was obvious and straightforward. My first homicide as the lead investigator would be no different. Fittingly, it was down in South District.

Benjamin Acero was drunk, and his wife was late coming home—again. When she finally arrived, he confronted her in angry slurs while their eight and ten-year-old children slept peacefully on the other side of their modest three-bedroom home in Cutler Ridge. She denied having the affair he accused her of, but as they wrangled through the night, Benjamin pulled a .22 caliber pistol from the closet. Julia Acero's called her friend Luz as Benjamin ranted at her. The woman could hear the fracas in the background.

"Are you alright? Is everything ok there?"

"Yes, yes, Luz..we're fine."

Then, with Benjamin roaring insults to her in the background, she whispered into the phone, "Luz, I'm *not* alright...help me...he's going to kill me..."

Moments later, Benjamin Acero fired a round from the pistol. In his drunken state, he missed, hitting the couple's waterbed. His second shot struck Julia in the chest.

Back in 1985, we still had 411—Directory Assistance, and the operator got a call from a man who had clearly come unglued.

"I shot my wife!" he wailed. "Help me, I shot my wife..."

With the calmest of voices, the operator said, "You've reached 411. Please hang up and dial 911."

Benjamin must've have certainly missed the comic nature of the exchange, and made the same frantic call to 911, who dispatched two uniform cars along with Fire-Rescue.

When the officers got to the front door, Benjamin was there, a sobbing mess. "I shot my wife!" he confessed for the third time in the space of five minutes.

After our team's arrival, Remmen went with me to Station 4, a place I knew well, where Benjamin was in custody. I opened the door to the interview room and saw a slightly heavyset, disheveled man with puffy, bloodshot eyes. I stuck out my hand.

"I'm Detective Nyberg," I said.

He returned the handshake. "I'm Benjamin, and I shot my wife."

Well, so much for two of the most difficult things in Homicide: making a next-of-kin notifications, and getting a confession. They would all be much harder after those two debuts. A fresh homicide case was either an "open pending" (which we called a "whodunnit") or CBA (closed by arrest), which Remmen liked to call "grounders." My first grounder couldn't have been easier, with Benjamin Acero continuing to make confessions all the way from Station 4 to the Homicide office, wallowing on the floor of my detective car, croaking "I shot my wife" over and over. Then we had a parade of witnesses like the victim's friend, Luz, the phone operators, and the responding officers. It was a sad situation the two kids woke up to—Mom dead, dad going to jail. They ended being taken in by their grandparents and went to live in Ft. Myers.

My second CBA involved two simpleton, ragtag brothers who didn't want to pay rent or be evicted went to the landlord's house and shot him. Most people shot once in the leg survive, but in this case the bullet nicked the femoral artery, and he was lights out in less than a minute, according to the M.E. The court case went pretty smoothly, overseen by a sharp and likeable prosecutor named Bill Howell. Both brothers got convicted and sentenced to life. Calm seas do not a good mariner make, goes the saying, and every new detective gets truly tested on his or her first whodunnit. Mine would come on the last day of August, 1985.

I spent two and a half weeks with a knot in my stomach that September, because we hadn't closed this sonofabitch yet. We had scoured every neighborhood in the north end, posted flyers, scoured the streets looking for info. Not a peep came back from the community, and that's not promising.

On the night of the homicide, we stood on the front steps of Modernissimo Italian Furniture, a large outlet just off the Palmetto Expressway in Miami Lakes, trying to decide just who was telling the truth. Jorge Palomo, the owner of Modernissimo, was at the Medical Examiner's Office on a metal table with a single .22 caliber gunshot wound to his chest. He had just had a meeting with his two business associates after closing, in the office of the two-story showroom, and according to the two survivors, they were accosted by robbers.

"It was three black guys," the manager told us. His shirt was torn, and his wire rimmed glasses bent. He claims this was from being roughed up by the three vicious bandana-wearing men. They made him and the company VP crawl on the floor, kicking them and jabbing them with the butt of a shotgun, demanding them to open the safe. They never got anything from the safe and had to settle for the men's wallets and watches.

"We don't even know the combination. The treasurer is the only one who knows, and she had gone home. They didn't want to believe that. They called us 'white pig' and told us to crawl. I thought they were going to kill us."

We did our scene work, finished up the statements late that night, and went on our way. Surely, we would get something in the coming days that would break the case. But we hadn't. Did the manager and the VP have a falling out with Palomo? Were they ripping him off and he discovered it? Did they do him in and concoct this elaborate robbery story, torn shirt and all? We couldn't discount it, not yet, and with each day that the robbers weren't found, that conspiracy theory howled louder.

Jorge Palomo was supposed to fly out of Miami the very next morning, back to his home in El Salvador, to celebrate his son's tenth birthday. Palomo was a big businessman in El Salvador and he had bodyguards shadowing him there wherever he went. He came to Miami without any protection, figuring that it was safer than the tumultuous and desperate streets of his country's capitol, San Salvador. Instead of celebrating with his young son, Jorge Palomo's cold body was being cut open.

I watched as the M.E. doctor's scalpel made ag a large "Y" cut under his clavicle from one armpit to the other, then down the middle to the lower pelvis. After he was opened up, I watched as the doctor pointed disturbed areas of tissue, the path of destruction the killer's .22 projectile took, front to back, slightly upward, and "riiight through the aorta," the doctor muttered with a with a small smile.

"Poor fellow didn't stand a chance after that." Dr. Jay Barnhart wasn't being disrespectful. He always had a smile on his face. Doctors like it when they can easily detect the cause of death, and this one would be simply typed, "perforating gunshot wound of the chest."

The lead investigator on a homicide attends the autopsy. That was the rule. You went there for several reasons, not the least of which was to give the doctor a briefing, though he already had a report we called the "M.E." sheet. The doctor would stick a needle in the heart, fill up a purple-topped test tube with blood, and give it to the detective as evidence. The lead then took that victim standard to the Crime Lab, where it was impounded for future comparison of any incoming unknown blood samples collected during the investigation.

Palomo had a small semi-circular bruise mark in the middle of his chest that looked exactly like the face of the barrel of a .22 caliber weapon. That and the soot on his shirt told us this was a "contact" wound.

One Sunday afternoon, after pounding the pavement for the better part of the month, our team sat in the office, working on reports, catching up on case file organization, and drinking coffee. Someone came singing down the hallway, and moments later a young effervescent uniformed officer came bounding in with a smile. He held up a plastic bag.

"Good afternoon gentlemen! I have something you might be interested in!"

In the plastic bag were Jorge Palomo's credit cards.

Officer Ricardo "Ricky" Ceballos' relatively slow Sunday afternoon had turned suddenly interesting—and strange—when he saw a naked man on the side of the road, waving him down. Once Ceballos got him wrapped in a yellow plastic blanket all officers carried in their trunk, he listened to the man's wild tale. It started with an apology.

"Sir, I'm sorry I know it's wrong," he told Ceballos. "I picked up this prostitute. She said we could smoke some base and have a good time for eighty dollars."

Freebase cocaine was the most sought-after drug in the inner city. Cheap and highly addictive, it attracted users from all walks of life. The shapely black girl led him to a second-story apartment in Lake Lucerne, a place well-known for drugs and shootings. Once inside he was accosted at gunpoint, relieved of his money *and* his clothes, and shoved outside.

Ceballos got a backup and went to the apartment. This is something he didn't have to do. Most officers would have taken the report, called Robbery, and been done with it. The Robbery detectives would follow up with it later. Once inside, Ceballos and his partner recognized it as a base house immediately. Inside was a woman who looked like the hooker the naked man had described. The young officer also noticed a butane torch on a table and a bunch of wired-out grungy looking people in various stages of wakefulness, draped around the apartment like dirty laundry. One man was hiding in the closet, and Ceballos aimed to find out why. Looking around the closet where the man had been, he found a bunch of credit cards.

He held them up to everyone. "These belong to anyone?" He asked. No takers, so he impounded them.

Ceballos, a determined former Marine, went above and beyond. All he was required to do was put the cards in an evidence bag and write up a report. The next morning, a detective would pick it up and do the follow-up work. But instead, he went to the station and started calling the credit companies. He got quite a surprise on his first call to one of the credit card companies.

"This card is stolen," the rep told him. "In a *homicide* case. Want the case number?"

After Ceballos told us the story, our Sunday, and the rest of that month, became very busy indeed. Our first order of the day was to get a search warrant for the apartment, and by that evening, we were watching SRT (Miami-Dade PDs version of SWAT) storm their way inside apartment 201.

"Ok, clear," the SRT supervisor called to us a couple of minutes later, and we hurried up the stairs. When I got inside, all the characters Ceballos had described were flex cuffed on the floor, as per SRT search warrant custom. One by one, we knelt next to them and got their names.

"Willie Harper," one guy with an afro told me. "My wallet is in my back pocket."

I opened the wallet and found Willie's driver license. But there was something else there, in the billfold area. It was money, but not familiar looking in any way. I pulled a stack of peach-colored bills from the wallet. They read, *El Banco Central De Reserva De El Salvador.*

It was time for Willie and me to have a chat.

"I don't know nothin' about no dead man, detective...I swear."

Willie sat two feet from me in an empty Lieutenant's office. The interview rooms were all occupied with detectives interviewing the rest of the denizens of apartment 201.

"Willie," I told him, going over the circumstances with him for at least the tenth time. "You're just full of lies, man, and you know it. C'mon, our dead victim's credit cards end up in the apartment where you live, and *you* end up with his cash. Gimme a break. You and I both know you've never even been to El Salvador. You couldn't even find it on a map. And you got a wallet full of El Salvadoran cash."

Willie's defenses were slowly waning. He shook his head, looking at the floor, and said, "I don't know how you can put me in this shit, man. How can you say I'm involved?"

I thought, damn Willie, do I have to draw it for you? And at that moment, I decided to do just that. I tore a square piece of paper from the Lieutenant's notepad, drew a stick figure, and labeled it "dead man." I drew an arrow from the dead man to a dollar sign and labeled it "dead man's money." I drew another stick figure, and another arrow from the dollar sign to the figure, which I named, "Willie's wallet."

"Does this make it a little clearer, Willie?"

Willie Harper stared at the crude diagram for a couple of minutes. Then he asked for my pen. He turned away as he wrote on the piece of paper, then he turned back to me, and wordlessly pushed the paper across the small space on the table between us.

Under my third-gradish art work, he had written the words: *If I give you the names of people who did it, what happens to me?*

I was sparkling with energy at that moment, knowing that closing my first whodunnit was close at hand. Fish *on*. Now, to get him in the boat. I had to choose my words carefully. This was a critical moment that could turn a suspect inward or push the door wide open.

"I can't promise you what's going to happen, but I know this much, Willie. You being truthful will help you out. The justice system treats truth tellers much more leniently than people who refuse to help. That man didn't do anything to you or the other guys who were with you. He didn't deserve to die like that."

Willie was thirty, and I made a silent wager with myself that he had a kid.

"That man has a ten-year-old son. That kid will never see him again."

Willie stared at me and swallowed.

I had to roll the dice a little here and having been in the interview room with him now for about three hours, I sensed he was smarter than the others. I remembered that both the manager and the VP had told us that one of the three guys didn't hurt them. That one guy seemed to be just along for the ride. From the way he spoke, I figured Willie was that guy. Let's get the money and get out. Willie might even be angry at the other two.

"Willie," I said, leaning forward and speaking quietly, "you're not like the other two dudes. I can tell that from talking to you. I don't think you wanted anyone to get hurt. You're not that kind of person."

He stared at me, then the floor, then the wall, and scooted his chair closer to mine. No one else was even within earshot of our closed office, but Willie's voice dropped to a whisper.

"I'm only telling you man. No one else." He looked around as if his voice might somehow leak through a vent, or under the door. *Here we go.*

"Ok," I whispered back.

"These guys are bad, man. I know both their names." He exhaled long and hard and stared at the floor. "I know 'em. They do *lots* of robberies. All over."

"And it's only a matter of time before they kill somebody else or get killed themselves. You're lucky, Willie, that we caught you now, before you got messed up in more of their shit."

He looked at me and nodded. "Yeah. You right."

And the fish was in the boat.

He tossed his head toward the paper, which was now a creation we had both made. "You're gonna use that against me, ain't you?"

I had some quick thinking to do. I couldn't tell him *no*, outright, because I figured a prosecutor would definitely want to introduce it. Telling him yes might cause him to clam up. I stayed non-committed. I said nothing, but tore the paper up and tossed it into the waste basket.

"There, Willie," I told him. "Let's keep talking. What you told me is important, especially for you."

In the next few moments, the Palomo case was revealed, like stadium lights illuminating a dark field. Willie tied together peripheral roles of some of the baseheads in the apartment, but most importantly he gave us the two other names that would roll this case up tight: Rowland Tucker and Larry Miller. Tucker was the shooter.

The fringe players were talking now too, in the other interview rooms. A lot of what they said corroborated Willie's story, but being baseheads, most of them didn't know a Tuesday from a Sunday or sometimes even a sunset from a sunrise. They lived from pipe to pipe. A basehead's life was smoking, sleeping, finding ways to buy more shit, and then more smoking, more sleeping.

What they were able to remember was significant: Tucker and Miller came to the apartment one night, bragging that they had "stung a cracker" and had "gotten paid." That's when cash, both American and El Salvadoran, was dumped on the table along with the men's watches and Palomo's credit cards.

The notepad paper with my caveman-era flow chart didn't end up in a landfill. After we locked Willie up that night, I went back into the Lieutenant's office and fished out the shreds of paper, and carefully taped it back together. It went into our evidence list.

For the next week, we served two more search warrants, one of which was on Tucker's apartment. There, we got a watch, a shotgun, and a pistol, though it wasn't the murder weapon. That was still out there somewhere. We got arrest warrants for both the other subjects, and we snagged Roland Tucker at his girlfriend's house. Tucker was a tough nut. He had been in many interview rooms and had been to prison before.

"I know what you're trying to do," he said, refusing to look at me. "I'll just do my time. I ain't sayin' shit. Take me to jail."

Miller was nowhere to be found. When we went to his aunt's house down in Goulds, where I had patrolled in uniform. She told us he had "left town."

As empty-handed as we had been the first two and a half weeks of the case, we now couldn't stop the information and evidence from pouring in. Willie called me from the Dade County jail a week after I had booked him in.

"Hey. You haven't found the gun yet, have you?"

"No Willie, we haven't. Why—can you help with that?"

"Yeah," he said. "It's buried in my girlfriend's front yard."

We went to the girl's house, and Willie assured us she knew we were coming. She pointed to the spot, and we unearthed a .22 cal pistol in a plastic bag. Our firearms guys in the lab matched it to the projectile Dr. Barnhart removed from Palomo's chest. Things were really cooking now.

Not three days later, a call came from a small town in Alabama. They had Larry Miller in custody.

My parents had some good friends in Fort Myers, an hour and half away on the west coast of the state. They had a big house on the Caloosahatchee River, and three kids I knew from when they lived in Miami. Their dad was Dr. Wallace Graves, the medical examiner for Lee County and two other surrounding rural counties in the area. At nine years old, I had no clue what a medical examiner was. To get to Fort Myers, you drove west on Highway 41 (there was no I-75 at the time), and then north on local highway 29, through Immokalee, a small agricultural town of where black folks still picked vegetables for work. Immokalee would have been largely forgettable except for one large glaring billboard at the entrance of town. It showed a white-robed Klansman on a horse, and blared the words, "You're in Klan Country."

"Tiny little nothing town...people with small minds," Dad muttered as we passed it.

Pritchard, Alabama is a small, poor municipality. It was settled by African slaves who had been spirited into Mobile harbor illegally on the slave ship *Clotilda*. After unloading the runaway slaves, the *Clotilda* was burned and sunk to avoid detection. Thirty-two of the one hundred ten slaves from the ship returned to the region and established "Africatown," later incorporated as Pritchard. Just south of Pritchard was the much larger city of Mobile, home of "Battleship Memorial Park," where the WWII hero battleship U.S.S. Alabama sits moored in silent majesty. Festooned with Japanese rising star emblems from its exploits in the Pacific, it likely casts shade on the sunken remnants of the *Clotilda*.

"So, y'all drove all the way up here, from Miami?" the detective supervisor from Pritchard PD asked Jack Remmen.

"No," Jack answered him, with a small smile, "we flew up."

The supervisor exchanged glances with a detective sergeant, who wore a porkpie hat and tie, and leaned forward in awe.

"So," the lieutenant inquired, "y'all *paid* for two plane tickets up here?"

"No, no," I broke in. "The police department paid for it."

The Pritchard Sergeant's jaw hung open. "For true? *They* paid for that?"

"Yeah," Jack told them. "And for our hotel too."

"*Hotel?*" The two men exchanged looks of complete astonishment. "That would never happen here. The city barely has enough money to pay us. We might not even get paid on time this week," the sergeant lamented.

"What happens," I asked out of curiosity, "if someone commits a murder, for example, and then leaves your jurisdiction—hits the road?"

The Lieutenant was quick to answer. "Oh. Tank-o-gas rule." His sergeant nodded in agreement.

"Tank-o-gas rule?" Remmen asked.

"Yep. City of Pritchard pays for one tank of gas for your car. That's it. After that, you wanna catch the bad guy? Fine. You're on your own."

I was very happy that the Miami-Dade Police Department had a policy significantly more generous than the "tank-o-gas" rule, otherwise we wouldn't be here to extradite Larry Miller back to our jurisdiction for Murder and Armed Robbery charges. Miller fled to go hide with at his grandmother's house in Pritchard. Three of Larry's female cousins lived there, too. These girls were all in their early twenties and had never had any contact with the criminal justice system until Larry showed up. One night, he told all three of them about the "man they robbed at the furniture store" and how an accomplice had killed the man. One of the girls told the grandma, and she decided to have no part of harboring Larry. She called the police.

We had Willie Harper wrapped up. The prosecutor offered him a phenomenal deal: plead guilty to second degree murder and robbery, get twenty years—likely be out in fifteen—and testify against Tucker and Miller. Harper's attorneys were in love with the deal. But three weeks later, Willie rejected it. He dumped the agreement and decided to plead "not guilty." Willie's stunning one-eighty had us frustrated—and confused—but we figured that Roland Tucker must have gotten to him somehow and threatened to have him killed if he ratted on him. Willie was now afraid to testify. He wouldn't say this, and we could never prove it, but it was the only theory that made any sense. Willie couldn't be rejuvenated. We had lost him—a huge blow to our case—and he would be tried separately from Tucker and Miller, who would stand trial together with a bunch of wasted base-addicts as witnesses.

In just about every murder case, the defense tries to exclude the state's best evidence from trial at a "motion to suppress" hearing. If the state is listing the murder weapon, seized during a traffic stop of the defendant, the defense will try to get it thrown out. Same with a confession. Was it coerced? Were Miranda warnings administered correctly? The motion to suppress was a no-brainer when a defendant was facing life, or worse. There was no downside for the defense to give it a try.

Public Defender Brian McDonald watched me carefully as I took the stand. I looked over at Willie Harper, his client, and made a weight-lifting motion with my arms. Willie had bulked up considerably since he had been in jail. Willie, who still shared a little bit of rapport with me, nodded and smiled.

Ten minutes later, McDonald was on full frontal attack, and I knew exactly where it was headed.

"So, Detective Nyberg. You apparently like to communicate with non-verbal gestures don't you?"

"Objection," the prosecutor droned, "relevance."

"Judge," McDonald argued, "just a few minutes ago, the detective looked at the defendant and made a motion about him working out with weights. It is an important gesture, as it is part of the core of my argument today. It goes towards some critical things that happened during the interrogation."

The judge leaned his head slowly back and forth as he contemplated McDonald's point. Thomas Carney was a fair, very firm man who had no time for nonsense or emotional manipulations by lawyers.

"Ok. Overruled."

"Detective," McDonald went on, "you just communicated with my client in a non-verbal way, when you made that weight-lifting gesture, didn't you?"

"I did," I said.

Mc Donald nodded, and pressed on. "And you communicated with him in the same type of non-verbal ways when you interrogated him in the homicide office, didn't you, when you two discussed his involvement in this case. Right?"

"I may have." The cartoon I drew on the notepad just had to be a part of this whole charade, I knew.

McDonald quickly moved my re-constructed note paper, complete with stick figures and arrows, into evidence. When he showed it to the judge, McDonald traced his finger down the page to highlight the tears and taping I had done, and Carney nodded. I decided I needed to minimize impact he was trying to create in any way possible.

Brian McDonald handed me the note paper and turned around swiftly.

"Who tore up the note, detective?" he said, walking away from me dramatically. He wanted me to panic, or worry or hesitate, so I answered as soon as I heard the "v" in the word detective.

"I did," I said calmly.

I could almost see disappointment on the back of the defense counsel's head.

McDonald went on to make a passionate argument that, by tearing up the note and throwing it in the trash, I had made a non-verbal promise to Willie that it wasn't going to be used against him. It was a good effort, a reasonable one, but Carney kept it in. The note was really an afterthought. We had Willie's confession and his prints on an electrical housing he told us they climbed to access the side of the building without being seen.

Willie was found guilty, and Carney, not happy about him snubbing the plea, skewered him: Life in prison, with twenty-five years minimum mandatory on the murder, and fifteen on the robbery, to run *consecutively*. If Willie ever got out, he would be 89 years old.

Mom and I were riding in her gray Rambler on 64th street when I asked her, "Mom, does God have a sense of humor?"

I was eight or nine, and it had been about a year since she had given me a colorful King James Bible, with a picture of a slender, white-robed Jesus, seated and talking to a bunch of people who sat at his feet. Mom was raised very strict Episcopalian by her devoutly religious mother. My Dad was so far away from religion that the two of them could have been from different planets, much less different upbringings.

"Religion is for weak people, Ramesh," he used to tell me. "It's a crutch. That's all."

In some sort of truce or compromise, they attended the Unitarian Church in South Miami, and for a while I went to Sunday school classes there. Not much about Christ, the resurrection, or anything intensely Christian was discussed at these classes. I don't remember being confused, because neither parent was overtly explanative with me about the concept of faith. The Unitarian church served as a demilitarized zone for their two disparate views on religion. One thing I learned, from my own observations: my mother was far from weak.

"Yes," she said, smiling at me, "I think god does have a sense of humor. He gave us a sense of humor and lots of other wonderful gifts, so I'm sure he has a sense of humor too."

Later that night, she told me she was glad I asked that question. "What's important," she said, "is to remember that what we DO is always seen by god. If we act badly, and hurt others, we will suffer too."

I kind of knew what she meant.

After we brought Larry Miller back on our warrant, I went back to Pritchard again, to take sworn statements from the three girls. Gary Rosenberg, one of the prosecutors on the case, joined me on the trip. When it was time for trial, Rosenberg and his partner, Michael Cornely, were in a quandary. The three sisters didn't want to come to Miami, citing that they had somehow been tricked. "Those men" who came to interview them, they said, never told them they were law enforcement. They told the judge in Mobile that we disguised ourselves as lawyers trying to help Larry.

Our judge reluctantly agreed to a "writ of bodily attachment" but cautioned us: "The judge in Alabama doesn't have to honor it. It's not an order, it's a request. I know you need these girls here as witnesses for trial, but the judge in Alabama can do what he wants."

And he did.

The judge in Alabama sent deputies out to the home of Larry Miller's grandmother and promptly arrested all three of his cousins.

"You'll stay in jail," the judge told the astounded girls, "until the detectives from Miami come and get you, and then you'll go to Florida and testify in their trial."

We were as amazed as we were delighted. When Jack Remmen and I landed in Mobile this time, we went directly to the Mobile County Jail where our witnesses were locked up, just as the judge had said. These girls didn't have a parking ticket between the three of them, and here they were, wide-eyed and in handcuffs, boarding a jet to Miami.

The trial of Tucker and Miller was a disaster. Without Willie, we had to rely on the testimony of five strung-out addicts whose brains had been scorched by cocaine smoke. Freebasing was an epidemic, and those who counted themselves as addicts could be found in every walk of life, old and young, black, white, ghetto teenager or Brickell Avenue accountant. It didn't matter. It sucked everyone in and didn't let you out of enslavement unless you went to prison or died. These walking ghosts were so horrible on the stand it was pathetic, and on the guilt of the two most culpable subjects, the jury did what we feared most: on Tucker, not guilty. On Miller, a hung jury. We could re-try him if we could somehow make the case better, but that seemed a doomed prospect, with these zombies as witnesses. It was heartbreaking.

I woke up every day with a sick feeling in my stomach. After all our hard work, the murderers of an innocent man were walking free. Only Willie Harper—who had not even carried a gun during the crime—-sat in a prison cell. A month after the verdicts, King and I flew to Chicago to interview a witness in one of his cases. When we got back, Remmen met us at the airport.

He gave me a slow-motion punch in the arm. "Got some good news for you, buckaroo," he said in his typical deadpan way.

"Yeah? What is that?"

A smile crept across his face. "Rowland Tucker is dead. He was playing with a gun at a base house in Opa-Locka and shot himself in the head."

King laughed. "There *is* a god!"

Two months later, Larry Miller walked into a Citgo Quick Mart gas station down in Perrine. Checking to see if there were any witnesses nearby and seeing none, he pulled a gun on the clerk and demanded all the money in the register. The clerk pulled a 9mm semi-auto from under the counter and began firing. The tiny market filled with ear-splitting explosions and the acrid smoke of burnt gunpowder.

Moments later, the clerk, unharmed, dialed 911 as Larry Miller lay bleeding on the floor. He would survive, but Larry Miller would push himself around in a wheelchair for the rest of his days, paralyzed for life from the waist down.

It seemed Mom was right on the money about god.

Chapter Six

Whodunnits

Palomo was my first "whodunnit." They didn't give you one until you had cut your teeth on at least a couple of CBAs. Because it was the first unsolved assigned to me, those three weeks before Officer Ceballos came waltzing in with Palomo's credit cards ground my gut every morning when I woke up, thinking of how we hadn't solved this man's murder yet. It was also why, when the jury came back "not guilty" on Tucker and hung on Miller, the grind, the bitterness, was dug even deeper into my conscience.

But when the universe came to the rescue, and the sense of humor Mom told me about became reality, my idea of *justice* took on new complexion. Jorge Palomo's widow, Maria Palomo was a lovely, dignified woman. She had returned to El Salvador after the trial with what I am sure was her own brand of bitterness and disappointment. Thugs had killed her husband, robbed her children of their father, and had gone free. When the phone rang, she picked up on the third ring.

"Mrs. Palomo," I said, "this is Detective Nyberg."

Her voice was polite. "Oh, yes, Detective?"

"I have some news," I told her. I explained what had happened to Roland Tucker. I could hear her swallow and choke on her tears on the other end, and she cleared her throat.

"Thank you...thank you very much for this. It's very good news," she said, and I could swear I could *hear* her smile.

Freebase cocaine ruled the streets of Miami's ghettos in the mid-1980's. Joyce Burrows, a shapely, 26-year-old woman with a young son being reared by Joyce's grandmother, spent most of her time on the street now. With an insatiable appetite for the white paste, she roamed her Liberty City neighborhood in search of a cock she could suck or could lift her skirt for, anywhere, anytime, for twenty or thirty dollars. She would then find the nearest supplier (who was never more than a few blocks away) where she could draw that precious smoke into her bloodstream and get the rush she lived for. That, like so many other desperate women on the streets, was her life: get a fistful of bills for letting others use your body, smoke base, sleep, eat. Rinse and repeat.

One morning in an overgrown lot at the corner of 59th street and 22nd avenue, a pair of kids walking a worn grass path through the lot saw a naked woman. They stopped, unsure of what to do, until they realized the naked woman wasn't breathing. Joyce Burrows in fact, hadn't taken a breath since some time the previous night or early morning. It had been a panicked breath, as she fought in futility to free herself from a ligature someone had wrapped tightly around her throat and choked her to death.

"Sub-conjunctive hemorrhages," Dr. Valerie Rao pointed out with her pen pointing at Joyce Burrows' heavily bloodshot eyes. "And the ligature marks, which you noted on the scene, Ramesh," she went on in her thick Indian accent, "this poor girl was choked very violently, very powerfully. I'm sure we'll find a lot more during the neck dissection."

In 1986, the Medical Examiner's office was a tiny afterthought in the bowels of the enormous Jackson Memorial Hospital complex. Everything in the place smelled faintly like decomposition, right down to the paper clips in the reception area. Because of the skyrocketing murder rate we dealt with, the morgue was crowded with bodies. There were times that the freezer, where bodies were kept on gurney tables until autopsy, were so jammed with corpses that they were stacked *on top* of one another to save space. The day I went in for Joyce Burrows' post, three other cases had just come in, one being a horrific motorcycle accident in which two of a young rider's limbs had been torn from his body. The torso and parts were on a gurney shoved in a corner of the busy morgue.

Joel, a mustached and burly morgue attendant with a Brooklyn accent, looked at me in despair.

"This is incredible, Nyberg...I dunno what we're gonna do, where we're gonna put all this?" He motioned to the room full of bodies. He was on a tirade from being overworked.

"Can you fuckin' believe it?" he went on. "While I'm trying to figure out where to put one body, this guy comes in." In that moment of exasperation, Joel grabbed the motorcyclist's severed arm and tossed it in the air. He didn't even look as the bloody arm cartwheeled slowly in the air and dropped back down on the gurney with a thud.

"It's incredible, I tell ya." Joel stared at me and shook his head.

Great, I thought. Just when you think you're winning the battle against being de-sensitized to human carnage, someone flips a fucking arm in the air.

"Joel, help me find my murder from this morning," I said, gently shouldering past him before he tossed any more body parts.

Joyce had been beaten, but strangulation was clearly the cause of death. As Dr. Rao carefully exposed the layers of neck muscle and pointed to the pinpoint hemorrhages, she asked me about the circumstances. I explained it, and then she dug deeper, showing me the hyoid bone.

"The hyoid is fractured," she announced softly as she cut the bone away from the depths of Joyce's throat to keep as evidence. "Only with very heavy force does that happen."

We would develop a suspect, a light-skinned, odd-mannered local with a beat-up light blue pickup truck. Several people we talked to mentioned him as being a street associate of Joyce's. One of them even said he was parked nearby the scene early that morning. This suspect had been seen the previous night of the discovery in the company of another dude they called "Blowfish." We also developed another witness they called Red.

But the Burrows case had hurdles similar to those in the Palomo investigation: these "witnesses" were the neighborhood's bottom feeders and drug addicts. Blowfish, twenty-nine-years old, watched cartoons all morning before he went out to find drugs, and Red was a small-time dealer, interested only in making a hundred or so dollars a week hustling cocaine on the street to support his own habit and have enough left over to eat. Like the Palomo witnesses, a Monday wasn't terribly different from a Saturday (though I'm sure Blowfish knew Saturdays for his precious cartoons) and their perception of time was warped. The hands on a clock held no relevance in their lives. There was darkness, light, and freebase cocaine.

In trying to develop suspects, we reviewed criminal activity in the neighborhood and found three other unsolved homicides of black females, all within a mile or two of the Burrows scene—all strangled. My efforts on building case against our pickup truck owner now had a parallel aspect: who had killed these other girls? Was the light-skinned pickup truck guy a serial killer?

Within a week, "Red" was shot and killed in a drug deal. Our solvability score slipped down the ladder a bit. Two weeks after Red's untimely departure, a woman was being harassed and slapped around by a large black male outside a grocery store not a block away from where Joyce Burrows' body was found. An older man came to the young woman's rescue, and stood in front of the woman's attacker, demanding he stop. The younger, bigger guy gave the old man a brief pounding, and told him to mind his own business. The old man went to his car, retrieved a pistol, and shot the younger man in the chest, killing him. The deceased woman-beater was none other than Anthony "Blowfish" Ealy. Our two most promising sources—guys that we believed were in the company of Joyce and our light-skinned suspect on the night of her death, were gone.

Even with the case against Mr. Pickup Truck deteriorating, we continued trying to see if there were links between Burrows and the other girl. The City of Miami Police had two other cases that seemed to fit the criteria, and now we were looking at *five* black females, all between nineteen and thirty years old, all strangled, all found within two miles of each other in Liberty City.

I went into Remmen's office and showed him the other homicides.

"Lemme go talk to the L.T. about this," he said.

We continued trying to drum up witnesses in the neighborhood, and all we got were vague references to our first suspect and even less useful mentions of Joyce's brief and nameless companions she frequented, all to sate her freebase addiction. The other dead girls were heavy basers too. We didn't get any closer, and other cases were still arriving at a good clip along with the normal flow of accidental deaths and suicides. Many of the homicides were street level idiocy like the one that was Blowfish's undoing. Others were drug related homicides of every kind, from Colombian cartel hits involving millions of dollars to low-level dime bag rip-offs, like the one that got Red killed. But they all needed attention. They all required the manpower of our already overworked detective roster.

An open homicide investigation is a *project*. From the moment you're standing on the scene, looking down at the lifeless body, you've embarked on something you're not supposed to stop working on until you've either solved the case or completely run out of resources to help you do so. In corporate America, when you're given a project, you're rarely given a second one until you've completed the first. Not the case in police work. If it's your squad's turn, you're getting another project, whether you're "ready" for one or not. You didn't stop working on the other cases; you had to become a diligent time manager to make sure you kept following up whatever leads you had on all the cases you were working on, including the ones you were just assisting other detectives on.

In the 1980's, our "projects" were coming in fast and furious. At the center of the cyclorama of death and mayhem were young men in ties, who rolled up their sleeves, put on gloves, worked the scenes, took witness statements, pored over evidence, attended autopsies, and diluted the impossible onslaught with alcohol in Miami night clubs. The next morning, they started it all over again. The "rotation" policy was that each team took a turn being "up" for the murder, and when they got one, they wouldn't be up again until the other squads all got one. Once a month, you were the "on-call" team, and might get called out in the middle of the night. The rotations were cycling quickly, with an average of one homicide coming in per day. It wasn't uncommon for us to be on the phone with witnesses, out in the field, or taking bagged evidence to the lab, and the phone would ring. Someone on another team would answer it, and then call out, "Who's up for the murder?"

At times it would get stressful and we felt like were shoveling sand while a dump truck was pouring it at our feet in mountainous proportions. It was important to break the stress, and our squad was always finding ways to do so. Our old phone system was designed so that you could go back into the Centac office and call in to the Homicide office from another line. Our squad had been swamped that particular week, and I had been grumbling about the case load, having just gotten two suicide cases in the midst of all the paddling against the tide on the Burrows case.

One day, Mike Tabernero was one of the only guys in the office and was always quick to grab an incoming call, so I went back to Centac and had Detective Gary Lefebvre call in and pretend he was a uniform officer with a big case.

"Pour it on," I told Gary. "Make it sound like a monster case." And he did.

"Metro Homicide, Detective Tabernero," Mike answered dutifully.

"Yeah," Gary said, "this is Officer Johnson from Central...we got a triple homicide out here on 62nd street and 18th avenue. We need you guys to respond."

Mike grabbed his pad and started writing. "A *triple*, you said?"

I slowly walked up, watching him, and Gary was doing an Academy-award performance.

"Yes, there's um...three dead, and I think at least four or five wounded. We got people laying in the street...the suspects are at large..."

"Three dead, five wounded..." Mike repeated, scribbling on the pad. "What's the location again?"

I walked closer, feigning impatience. "What have we got Mike, what is it?" Mike covered the mouthpiece and waved me off.

"Another homicide?" I said, pacing, "are you fucking kidding me?"

Mike waved at me to quiet down as he wrote and talked to "Officer Johnson" about this monumental shooting.

"Fuck it!" I yelled. "Tell them we're not coming."

Mike looked at me, his eyes wide. "Nyberg! Shut up and let me get the information—this is a triple murder."

"A triple!" I poured it on now. "Oh great, just what we need. Tell them we can't do it—"

"We can't do that!" Mike said, "Will you *calm down*?"

Then I snatched the phone out of Mike's hand and yelled into the phone, "Fuck you, we're not coming!" I slammed the handset down.

Mike sat stunned, his eyes like saucers. "Holy shit...Nyberg has fucking *lost it!!*"

Just then, Gary Lefebvre came out from Centac, laughing hysterically, and I started cracking up.

Mike looked at Gary, then me, and shook his head. "You *assholes!*" he said, but he was laughing too.

The call that came in on May 1st, 1986 was no prank. The Joyce Burrows case was some four months old and still unsolved. We started branching out to drum up more intel, looking at other people our only known suspect had crossed paths with. We kept an eye on him too, as much as we could with our team rotating the incoming cases between us. And then, that May 1st afternoon, someone from the corner of the homicide office called out, "Who's up for the murder?" Well, that was us, Squad C, and that would be *me,* up next in rotation. It was time again to get a fresh pad, and head out to see who our next "project" was going to be.

H and R Hoist and Rentals was a crane and heavy equipment company up in the northwest section of the county. H and R consisted of a dirt compound for the cranes and machinery, and a couple of poorly maintained trailers that served as the company's headquarters. One of the trailers was the office of the company VP and manager, Jack Harold Wilcox, fifty-three years old.

Wilcox now lay on the office floor, cold and still, a single bullet wound in the back of his head.

Across the street from my house on Southwest 62nd Ct, my friend Don and his mother lived. A derelict 1950's era Plymouth sat in the front of the house, and just a few feet beyond that was large circular ditch in the rocky swale next to the road. When it rained hard enough, that ditch filled up. Don and I, as well as a few of the other neighborhood kids, had a huge puddle to play in. In the summer we got almost daily rains, and our muddy mini-pond was never empty. Don took flat pieces of plywood he would find in the alley and we would "wop-board" across the puddle; our version of surfing. When we weren't sitting inside the old Plymouth, bouncing on the sponging seats as if we were driving, we were splashing or wop-boarding around until we were breathless. My parents weren't huge fans of the puddle, as I would usually come home soaking wet and muddy.

I had a recurring dream at that age, with me playing at the edge of that mud puddle. I had it at least five times between the ages of eight and ten: I'm kneeling by the puddle and a car comes racing down the street. Inside are four Chinese-looking men; they look directly at me as they pass, and I watch the car race up 62nd Ct. The little car goes streaking past the stop sign across the intersecting road, and smashes violently into a large concrete wall. I am transfixed as I stare at the car. Out of the wreckage, the four men emerge one by one and look directly at me. Then, they are coming FOR me. I begin to run across the street to the safety of my house, but my legs turn to lead. I am straining to make it across the street, willing my legs to churn faster. I watch in terror as the four men, wearing tiny, sinister grins, advance towards me. They are gaining, but I'm barely out of the mud puddle. Then, I wake up.

The employee who found Jack Wilcox' body ruefully recounted to me what time it was and what he was doing when he entered H and R's main drive, in the middle of which was a large hole filled with the previous week's rain.

"I was cussin' at the mud hole," he said, describing his navigation around the giant puddle as he headed towards Wilcox' office.

When I was growing up, most Miamians I encountered were transplants from the Carolinas, Georgia, and other corners of the South. Many were former servicemen who had been stationed at Florida's numerous military bases. For the next twenty years, most of them would leave south Florida. You didn't hear phrases like "cussin' at the mudhole" very often in the 1980's. The southerners who stayed, it seemed, all went to work at places like H and R Hoist.

Earlier that day, some unknown person had also snaked their way around the rocky, muddy trail that was the entrance to H and R Hoist. That person had likely taken great care that no one was around when they finally made it to the office trailer. They maneuvered their vehicle back out to the main road, too, around that mud hole, as Jack Wilcox lay on the trailer floor dying.

Jack and his wife Frances lived in Key Largo, a good two-hour drive from H and R. It was worth the drive for Jack. He loved the water, loved boats and diesel engines, and had been a champion offshore boat racer in the 60's and 70's with racing legend Mike Gordon aboard Gordon's boat, *Fish Peddler*, named after Gordon's Miami seafood restaurant on Biscayne Bay. Jack's father, H.C. Wilcox, had a diesel engine shop in Miami on NW 27 avenue for decades. Anyone who knew diesel brought their engines there for troubleshooting and repair. Jack helped his dad work on diesel engines for boaters and heavy equipment owners alike. He built a reputation no one else in the local industry could touch. Later, Jack excelled at racing the "runabout" boats that became a popular racing design of the era.

"Jack is the finest racer I've ever seen in a runabout boat," Hank Langenskamp, a champion racer told the New York Times in 1971. To this day, professional racers gather in Key Largo to win the offshore boat racing trophy in an annual event called the Jack Wilcox Memorial Boat Race.

Frances Wilcox sat in one of the lieutenants' offices at the Homicide Office and fidgeted slowly with her hands. We didn't put next-of-kin in the tiny, dirty interview rooms, where we talked to suspects and witnesses. Families of murder victims deserved better surroundings. Frances' voice trembled slightly, as the voices of widows often do, but I would come to know that her tone always had a delicate, almost charming waver to it. She told me everything she knew about Jack, marveled at what a great, fun man he was to be around, of all the things he had accomplished, and of his love for boating.

"I don't know what I'm going to do without him," she told me.

Frances called daily that week to find out what was going on with the case. But we didn't have much to tell.

Investigating the death of a man as gregarious and well-known as Jack is a daunting journey, with trails and paths crisscrossing everywhere. They all had to be followed up. Jack knew lots of people. He knew his secretary, we soon found out, *quite* well.

Billy Roper founded the company with a guy named Michael Hipps. Hipps and Roper (H and R) split; Roper bought Hipps out and partnered up with Jack. What better asset to have in a heavy equipment company that provided man and materiel to construction crews than Jack Wilcox? The company scuttlebutt, Roper told us, was that Jack was dallying heavily with the company secretary, Denise. He found mini-cassette tapes Jack had recorded on a hand-held recorder in his office. The tapes were made for Denise, recounting their wild and steamy escapades—some on Jack's office desk—while on the long drive back to Key Largo.

In an interview room, Denise sat staring at me, wide-eyed as a lemur as she answered each question. The next one I had to craft carefully, so that it wouldn't sound too harsh.

"Did you have...more than just a professional relationship with Jack?" She froze, her eyes getting even wider. In a hoarse whisper, she said, "Yes."

Investigations, if they are moving in the right direction, eventually start eliminating people. But in the early stages, it can often widen the pool of suspects. Now that we knew about Jack's affair with Denise, the suspect list technically consisted of, Denise, her boyfriend—whomever he may be—Frances Wilcox, Billy Roper, and Michael Hipps. Those were the prominent candidates because the possibility of a random robbery seemed so unlikely.

Roper was starting to act odd. Just three days into the case, Denise called me and told me she had an interesting story to share. Billy Roper invited her to lunch the day after the murder. During their outing, he launched into a bizarre tale that had her head spinning.

"He told me that Jack had been running drugs for the Nicaraguan mafia," she reported.

It was a startling and bizarre tale. Drug smuggling was synonymous with the decade, to be sure. Colombians and their cartels were well known, and Jamaicans had recently gotten very busy in the cocaine trade. But none of us had ever heard of a Nicaraguan organization having any significance in the drug export trade. Denise described Billy Roper as "rambling" and not making a lot of sense. It was intriguing, to say the least.

Then there was a guy named Brett, a mechanic who had a dispute with Jack on the phone about some diesel engine parts. Jack wanted him to pay for them, and the guy said they were no good. Bring the parts to me, Jack said, and I'll look at them. Brett was supposed to show up the day of the murder. We hadn't yet found Brett, and no one else could confirm if he had shown up or not.

The evidence didn't do much for us; a single expended .25 caliber casing. Blood evidence that indicated that Jack was shot while sitting at his desk, and then pulled off the chair, onto the floor. We got an unidentified fingerprint from a table against the wall opposite Jack's desk. No one had seen anything, or anyone. Denise had a decent alibi, as did Frances, though ostensibly she could have hired a killer, had she found out about Jack's affair. Billy Roper was the only one whose alibi couldn't be proven or disproven. The Nicaraguan Mafia stuff was unsubstantiated, if not pure folly. Jack had no connections we could find to organized crime that we could readily find. He was a good ol' boy Miamian with roots in the boat racing business, though we knew that the boat racing business was a wealthy man's sport, and drug smugglers were known to be in the industry. Wilcox loved his bourbon, his house in the Keys, and his family. Denise had to be included in his favorite past times as well. After a month, we were no closer to solving Jack's murder than we were solving Joyce's.

All we knew was that, for a brief few seconds on May 1st, 1986, the rippled image of the killer's vehicle—maybe even the killer's face—-was reflected up to the sky by the ragged mirror of H and R's gatekeeper—the mudhole.

Jack Remmen nodded towards the door that led across the hall, where Captain Wayne McCarthy's office was.

"Let's go. Captain wants to meet with us." The *Captain?* What was this?

Fifteen minutes later, I learned that I was being pulled off of Squad C – "detached," it was called—and paired up with a Cold Case Detective named Greg Smith. Smith and I were to work the murders of the black females I had found in my research, to try to determine whether we might have one offender (a "serial killer") or whether the deaths of these girls—there were *seven* now—were all coincidence. I looked at Jack Remmen after we left McCarthy's office.

"What about the Jack Wilcox case?"

"What about it?" he said, "Is there something I don't know? You close to charging somebody?" He and I both knew the answer to that, so I said nothing. Clearly, the possibility of a serial killer in Miami was priority.

The next day, we had another meeting, this one at the Medical Examiner's Office, with Doc Davis and a supervisor from the City of Miami's Homicide unit to go over the unsolved murder cases Joyce Burrows, Cynthia Driver, Leatrice Knighton, Joann Hamilton, Kathleen Fox, Weida Brown, and Cynthia Phillips (the City of Miami's case).

Sifting through the photos, the stillness of death was never lost on me. This was especially true on the scene itself, but by now I had been on enough death scenes that even just viewing the photos brought me there: the absence of the rising and falling chest, the unblinking eyes, even as flies buzz around them. You looked at a body, and you tried to piece together their last moments. You tried to picture them laughing, or crying, or just walking, waving down a car, walking down a bushy path to a dark corner to make a few dollars, sitting in a crowded base house, sucking on a homemade pipe fashioned from a crushed beer can. Then someone wrests the life from them, and the motionless husk is left.

That's when we show up. The husk is ours. We study it, cut it open, study it some more, try to make it come alive again. It was a play on a stage, except we only get the final scene, frozen in time. We have to figure out the previous scenes and what the characters were doing in them.

"So," Frances Wilcox asked me during her weekly call, "what else have we found out?"

I told her that Billy Roper was acting weird, that there were still people to talk to, that nothing had transpired with the mechanic, and, oh yeah: I'm off the case.

"But, why? I mean, because of these...hookers?"

"Yes," I tried to keep my sigh from sounding too deep. "Look Frances, it won't be forever. I could have told you we're going to be working the case every day, like we were, but I'm just not going to lie to you like that."

Her silence on the other end was deafening. Then, finally, in her sharp, trembly voice: "When do you think you'll be back on it?"

"As soon as we figure out this mess. As soon as we can decide whether we have a serial killer on our hands or not."

She and I both knew that wasn't soon enough.

Greg Smith and I ran down lead after lead in every one of those cases. Some of those leads were lukewarm, others flat out cold. These cases, like Joyce's murder, had been set aside during the onslaught of incoming homicides. None of the lead detectives had forgotten them, they had been forced to set them aside to handle new arrivals. In between interviewing people we found in the reports, we would go out late at night and interview hookers in Central District. It wasn't long before we knew their haunts and knew almost all of them by name.

There was always a cluster of them around 17th avenue and 79 Street. We widened our inquiries, going into the City of Miami from Biscayne Boulevard and 79th down as far as 36th street. Pockets of girls worked out of old hotels like the Seven Seas, the Sinbad, and The Biscayne. Most of these young women were dirty, infected, and desperate. They would risk getting in a car with a total stranger because if they could make thirty bucks they could keep scoring base. Even a five-dollar blowjob would get them a hit or two on a pipe in some dingy back room or alley somewhere. Many of the girls got to know us, but the ones who still saw us as a threat would see our unmarked K-car roll up, yell "99!" (ghetto code for police) and scatter.

One night we caught up to a few of them at the corner of 17th and 79th street and convinced them we weren't there to arrest them. The others slowly warily of the shadows when they saw us conversing. Soon we had a group of four or five. We asked them if anyone had tried to hurt them, if they heard anything about someone choking girls, anything that could help, and we showed them Joyce's picture.

"Uh-huh," one girl said, nodding. "I seen her. On 22nd. What happened?"

The girl cried when we told her she was dead, and we made sure she got our business card. These young women came to trust

Greg and me and were opening up. None of them, however, had anything concrete. None of them knew first and last names of their johns or even the other girls.

"Come back on Friday night, about one in the morning," she told us. "There's a lot more girls out here then."

We did, and this time we stopped at Dunkin Donuts to pick up a bunch of coffees and two dozen donuts. When we pulled up, the girls all started scattering again. Then, Greg and I got the goods out and put them on the hood of the car.

"Hey, we got donuts and coffee!" We called out to them. Greg and I grinned at each other as they stopped and started walking back to us. There we were, two detectives in ties, at 1:30 in the morning, having donuts and coffee with a bunch of prostitutes on a dark Liberty City street. The girls got talkative and one of them told us about an apartment down off 71st street where Joyce and others go to smoke. They told us some people there know what happened. Information like this always got you a little charged up, but we also had to remember that these were base addicts telling us this, and you never knew what was accurate and what was bullshit. At least this small crew knew they could talk to us.

"Thanks for the donuts, ninety-nine," one of them called as they walked away.

The next night, around midnight, Greg and I parked around the corner from a cluster of rickety old apartments and walked the alley between the two buildings. We found the apartment and heard some people talking and inside. It smelled like weed. We knocked on the door, and someone cracked it open about an inch, looked at us, and slammed it shut.

"Fuck it," Greg said, and kicked the wooden door in. We burst in with our guns out and saw a guy run out the back door. We let him go, as we had two other people inside. We kicked in another closed door and a woman sitting on the toilet, stark naked, screamed when she saw two cops with guns.

When things calmed down, we got their names and talked to them. The naked woman put a towel around herself and begged us not to arrest her. We it was a know what was in the apartment and that we didn't care. We just wanted to find out what happened to this girl. She looked at the picture and nodded. "I've seen her here."

But that was all she knew.

And so it went, week after week, interviewing street girls, pimps, and johns, with little else but the occasional nod of recognition. We were showing pictures of the other girls too, to try and jog someone's memory. One girl told us she knew someone that could help, but two days later she was killed in a shooting. Every street whore in the area knew the tall salt-and-pepper detective team of Smith and Nyberg. We talked to several girls three or four times.

Nancy Williams was a rare white girl in the area who liked Biscayne Boulevard but could be found just as readily with a gaggle of black girls over on 17th, where we had our donut party. She was lanky, with red sores on her face and stringy brown hair. One night, she was on 79th street, wearing a pair of tiny shorts. Her pubic hairs were so long they were sticking out from the legs a good three inches. How anyone could be desperate enough to drop their drawers and *pay* for that kind of company was mind-boggling to me. But Nancy was a street vet and seemed to know everyone. We ran into her many times, so much that when she saw us she would wave *us* down.

"Nyberg," she said to me one time, looking me up and down, "I'd like to sex your ass one day."

I just chuckled at her and held down my vomit.

Nancy said she knew pimps who knew girls who knew what happened. But we heard that from others. Shreds of information, like the smoke from a base pipe, just seemed to curl off into a corner and dissipate. The jumbled, desperate galaxy of freebase cocaine and street sex in Liberty City left us empty-handed. The players were all so focused on the next hit of a pipe that, even if they did know something, they didn't care enough to tear themselves away from their next fix. We were beginning to think that the truth about Joyce's murder—as well as the other victims—lay in the grave with Blowfish and Red. Our main suspect also knew the truth, but after a brief interview with us, he was no longer talking.

Of the seven murder cases, Leatrice Knighton had the most promise, because her murder was the most recent before Joyce, and she had lived just a half mile away from our crime scene. We finally developed a suspect named Laudell Allen. Leatrice's family said Allen had been stalking her weeks before her body was found. After some bloodhounding, we followed his trail all the way to New Mexico, of all places. Allen had found a job from someone he knew out there and gotten arrested for robbery. He was in custody, so that would make things easier once we got out there. The more we talked to people in Leatrice's circles, the more they had to say about Laudell. He was looking strong as Leatrice's killer. We found absolutely nothing, however, that would link Allen to Joyce's murder. Greg Smith and I headed west, landed in Midland-Odessa, Texas, and drove past miles of tumbleweeds and cotton fields out to the desert town of Hobbs, New Mexico to talk to Laudell Allen—and anyone else Laudell had spoken to.

The band at the Brass Bottle was *really* good.

They were into their second set, doing *Heard it in a Love Song* by Marshall Tucker, when Greg and I were into our third or fourth Jack Daniels on the rocks, enjoying the music and drawing a stare or two as the newcomers to town. The Brass Bottle was clearly the place to unwind in Hobbs, New Mexico. We had just gotten back from Lovington, about a forty-five minute jaunt north of

Hobbs, after interviewing seventeen of Laudell Allen's former and present cellmates at the state prison there. The prison personnel there treated us like royalty. The Lieutenant even moved out of his office for the day and told us to hold the interviews there. We gave him a list, and he made sure that his people brought the inmates in, one by one.

Conducting prison interviews is like panning for gold. Most of the time you won't get anything. But every so often, someone has a nugget that can make your case. Lovington didn't yield much except one fellow who said that Laudell had confided to him that he had "done something pretty bad" in Miami, and that itself was worth the trip. Now, we had worked up a thirst, and we had asked the Detective we had been working with, Tony, where to go.

"Brass Bottle," he told us. "I'll try to meet you there." We got there around eight, and Tony paged us a few minutes afterward, apologizing that he couldn't make it. Greg and I, however, had been on trips to small towns several times, and we were comfortable being the new kids in town. It was the night before Halloween. The Brass Bottle had a few spooky decorations around and we sat at one corner of a sawdust covered dance floor, toasting our success at the prison with Jack Daniels.

Our server, a short, chipper brunette in a black short skirt, learned a little more about us each time she came by, whether she wanted to or not. That's the way it always was with Greg. He loved to talk to people—anyone—bartenders, taxi drivers, a drunk sitting on the corner, it didn't much matter, and he spoke to everyone the same way. You could be millionaire businessman, or a hobo; Greg would likely learn your first name, and call you that from that point on.

Late into the night, the band was still going with some Eagles, ZZ Top, and we were singing along, tapping our feet. She brought us another round (we had lost count at that point), and Greg smiled at her and said, "You've got the nicest set of legs on anyone I've ever seen, dead or alive."

"*Whhaat*??" She said, her hands on her hips, amused and clearly curious.

Greg nodded and chuckled. Oh, here it comes, I thought to myself.

"Yeah, see," Greg said, pointing at me, then himself, "we're homicide detectives. So we've seen lots of legs, dead ones and alive ones."

I'm pretty sure I muttered something like "Oh good god..."

And the conversation was on. She was enthralled.

That was Greg, and when he had a little bourbon in him, it was bound to be an entertaining evening.

We needed more than just the statement of Allen's Lovington State prison cellmate. We went back to Miami and pounded the pavement some more, talking to all of Leatrice Knighton's street friends, as well as Laudell's. When we told them that Laudell was in prison in a state far away, they were more open to talking to us, and we secured two damning statements Laudell had made to his drug contacts in the area. He told them both that he had to get out of town because he had "done something to that girl on 53rd street." Between those statements, some physical evidence Laudell had left on the scene, and the statement we got from the prison, we were able to secure an arrest warrant. It wasn't a great case, but it was enough. We were eager to talk to Laudell now and see what he would say and see if he might have some involvement with the deaths of our other victims. In trying to solve Joyce Burrows' murder, we had solved another one. But that was the mission of our Cold Case squad.

We went back to Hobbs in late November, the night before Thanksgiving, Tony invited us to the police station for a potluck, a Thanksgiving eve tradition at Hobbs P.D. The families of the officers came and brought home-cooked dishes, and the most memorable one I had was an excellent—though fiery—elk meat chili. We cooled our stomachs with a brief trip to the Brass Bottle, and on Thanksgiving Day we gave thanks by extraditing Laudell Allen back to Miami to face murder charges. The long drive from Lovington Prison to Midland-Odessa airport was flanked with huge stretches of cotton fields, devoid of trees. It felt like you could see for miles. Greg cautioned Laudell not to try anything dumb and jump out of the car to run. Laudell looked out the window of the car at the tree-less horizon.

"Where would I go?" Laudell said with a grin. "Y'all would be able to see me runnin' forever."

Chapter Seven

Sweet Dreams and Flying Machines

I often helped Dad in his shop, where he cut sections from large sheets of copper with a pair of metal shears. He hammered them into shapes, used a torch to weld and add color to them. I would get to hold the pieces with a pair of tongs and dunk them into a bucket of water with a satisfying hiss.

He was making a bird. A gull in fact, and he was taking great care to piece the gull's wing together. "You see," he told me, holding up the finished wing so I was looking at the edge of it, from the side, "the shape of the wing is larger in front, and tapers down. It's smaller in the back." Then he took a piece of paper and drew it, showing me how the air flowed over the wing, and caused lift. "That's how airplanes fly," he said. "Their wings are shaped like bird wings."

I was sitting at my desk in the Homicide Office when Dad called.

"Ram...Mom's got cancer. Pancreatic cancer." My dad never cried, but his voice was breaking. "They say she has three months to live."

Mom had gotten a biopsy a couple of weeks before that phone call for the persistent, debilitating pains she had been having in her lower back and abdomen. I knew nothing about pancreatic cancer, but I was about to learn. I didn't know what to say to my father. I was too stunned.

"Are you coming over later?" He asked, his voice shaky.

"Yes of course. I love you Dad," was all I could muster before hanging up.

Not long after that, Dad and I had a meeting at the oncologist's office, so he could explain the unexplainable. My sons, Erik and Greg, were eleven and nine, respectively. I talked to them about their Grandma's now-shortened future. I cannot remember, today, what I said to them.

The time was coming soon, we all knew it, when Mom's life would exist in a bed while we all waited for the end. Until then, you never would have known what was on the horizon. She got up at the same time every morning and went to school, and as long as she possibly could, made sure that South Miami Middle School had Dr. Rasamma Nyberg, their principal, in the office, in the hallways, in the meeting rooms, greeting kids at lunch, and doing what she had done for thirty-seven years.

It was going to be an odd Mother's Day. Indeed, though no one would say so, it would likely be our last with Mom. Dr. Kroner had told us that at best she had six months to live, but here it was, May 11, 1996, the day before Mother's Day, and she had already beat that prediction at seven months and counting. That day at school, however, she fell. Her legs and her strength, she said, just kind of slipped out from under her.

I was standing by her bedside in her hospital room and she was smiling weakly, talking to me and Vivian. The TV was droning on with some "breaking news," and I couldn't help but catch the image of a helicopter hovering over the Everglades and at the same time hearing the words, "*...airliner apparently crashed...*". The story unfolded then, and the reporter was talking about a jet—a large passenger jet—that had left Miami International and crashed minutes later. Arriving news helicopters couldn't see anything or anyone except for some unidentifiable debris in the shallow, mucky waters below.

I stood there and glanced down at Mom. I knew at that moment that I would be going to work, and that I would be there for quite a while.

It would later be named "Forward Base 592", and from our HQ building it took about an hour and half to get there. The drive was forty-five minutes to a staging area on the north side of US 41, 12.3 miles west of Krome Avenue, then another twenty minutes north on the L-67 canal, courtesy of the Florida Marine Patrol, who would be our taxi service for the next month. By the time we got to the staging area, at least ten or twelve uniform cars and another five to six Fire-Rescue trucks were there. Live-broadcast television crews were there too, from all the local stations, some from around the country. By day three, it seemed like every news media truck in the nation was there. It was like a live-eye convention, a veritable village of cameras, trucks, and reporters. In the middle of the flat, swampy wilderness of the Everglades, the foreign beehive of activity was surreal. It would one of many surreal images still burned in my brain.

After picking us up at the staging area, the Florida Marine Patrol boats (the "Grouper Troopers" as we nicknamed them) would pull up to a spot along the L-67 levee access road, a bumpy strip of dirt and rock used for the South Florida Water Management District to test Everglades water levels. The clearing in that turnaround of the road was just big enough for the Fire Department's tents. From that spot, it was another fifteen-minute airboat ride east and south to get to the crash site.

We got briefed on what we were doing. It was going to be a bitch, that much was clear.

"It's hot and you'll be wearing biohazard suits," a commander said as he stood in front of us in one of the big tents. "There's gators, there's snakes, and there's a really big mess out there."

The "really big mess" was what was left of a DC-9 jet carrying 111 human beings, that had basically gone into a shredder. ValuJet Flight 592 left Miami International Airport that morning on its daily trip to Atlanta. After seven minutes in flight, the tense voice of Captain Richard Hazen could be heard requesting a return to MIA.

"We need to return to MIA. Smoke in the cockpit, smoke in the cabin," he said tersely. After that, there was some unintelligible noise when MIA tower tried to raise Hazen again. Then, nothing. They had lost contact.

A fisherman a couple miles south was in a small boat casting for bass when he caught sight of a jet plane sailing earthward. Then, a rumble of thunder and a plume of water, debris, and smoke. The fisherman happened to have a pilot's license.

"No," he told the dispatcher. "Not a small plane. It's an airliner."

But how? Why? We would find out soon enough.

The news helicopters had beaten everyone to the scene. They were the ones sending the images I saw from Mom's hospital room. They were reporting that there was "nothing" below, and that all they could see was a "big hole" in the swampy, grassy waters below.

"The plane," one reporter said gravely, "has disappeared." These comments would give rise to conspiracy theories that persist to this day. There are people who still believe that the plane and the people really did "disappear." When we arrived at Forward Base 592 and took that first ride out to the crash scene, it was horribly evident that this was not the case.

My first memory of ValuJet was the smell of jet fuel. We had just left the base in our airboat, about fifteen of us, all with specified roles. Some of us were designated to pick up the body parts, and others were there to hold open plastic bags, and hold a small tag, with a body part number written on it, while a third team member—these were Crime Scene techs—photographed us holding the tag next to the body part. Then we put the remains into the bag and affixed the tag. At the end of forty-five-minute relay, the individual bags were put in a large green zippered body bag. After our arrival and disinfection spray-down station, the body bag was carried to a canopied area and placed with other body bags from other relays. At the end of the day, all the body bags carrying what was left of the one hundred eleven Mother's Day weekend travelers were helicoptered thirty-six miles east to the Medical Examiner's Office.

The smell of the jet fuel emerged just a minute or so after the airboat took a gentle swerve turn to the right past a stand of tall sawgrass and water lilies. A few minutes later and a couple more zig-zags through the swamp, the "debris field" came into sight. If only those news helicopters could have been down where we were, at snake's eye level. My eyes skimmed an area of about seventy-five yards in all directions, dotted with clumps of sawgrass. Floating in the coffee-colored water were suitcases, clothing, hands and feet, and—right next to the boat bobbing gently against the hull—chunks of human flesh. We would find hundreds upon hundreds of those over the coming weeks. We would find, too, disembodied feet and hands. Dozens of them. We learned that they come off at the wrist and above the ankle during impacts as great as ValuJet 592 experienced. Most of the men's feet were still in tied shoes or loafers. Many of the women's feet, which had presumably been in less secured footwear, were bare. Greg Smith found a woman's slender, unscarred hand—complete with meticulously painted red fingernails and a wedding ring—floating just a foot from the hull of our airboat.

In that first relay, I remember all of us just looking, taking it all in. It was jarringly unfamiliar, even to us who had been on all kinds of death scenes. You drive to a case, and it's a decomp; you get ready for the smell. You've done it a bunch of times, and you know it will be gross. You know there will be maggots, the stench, the bloating, all that. You go to a suicide, and even with the barest sketch of information you have, you can kind of picture what the victim will look like. You've been there. It's familiar. You take a deep breath, and you know how to handle it. This, we had never seen.

When the driver cut the noisy propeller, we heard nothing but a gentle sweep of wind through the sawgrass. We all sat there, silently looking out over an expanse of floating clothes, body parts, and an occasional length of twisted metal trapped in between some weeds, as jet fuel trailed gently across our nostrils. It was so starkly unfamiliar that it was disorienting. Silently, we surveyed it all and then, as if someone had flipped a switch, we went to work.

The only ones allowed in the water were certified police divers, though where we were, the divers were in mostly waist deep water. They waded ahead of the airboat with long poles and fished out whatever was in front of them: a hand, a foot, a chunk...and carefully brought it to us at the edge of the boat. Tag, click, bag, and then the next body part would be served up. We were instructed to leave airplane parts in place, and one team member oversaw the procedure of placing a red flag where the plane part was. The FAA and NSTB investigators, in their own airboats, buzzed around picking those up, by the hundreds. Conversely, they put blue flagged poles in the ground when they found a body part, for us to get. There was very little talking, just everyone carrying out their role. The photographer might every so often say, "Hold it higher...that's it..." *click.* Otherwise, the conversation, the banter, the silly ribbing and jabbing we did with one another on homicide scenes was markedly absent. In this new work environment, we were all rookies. We were all absorbing and mapping the visuals of this jarring scene.

The Miami-Dade Police Department's Psychological Services office sent a counselor out. The department anticipated, wisely, that some of us might, "take a hit" (as the counselor told us).

During a briefing we were told do *not* pick up any personal items that may have belonged to passengers, unless it was a piece of jewelry, credit card, or something that could aid in the identification process. If you pick something like that up, we were warned, you're in danger of "taking a hit." Some of us joked quietly about it. But we all knew what they meant, and we all knew that taking a hit was a possibility. *Don't pick up personal items.*

When our forty-five-minute relay was done, we roared back to the base, our green zippered bag bulging with dozens of bags of flesh, hands, and feet. These fragments, I remembered thinking, used to be parts of living, laughing, dozing people, all going to Atlanta to see someone that loved them. This entire experience, I thought to myself, is one big "hit."

In between relays, we enjoyed the air-conditioned tents that the Fire Department had brought out. We lounged, dozed, ate sandwiches, and hydrated (we were sternly reminded to hydrate, and there was an endless supply of water, Gatorade, and soft drinks helicoptered in every day). We were also learning more, as the days wore on, about what happened and what we were looking for. We were all getting better at expecting what was floating out there, waiting for us. We were all losing our rookie status.

At one of the briefings we were getting daily now, we were shown an oxygen canister. This was a small cylinder that resides above the heads of passengers and supplies oxygen to those masks that are supposed to drop down during a loss of cabin pressure. There were, apparently, a whole box of them in cargo hold of the aircraft—and they weren't supposed to be there. The prevailing theory was that these canisters activated in the cargo hold and were like flamethrowers. It would have been a matter of a couple of minutes before everything in the cargo hold was on fire. We weren't supposed to pick up airplane parts, but finding a canister or any airplane part that looked scorched, was a big deal, and we were to let the FAA investigators know right away.

At the end of the day, as the shadows on the Everglades lengthened, we were ferried back to the staging area by the FMP boats, or, if we got lucky, we could hitch a ride on the chopper if they had a spare seat. I had a routine I followed for those three weeks: get off the boat, get in my car, and drive to Baptist Hospital to see Mom. Each day, as I made the long drive east on Tamiami Trail, the enormity of this experience became more deeply internalized, until my visits to my Mother crystallized into the realization of an immense privilege I had been given: a blessing, a golden chance that the families of those passengers—now tattered, floating, and stuck in the sawgrass roots in my rear view mirror—never got to have. One minute those folks waited in blissful ignorance for the arrival of wives, husbands, kids, grandparents. Then, the sudden, impossibly cruel news slammed into them: the plane and their loved ones are no more. They don't even get to have an open casket viewing.

They also didn't get the luxury I was getting: to *know* the end was coming, and to say a long, sweet goodbye.

When I was eight, I had a sandpile I liked to play in on the side of the house. It was a little different every day. Sometimes it was littered with small leaves from the Surinam Cherry bushes nearby, and I had to brush them off. I liked it clean and smooth, devoid of any other obstacles. A white, sandy dune, so I could set up my little plastic soldiers, and formulate complex battle scenes on the feathery slopes. Sometimes, families of black ants would invade the sandy mound, and they served as a live enemy that my soldiers could pursue. I had many toy soldiers and some toy trucks. But when we moved—or when I grew older—I'm not sure which, all those things disappeared. Your toys, the things you treasured and used to bring your imagination to life, get lost. They leave you.

I never thought of it the other way around: that a child could leave the toy, orphaned, with no one to play with it.

It was perhaps the second or third relay of the day. Every day, it was the same, and we had become used to it: the roar of the airboat engine, the smell of the jet fuel mixed with the smell of decomposition, which got stronger each day. More feet, more hands, more chunks of flesh, now getting grayish and mottled with rot. The airplane parts were being carted to a makeshift hangar about half a mile down the levee road and were being assembled on a wire frame mockup of the DC-9.

As horrid as the whole thing was, we had learned what to expect, and we were in our rhythm now. We had added the sights and smells of this experience to our already macabre mental inventory. The laughter and the mutual tormenting that defined our camaraderie returned. We were doing our homicide detective thing. If anyone was taking "hits", they weren't showing it.

There I was, looking out about ten feet at a man's sneakered foot one of the divers was about to fish out of the drink and serve up to me for bagging. I reached out and got it, and I held it up for the photographer. As I placed the body part in the bag and tied on the tag, something green caught my eye. I completed my bagging task and looked down into the water. There, bobbing gently against the hull of the airboat, was a little green toy shovel. It was the kind of shovel kids played with at the beach. It floated there, as if to taunt me: *Don't pick up me up, you could take a hit.* I stared at the shovel. It was just like the shovel my boys had. The realization hit me like the kick of a Remington shotgun at the range. There was a little kid on the flight. A kid small enough to still play with toy plastic shovels, no bigger than a salad fork. The little kid was in pieces now. I may have picked up parts of him already.

I looked over the expanse of the Everglades, and then back at our guys in the water, wading slowly. That little boy or girl had been on Flight 592 smiling, or sleeping, or being a nuisance, who knows what. He had probably played on South Beach during his family's trip there and made sandcastles with that shovel. All I had to do was unzip the top of my biohazard suit, and quickly drop it in there.

Don't pick up any personal items, you could take a hit.

My heart was in my throat; my mouth was dry. Someone would want that little shovel. Someone who held and played and laughed with that little child would treasure it. Was I going to get it to the family? We would know all their identities soon enough. I silently cursed our relay rules. My psyche battled fiercely at that moment, of whether to break the rules and take the shovel. It was a child-less shovel. It would be coveted by a child-less family member. I felt palpitating, choking stress in my neck. All the while, the shovel, bobbing with the tiny waves and ripples around the waterline of our boat, taunted me. Nyberg, I said to myself, you're *taking a hit*. But if I *didn't* take it, wouldn't there be a "hit" there too? I don't know how many times I swallowed and fought with the decision before our airboat pilot cranked up the engine again and we pulled away, leaving the shovel behind in our wake. I didn't look back, and I prayed that I wouldn't see it again.

One morning in June, Mom's hospice nurse told me it was going to happen any hour now. Her vitals were diminishing, and we should be ready, she said, for her to go tonight or tomorrow morning. It was that close. We were as ready as were going to be.

Almost three days later, we stood next to the bed, Mom dozing deeply in a morphine dream. The hospice nurse shook her head. "I don't know what she's waiting for," she said, perplexed. "She's hanging on, for something."

Then, on June 18th, early in the morning, Mom's breathing came in long, delayed gasps. Several times, when it seemed like she would not inhale again, she did. And then, mercifully, the ragged inhalations stopped. I remember reading that the hearing was the last thing to go before the brain completely shuts down, so I said in her ear, "Have a wonderful journey."

Well after the van wrapped her body up and took it away, it dawned on me. June 17th, the day before, was the last day of the school year. She hadn't read a newspaper or watched TV in at least a week, but it made sense to me that she somehow knew. School had to be closed and everything taken care of before South Miami Middle School principal Dr. Rasamma Nyberg could go.

****

Art Nanni took us out on his boat to Sands Key, the northern neighbor to Elliot. Sands had a semi-circular cove where, countless times, our family snorkeled, fished, or just anchored up for lunch. The mangrove-infested coast of Sands had a hidden inlet that led to another small cove in the island's interior. We would tie the sailboat to a nearby pine tree, hop ashore, and explore the place, including the deserted Atlantic beach side, more times than I could count. Mom belonged in the green, shallow waters of Sands Key.

The turtle grass on the bottom leaned gently with the current, and schools of silvery mangrove snapper slipped around and away as the anchor splashed, sunk, and then caught us on the sandy bottom. I said a few things—though I've forgotten what they were. "We're all here, Mom," I remember saying before opening the box and letting her ashes spill out into the bay. After that, I kind of got tongue-tied, and didn't know what to say. But it was ok, Mom and I had talked whenever the morphine would wear off and the pain would wake her up. She would speak in a near whisper and smile weakly at me. Everything had already been said.

There's a trade-off with everything in life, and apparently, in death. Mom suffered, and we had to watch. She didn't get to go quickly, but she didn't have to plummet from the sky either, blinded by smoke and wrung with terror, with no time to whisper to any of us. And we got our long, sweet goodbye.

After ValuJet, I had several dreams about plane crashes. They were all slightly different, but in each one an airliner is half in, half out of water. The fuselage is awash, and I'm trying to get to the survivors, or at least get to the plane to see if there are survivors to rescue. But there must be, because the plane is intact, it's not shredded into metal confetti and spread across the Everglades. No, it's half in a lake, and half sticking out. It's half in the surf of a sandy beach, on and half underwater. That told me there's hope, and I'm trying to get into the plane, but the dream never finishes. I had several dreams just like that.

About a year after the crash, I had a witness to go interview in Atlanta. I filled out the paperwork, got the approval, and one fine Monday morning I sat at the gate of AirTran, waiting, and smirking, because I knew what AirTran was; it was the former—and now defunct—ValuJet airlines, reformed under a new name after being battered into financial submission by the storm of Flight 592 lawsuits. It was still the bargain-basement way to fly, and that's why the County chose this flight for me. True to form, the crew was late—the *entire crew*—because there had been some sort of mix-up. People were grumbling and moaning and stressing out. Finally, the gate agent announced that a new crew was coming in. I hated changes when it came to travel plans. They were never good. Changes brought uncertainty. Changes absently got oxygen canisters tossed into cargo holds.

Finally, the crew arrived, and I joined the long line of passengers shuffling slowly through the jetway. Just I was about to reach the open hatch, someone to my left nudged me. It was a man in an airline captain's uniform, holding a cup of coffee. I have no idea why he picked me.

"Where's this plane goin'?" he said, looking at me, and then inside the plane.

"Um, Atlanta," I said, looking at him. The old woman in front of me turned around and looked at him too.

"Oh," he said. "I think I can find that." He pushed his way through to the cockpit and sat at the controls.

The old woman's eyes bugged out. "Oh my god!" she said in a shaky voice. "*That's* our pilot?"

I laughed, thankful for a pilot experienced enough to have a sense of humor, and all my fears about being on the imposter airline that was once ValuJet vanished.

"Don't worry," I told the woman, "I think we're going to be fine."

Gallows humor. Apparently it was shared by cops and airline pilots alike.

Chapter Eight

The Secrets of the Redland

"The Redland" is a sprawling stretch of farmlands in southwest Dade County. Houses were scattered in the region, most of them on 5-acre lots. It was a place where people could enjoy a more "country" style of life but still be just a forty-five-minute drive to Miami. In the early 1980's there were patches of housing developments starting to show up. For the most part, though, one could drive for miles and pass nursery after nursery and farms growing everything from pole beans to tomatoes, and everything in between. There plenty of groves too; mangoes, avocados, limes, and a host of other tropical fruits. It was a fun and interesting place to work in uniform patrol. It took forever to get to calls because everything was so spread to the wind, but that was part of South District's charm.

There were isolated pockets of humanity here and there, with quaint signs and names like the lone bar and grill out on Redland Road, called "Faraway Joe's." The reddish soil that gave the Redland its name eventually gives way to the Everglades, and from there, it's all sawgrass, water, and oolite rock all the way to the west coast of the state. Just south of the Redland was the city of Homestead, a place with a definitive country personality, complete with country-western bars and its own annual rodeo.

The seamy side of nearby Miami—and the lure of easy money—had a way of seeping into every neighborhood. Not even the Redland was immune. Those farm fields and quiet roads had their own dramas and secret criminal enterprises. With its many barns, greenhouses, remote airstrips, and myriad of places to covertly grow and store product, Redland provided everything the modern smuggler needed. Because it's such a large area, law enforcement took a long time to get anywhere, and we just didn't have enough people to cover everything. For uniform officers in South District, Redland was part of "area 2", and we might have three or four patrol units working the vast area. When things got busy along U.S.1, the deep western reaches of the Redland often got ignored entirely, and from U.S.1 it would take a good fifteen minutes—even running lights and siren—to get to, say, Faraway Joe's.

In 1982, the typical Homestead resident was either a white, middle-class, and countrified (complete with pickup truck, Rottweiler, and John Deere tractor), or a poor Mexican migrant who spent his day picking corn and tomatoes all day, and his nights drinking beer in one of the migrant camp cantinas or Mexican bars. The migrants used to get pretty tanked up on the weekends, and we could just about count on at least a couple of calls to one of the migrant camps for a machete fight, a shooting, or some other brand of violent drunken brawl.

I didn't get in a ton of trouble as a kid, but when I did, it often had to do with me not wearing shoes. Footwear, when I was eight or nine years old, was an afterthought. I would dash out of the house to climb trees or play touch football with my friends across the street, and sometimes just forget to put them on. Or I would go out with them on, and kick them off before tree climbing, because, well, it's just not the same with shoes on.

Dad got very annoyed when I cut my foot once, running around on Soldier Key, where we had tied up the boat for one of our picnics. I never wore shoes on the boat, so when I went ashore it never dawned on me, until I felt something sharp and fell on my butt, foot in hand, to see blood oozing out from underneath my great toe. Jagged oolite rock will do that.

"Dammit Ram," my Dad would growl. "You never listen when I tell you to wear shoes."

I remembered that day on Soldier Key when we pried open the driver's door of a charred pickup truck, sitting on a dirt road, deep in the Redland. Our long-sleeved shirts and ties must have looked wildly out of place out here. It was nice, though, to be on a homicide scene and not worry about neighborhood onlookers or news media people. We didn't even have to put up crime scene tape.

There was someone inside the smoldering truck, and though he had been roasted pretty well, we could tell a couple of things: he had been shot in the side, and the pickup truck had been set on fire. The torcher wasn't up to speed on fire science, as he had rolled up all the windows before setting the fire inside the cab. The fire didn't live long enough to completely destroy the vehicle, but it provided enough heat for Juan Garcia's body to swell and his intestines to bulge out of the large gunshot wound on his left side. We also noticed that the dearly departed Juan Garcia was barefoot.

From the tools and mud and other stuff in the bed of the truck, we could tell he was a migrant worker. There was nothing around but farm fields, and it was late in the afternoon when a guy driving a tractor had seen the smoke-enshrouded truck and called police. There was a pair of muddy work boots in the bed of the truck. But why had he taken them off, and driven barefoot? No one did that around here.

Our interviews with the victim's roommates shed some light on the case. Garcia had been at the Nueva Era Bar, a popular Mexican unwinding spot on the northern end of the Redland last Friday night, when another migrant worker complimented him on his black leather western boots. Over a couple of beers, the unidentified offered to buy them.

"I'll give you $10 for them," he told Juan Garcia in Spanish. But Juan liked his boots. No, he told him. Not for sale. The man made a higher bid, but Garcia still refused to sell.

Our witnesses said that this other male was quite pissed off. He wanted those boots, and he told the bartender as much. In his statement to us, the bartender corroborated the stories of the other witnesses. Yes, this dude was furious that Juan wouldn't sell the boots to him.

It took us a few days, but one of Juan's buddies thought the guy's name might be Vidal, and he took us to a small farmhouse where this "Vidal" lived. The landlord of the place confirmed his tenant's name: Vidal Salceiro. We got a Florida ID card and picture from the state and we went back to our first witness with a photo lineup. He nodded and tapped the Vida's picture.

"This is the guy here. The one who tried to buy the boots." The witness turned us on to another witness, Manuel Chamorro.

"Manuel can tell you more," our guy said. Manuel told me that Vidal said to him that he was going to get those boots from Juan "if I have to kill him."

If that was true, then Manuel was what the legal system called a "material witness." Those few words from Vidal provided a significant connection to the victim, and helped prove motive. You wanted material witnesses, as many as you could get. In cases like this, they were usually few and far between. Manuel was important. Our source didn't know where Manuel lived, but he said finding Manuel at the Nueva Era—where this tale began—was a fair bet.

Manuel, it turned out, liked to play pool in the back on Friday nights. We thought it would be good to have uniform along, so we contacted my old cohorts in South District and told them we were going to pay a visit to the Nueva Era to find Manuel. Chris Bimonte, a fine officer I worked with in uniform, was there to assist, along with a couple of other uniforms guys. One of them knew Manuel and could point him out. The place was jammed, and a *mariachi* band played in the tiny front restaurant area. A small hallway led to the back and we shouldered our way through the crowded seating area, getting lots of stares from the patrons. The band was cranking out some lively Mexican tunes, and Bimonte nodded to the rear, where the pool room was.

One of Bimonte's squad mates went in before us to see if he could spot Manuel, and there was a sudden commotion on the radio. Bimonte yelled and waved for us to follow him. When we got back to the pool room, the officer had Manuel handcuffed and breathlessly told us that Manuel had been carrying. When he spied the brown uniform coming in to the pool hall area, Manuel tried to ditch some small bags of cocaine in the tiny bathroom nearby. So, our prospective witness had a little side business in the pool hall, it seemed. Manuel didn't want to go easily. Maybe it was the coke, or all the Budweisers he had downed that night, but he wanted to fight, even after he was cuffed.

I had one arm and a uniform guy had the other as we hustled Manuel out of the pool hall area to get him outside. He was still fighting when we got into the restaurant area, pushing with his legs, twisting, and shouting expletives in Spanish. At one point he shoved so hard with his legs he sent me and Bimonte careening towards the bar where the *mariachis* were playing. The patrons watched from their seats and continued to eat and drink. What should have been a routine arrest had turned into a maelstrom of noise, chaos, and lively Mexican music. I found myself pinned against a grandly-festooned *mariachi* guitarist, both of us pressed up against the bar, momentarily unable to move. The guitarist, with his fancy hat and gold uniform, was inches from me. He looked at me with eyes bulging but *continued playing*. The other band members watched, and they too, never missed a beat, strumming and yipping as we knocked over tables and chairs—and nearly crushing their guitarist—on the way to the front door.

We got Manuel out of there and pushed him, struggling and cursing, into one of South District's patrol cars. Before we left, we could still could hear the joyous strains of the *mariachis,* playing faithfully from inside the Nueva Era bar.

––––––––––––––––––

I was the lead investigator in fifty-five homicide cases while in Homicide rotation. They each have a story or more to tell after the yellow tape came down and we got to work. Juan Garcia's murder wasn't front page news; he was a migrant worker, trying to get to the next level. It was memorable for me, though. I had worked in South District and had dealt with migrant workers many times. I felt right at home, and the scene at the Nueva Era can never be erased from my memory. But we weren't done.

Manuel came down after whatever high he was on, and spoke to us calmly, even respectfully. He wouldn't be a great witness in trial, but right now his testimony weaved nicely into the framework we already had, and his statement pushed us over the probable cause hill we had to scale. He admitted to knowing Vidal. He admitted, too, that Vidal told him, triumphantly, that Juan Garcia's black cowboy boots were now his. How? Manuel asked him.

In Spanish, he told Manuel, "He is now ashes." Manuel had just gotten an upgrade to a *blue-ribbon* material witness. The cocaine in the pool room was a small hurdle, and one the prosecutor would have to overcome. We were set. My next trip was to a judge for two warrants: one for the arrest of Vidal, the other for a search of the farmhouse. The place wasn't far from where we had found Juan's charred pickup truck and barefoot body. A long meandering grass driveway led to the tiny house, nothing more than a dingy little shack bordered by corn fields. The "element of surprise" would be tough. Vidal could see us coming a good two hundred yards away. Vidal's failed attempt to burn up the car and the comical arrest scene at the Nueva Era with the *mariachi* band had given this case a twist of absurdity, but it wasn't over.

When you serve a search warrant, the law requires that you read the warrant out loud, even if there is no one there. The spirit of the law behind this procedure is this: you may believe there is no one there, but there *could* be someone hidden away beneath the floorboards, in the crawlspace, or hiding in a clothes hamper. If that's the case, they are afforded the right to know why the government has been able to circumvent their Fourth Amendment protection against unreasonable search and seizure. As such, you are required to read the warrant *out loud*, regardless of whether or not you see anyone present.

As the crime scene guys started to take photos, I stood outside the rickety little house and started the flowery speech of the search warrant. The phrases are laced with old-time language about "summoning the Sheriffs of the State of Florida," peppered with "heretofores" and "therebys." If some Mexican migrant was huddled underneath the floorboards of the place, he would have no fucking idea what all this legal-ease prose meant, but we still had to read it.

As my recitation of the warrant language progressed, I got into it. There was a flock of geese about ten feet to my right. I turned to them, put my finger in air, and continued reading, barking out the "wherebys" and "therefores" with increased emphasis. They were, after all, my only audience, save for a tall, gangly female Crime Scene Tech named Kim Haney. I heard Kim chuckle as the flock of geese moved away from me, honking warily. I walked after them, shaking my finger in air, the ornate language making me sound like a congressman from the 1800's making some dramatic proclamation. The geese became increasingly agitated and waddled rapidly off together, quite pissed off at me, honking angrily and flapping their wings. I pursued them, and Kim snapped several pictures of me pursuing the geese, which by the end of the warrant had reached a state of near panic.

We got inside well before I was done with the geese. The reading was a formality, and there were no neighbors around to see if we had gone in prior to the reading or not.

Kim Haney was still laughing about the geese when another detective on my squad called out, "Ram, check this out." Inside, the stove in the farmhouse's miniscule kitchen was still warm, with a small pan of beans steaming. The back door was open. The thick cornfield behind the house was a good five feet high and Vidal was short. We called for a chopper to see if we could spot Vidal, but he was long gone. Most likely he had peeked out his window and seen us coming down the long drive. He was hightailing through the corn long before my address to the geese even began. I figured we would get him later. Standing neatly on the floor of the kitchen, next to the stove, were a pair of black cowboy boots.

It would be literally years before we found Vidal. Where the hell had he gone? We made a wanted flyer and posted it all over Homestead and the Redland hangouts Mexicans would frequent. The warrant was in NCIC, routine with all our murder warrants.

An FBI agent, perusing a newspaper one morning during breakfast at his home in Connecticut, recognized Salceiro's name from an NCIC printout posted in the FBI office where he was stationed. Vidal, it turned out, was a homicide victim in the small Connecticut town where this agent lived. Central American migrant workers moved through once a year to pick apples and other crops. Another migrant had stabbed Vidal to death in a dispute. No one in the tiny township thought it worthwhile to run Salceiro's name in NCIC, so they never knew he was wanted for murder. We didn't know until that day that he was dead.

Juan Garcia and Vidal Salceiro both left the world the same way: without their favorite pair of boots.

I don't remember the kid's name. I don't even remember what he looked like. But he had a knife, and he was older and bigger than me.

Somehow, I had ended up on his bike, and he was pedaling through the narrow, tree-shrouded streets of South Miami, telling me he was going to kill me. I was being, I thought "kidnapped." I remember having a sick feeling in my stomach. Here I was, no more than eight years old, and I was never going to see my Mom and Dad again. I remember tears filling my eyes, wishing I could somehow call out to them. I would glance at each intersection as my captor pedaled through them, telling me not to try and escape. Would Dad's light blue Ford station wagon happen to be nearby? Could I yell out to him, and be freed from this sickening, saddening end to my life?

Just as shrouded in confusion as its inception is the end to this event. The bully with the knife turned his bike around, mumbled something, and let me off, his little game at an end. I walked home, more relieved than I could ever remember. I couldn't help but think, though: what if he HAD killed me? How long would Mom and Dad be looking for me? How would they find out? It was too distressing for my young mind to explore, so I just high-tailed it home, and the white gravel of our front yard under my bare feet, in the shade of the umbrella and ficus trees I loved to climb, never felt better.

Catching up to Juan Garcia's killer was another example of how things can take a little longer in the Redland. When a ten-year-old Redland boy disappeared, everything took too long.

Jimmy Ryce clambered down from the school bus on the afternoon of September 11th, 1995, as he had done every school day that year. At the corner of SW 167th Avenue and 264th street in the Redland, he had barely two blocks to walk to reach the front door of his house. The bus driver glanced his way, watching Jimmy amble south along grassy swale of 167th avenue. Then she put the yellow school bus in gear and left.

It was the last anyone would see of Jimmy alive.

It didn't take long for the alarms to sound. Kids in the Redland didn't go missing; 10-year-old kids don't *ever* go missing, unless it is a parental abduction linked to a custody dispute. Abduction of children—out of the blue without familial involvement—aren't nearly as common as Hollywood would have the public believe. Jimmy Ryce's parents were married and together. This was not a dysfunctional household; they were used to seeing Jimmy bounding in the door after school every day.

All of South District was looking for him and before nightfall the BOLO had been put out numerous times. Every brown gown in existence, and every cop in all thirty-two jurisdictions of our vast county—knew Jimmy's name. By next morning, his disappearance was statewide news, and by noon the nation new Jimmy's name. Dozens of residents in the Redland were already participating in search teams, combing the fields and woods for him, hoping for a clue. It wasn't long before Homicide was mobilized, along with dozens of other detectives from various units like Robbery and Sexual Battery, to handle every lead our rapidly assembled task force could think up.

Jerry Crawford and I were assigned to interview an interesting guy who lived on the next-door property to Donald and Claudine Ryce. When we learned of this guy, it made our spine tingle: he was a boat mechanic named Ray Sutton. The Ryce's neighbors owned Redland Construction Company, and had known Ray since he was a child. They let Ray live in a small guest house at the western edge of the five-acre lot, and allowed him to run his boat maintenance business there. The bald, stocky Sutton had a jovial persona and thick hands, toughened by years of boat repair, and he was missing half of right index finger was gone, severed in a machinery accident.

The oddity of Ray Sutton was that his friends and neighbors never saw him with women. The background check we ran found no criminal history but did find one thing that chilled me to the bone: Ray's 40th birthday was September 11th, the day Jimmy disappeared.

"Sure, I'll talk to you," Ray said to Jerry and me. "And yeah, I'll sign your consent to search the house," he said, nodding to the paper I was taking out of my clipboard. "FBI's already been through the place, but you're welcome to it."

Ray carried himself with kind of a jolly cynicism. Though he looked intimidating at first, he had an easy smile, and a folksy gift of gab. He was cooperative yet grumbled just enough not to sound overly eager about it. Ray wasn't reluctant to help. Rather, it was annoyance with the incessant and repetitive law enforcement presence at his home. True to form, the FBI agents working the case didn't bother to ask us if we had searched or ask if it was going to interfere at all with our homicide investigation. We were used to stepping on each other's toes, but it seemed as if we were the only ones that actually cared about the overlap of work.

We brought Sutton to Homicide, examined his fingers—all nine and a half of them—and took photos, prints, DNA, the works. He even agreed to a polygraph, which he passed. By the time we cut him loose, I wasn't as convinced as I was earlier in the day that Ray was a pedophiliac monster and that Jimmy Ryce was his 40th birthday present. He didn't throw out theories about others, and he didn't loudly voice his innocence.

"I know y'all gotta do all this. I get it," he said. "I just hope you get whoever did this. The Ryces are good people and they don't deserve this."

It seemed like a normal way to act, but Jerry and I agreed that we had to keep Sutton on our radar, regardless. If he did know something about Jimmy and was hiding it, he was one cool customer. That wasn't impossible with true sociopaths; but, was he one?

The investigation had become massive in no time. The FBI and FDLE were actively involved, which was to be expected. Who knew where Jimmy was? His abductor could by this time easily have crossed state lines. We had nothing, so the leads we were handling were vast and hopeful. We really were turning over every rock. Leads were being disseminated to dozens of detectives and agents.

One avenue the task force wanted to explore was previous sexual offenders. Most of us in Homicide were given ten or twelve folders, each one containing the criminal history of a sexual offender from Miami-Dade County. Our task: find out where they were at the time of Jimmy's disappearance and go interview them. If they have an alibi, cross them off and go to the next one. I looked through my stack of folders and was stunned. The abundance of sexual offenders in one district was staggering. So many of these guys were in the south end, and I was just one detective. One guy I interviewed owned a small retail electronics outlet in Cutler Ridge. Another was a mechanic. And then, there was Michael Renwich.

Renwich had been arrested recently for sexual battery on a minor, and lewd and lascivious behavior on another. L and L was a crime that you could be charged for if you exposed yourself to a minor, or basically did anything overt of a sexual nature, short of touching a child. Once you touched, you were in the "sexual battery" realm, and that was far more serious. I planned to interview Renwich at his home—he had just begun serving a six-month house arrest sentence on the L and L and wore an electronic anklet that alerted authorities if he left his home for any reason. In the interim, he had been charged with a trio of sexual battery cases on minors. Before the interview, I reviewed the police reports of his last report. It was an investigative report I was reading, written by one of our Sexual Battery detectives. Six pages in, I dropped the report on the floor in horror.

I was still living at home with my parents, going to Miami-Dade College, studying music, when I learned of Brian Jensen's death. Brian was a quiet, slender 14-year-old who lived with his mom, dad, and older brother next door to us. He used to play with their dog in their back yard, and we would see him over the back fence and say hi. His parents were disarmingly nice people; unassuming and laid back. Brian's dad was one of the most pleasant guys you'd ever want to meet. He worked hard and worked a lot. There were weeks we didn't see him around. So it was a jolt when we learned from Jackie, Brian's Mom, one afternoon, that they had found Brian hanging in their garage. It was the first exposure to suicide I had experienced. Little did I know how intimately familiar with suicides I would become just a little while later in life. Poor Brian, I remember thinking. What on earth went through his young mind to do such a thing?

In the sexual battery detective's report, Renwich described in detail his pattern, his strategy to getting close to young boys. He would start by befriending the mom. Mow the lawn a few times, bring her flowers on Mother's Day, and then, something like "hey, how about I take junior to a movie if he's not doing anything?" It was a devious, patient, well-crafted attack plan. Lull them, bring them close, then capture the prize. The report named names of his victims Renwich had taken sexual advantage of. One of them was Brian Jensen.

I wasn't sure at that moment—with my head in my hands—and the pages of the report on the floor, what was meant by the "oh, god!" I blurted out to an empty room when I saw Brian's name on the report. Did it mean that I could not follow up this lead? Did it mean that I wouldn't be able to impartially sit across from Michael Renwich without wanting to strangle him? Did it mean that I could never look at Jackie Jensen again the same way, knowing now what might have led her son to make that awful decision that day?

Sitting across from Michael Renwich wasn't as excruciating as I thought it would be. I actually *wanted* to see him now, the way someone wants to get close to a train wreck or a shark. I kept the goal in mind: this guy *could* be Jimmy Ryce's killer. One thing I knew we would not do is talk about Brian. Thankfully, it wasn't relevant. All that was relevant was whether Renwich had the opportunity—the means and the motive were already well established—to abduct Jimmy Ryce that afternoon. As it turned out, he did not. The day Jimmy disappeared, Michael Renwich was sitting in a jail cell, having been arrested three days prior, on the charges he was currently awaiting to resolve, either by plea or trial. I will never forget what he said to me. It changed the way I thought about sex offenders, and their victims. And Brian.

"I hope they don't let me out," Michael Renwich told me, looking down at the table that was between us. "Because if I get out, I'll do it again. There's no way I can stop myself from doing it again."

He looked up at me, his eyes pleading. "Can you do whatever you can to make sure I don't get out?"

I would. Oh, I would. It's too late for my neighbor's son, but hell yes, I'll do whatever I could to keep him and other predators like him on the inside, where they can't get to the Brian Jensens of the world.

For all the manhunts, surveillances, civilian-led field searches and researching of creatures like Michael Renwich, it was a completely unexpected event that led to finding Jimmy. A Redland woman who rented her trailer to a guy named Juan Carlos Chavez hadn't received rent, and Chavez wasn't answering the door. She finally forced the lock, and went in. There, on the floor of the trailer, was Jimmy Ryce's backpack.

It wasn't long before the lead team found Chavez, and he started talking. He wasn't in custody. A backpack of a missing child isn't enough to charge anyone, so Chavez came with detectives to Homicide on his own free will. The interview of Chavez would last almost *three days*. Local media got wind of the situation, and defense attorneys from the Public Defender's Office were in an uproar. They called our office repeatedly, demanding that we release Chavez, or let them talk to him. The kicker was this: Chavez was not under arrest. He was "free to leave." Then, they demanded, why didn't he? Surely we were keeping him there unlawfully. Charge him, they snarled at the lead detective, or let him go!

Chavez' unwillingness to leave our Homicide Office made perfect sense. Everyone in south Florida by know knew his name and his face. Had he gone back to the Redland, there were scores of people, friends of the Ryce family and others, who would have loved to have had a piece of him. I could totally see Ray Sutton, who had convinced us that he wasn't a killer, taking Juan Carlos Chavez' life and thinking nothing of it. There was no doubt in anyone's mind—Chavez' especially—that the safest place on earth for him at that time was in an interview room at our Homicide Office.

Any time you are interviewing a subject, you document everything: times, the subject's appearance, every word they utter, when they were given a bathroom break, coffee, cigarette, snack…it all had to be carefully logged, because it would all come under fire during a motion to suppress hearing. Luis Estopinan, the lead on the case, along with his team did a superb job of chronicling every detail of that long encounter, from the very first contact to the time they finally got Chavez to admit to the rape and killing of Jimmy.

After killing him, Chavez buried Jimmy Ryce's remains in a planter on his landlord's property. The confession was long, detailed, complete, and, thanks to Estopinan and his team, constitutionally sound. It passed all the rigors of the motion to suppress, and Juan Carlos Chavez was convicted and sentenced to die in Florida's lethal injection chamber.

It would be nineteen years—February 12, 2014—until the Ryces were able to travel to Starke, Florida, a tiny prison town north of Gainesville, to witness Juan Carlos Chavez being put to death.

Chapter Nine

Flyboys

It was August of 1972, and I was standing on a hot, potholed tarmac at Marsh Harbour, Abaco, Bahamas, trying to get my sea-legs. I had spent almost three weeks living on a sailboat, and what a time it had been. Now school was starting and I needed to get back to Miami. I soon learned that the crooked-toothed man who sold me my ticket—and carried bags—was also the pilot. Marsh Harbour International Airport was a weedy airstrip with a little concrete shack at one end. It was an "international" airport because it had flights from the Bahamas to the United States. The cheerful Bahamian man ran the whole place. I waved to Dad and the rest of the crew I had come over with, and the pilot cranked up the twin-engine prop plane. Off we went—I think there were two other passengers—heading west to Florida. I watched the tiny airfield disappear and marveled at the crystal blue-green waters I had spent three weeks sailing and snorkeling in, from six thousand feet above.

Almost as much as the fishing, lobster diving, snorkeling and sleeping under the stars on the deck, I loved the sailing journey from Miami—all eleven hours of it. A fierce but favorable sea swept us eastward after we left Miami Marina on our way to West End, the town at the westernmost tip of Grand Bahama Island. The strong west wind kept us at an average of nine knots, a blazing clip for a 32-foot shoal draft sailboat. When it wasn't my turn on the tiller, I was navigating. I learned how to use the RDF—the Radio Direction Finder—and use the transmission signals from Jupiter Inlet and Nassau to line up vectors of their signals on the compass rose and get a cross-bearing: a small penciled "x" on the chart, to mark where our little sailboat was on the roiling deep blue waters of the Florida Straits. It was an adventure I would never forget. I was stimulated with the idea that I knew how to find where on the planet we were with this small, cereal-box size instrument, just by the repetitious morse-code beeps from some distant, invisible points on land. How, I wondered, had they done it in the old days, without electronics? It was wonderful and alluring in its electronic charm. I wanted to navigate all the time and take that RDF with me everywhere. It was the coolest thing I had encountered in my young life. Navigating the earth, I thought. Pilots of all kinds were lucky people.

One March afternoon in 1986, Remmen came up and said, "You're up for the next one, aren't you?" I was.

"Saddle up. We've got one way out in the south end, in the middle of nowhere. Not sure what we've got yet, except that there's a body and an airplane out there."

Homestead and Florida City are the southernmost municipalities in the County, defining the southern end of the Redland. When you leave Florida City on U.S. 1 southbound towards the Keys, there is a bar called the "Last Chance Saloon," the last place in the county to buy liquor or food until you reach the marina at the county line. Between the Last Chance and County Line Marina, you're on U.S. 1, arrow straight for fifteen miles, flanked by nothing but scrub and marl. This land gradually dissolves into the brackish marsh of the Everglades, a segment of which contains the largest crocodile sanctuary in North America.

Midway between the Last Chance and the end of the Florida peninsula is a large canal called Aerojet, built by a company of the same name and contracted by NASA to accommodate a rocket building project in the early sixties, as the United States pushed the cold war space race with the Soviets. The idea was that Aerojet General—one of the country's largest rocket propulsion manufacturers—would build the canal to ferry the large rocket parts from the assembly and testing site that was being proposed in the Everglades, to Cape Canaveral for eventual final production and launch. The initial testing in the area resulted in hydrochloric acid fallout in the region, killing acres of crops in farms in and around Homestead. Vehement complaints from farmers led to the abandonment of the site.

Remnants of the facility still sit west of the C-111 canal, which cuts a wide swath south through the Everglades and then east to Biscayne Bay. Christened the "Aerojet Canal," it was the largest of the Everglades canals not designed for "flood control." That was the phrase early Florida power brokers used to sell the idea of what was in truth a monumental plan to *drain* the Everglades entirely and re-purpose it for farming and housing development. In the process, they created a vast network of canals with accompanying levee access roads, tailor-made for remote smuggling operations.

A South Florida Water Management District employee opened the gate to the levee road just off U.S.1, to let us in, and we drove the rest of the way in our K-Cars, bumping over the rocky trail to another levee road which cut north, one of the connecting canals from Aerojet. It was a SFWD testing employee who had found the scene. He was taking water samples and depth recordings from the canal when he saw the mangled, burned remains of a Piper twin engine aircraft. When his supervisor came out, they walked a little further down the road and smelled something bad. About two hundred yards north of the airplane, underneath a small canopy of dead branches, was a human body, decomposing—and *headless.*

The plane was on the west side of the dirt access road, facing south. The landing gear was crumpled underneath the fuselage and the interior cockpit area and seating section were thoroughly burned. With a crashed airplane, we had to notify the F.A.A., and they sent one of their investigators out. I didn't know it then, but F.A.A. investigators were knowledgeable beyond just the mechanics of plane crashes. The guy who met us out there was well-versed in the routes and people involved in the illicit drug trade as well.

While the F.A.A. investigator inspected the plane, I went with our crime scene photographer and started taking the branches off the body. It was a male, decomposed a couple of days at least. Where the head was supposed to be, a bloody stump with part of the spine protruded. When we examined closer, we could see some red hairs on the skin where the scalp would meet the back of the neck. We checked the body's pubic hairs while we completed the examination and confirmed that our dead guy was indeed a redhead. He wore a denim jacket and a pair of blue jeans, with a distinct oval belt buckle. In the middle of the buckle was a bald eagle in flight, surrounded by the words "Pratt Whitney-Dependable Engines." Pratt Whitney manufactured reciprocating airplane engines typically found in propeller aircraft. Was he a pilot? Or someone accompanying the pilot? There were a dozen questions swirling in my head at that moment. Things became a bit clearer when we searched the body. A can of "Deep Woods Off" bug spray was found in his jacket pocket, and we dug a set of keys—one to a Ford vehicle—out of the pocket of his jean pants. But no wallet or ID.

About another hundred yards to the north of the body, we found a small campfire, a few empty beer bottles, and some cigarette butts. This guy, either alone or with someone else, was likely part of the offloading crew, and waited for the plane to land. Now, how did the plane crash, and how did this red-headed fellow die? Below the neck, there was very little on the body to help us. No stab or gunshot wounds. With a crashed plane nearby, the working theory was that he was killed somehow during the crash. After we got all the photos and put that distinctive belt buckle in a plastic bag, the M.E. drivers arrived and zipped the victim up along with the jawbone and facial bones we found nearby. Standing on that elevated access road, I looked around to see three hundred sixty degrees of marl, oolite rock, and lignum vitae shrubs growing in shallow ponds. Sawgrass whispered in the breeze, and I had to wonder what we might be missing. As we did on most homicides, we called the chopper for aerials. This time, I went up with the photographer. Six hundred feet up, the temperature quickly got cool and comfortable, and we cruised slowly around, looking for an abandoned vehicle, maybe some dumped drugs, anything that could help us. All we saw was a flock of roseate spoonbills, roosting in a small hammock about a quarter mile from our scene, oblivious to it all. It was a beautiful sight.

Back on the ground, the F.A.A. investigator waved me over. He pointed to a small container with some greenish looking liquid in it. "I just took this out of the gas tank. Green gas. They fueled up in another country. We don't have green gas here."

That wasn't all. "The filler cap was open, and it looks like they took some gas out and torched the plane. They probably wanted to make sure there was no trace of residue."

I told him about the body, and he thought for a moment. "I know of a red-headed pilot. Danny O'Neal. FDLE knows about him. He's smuggled a bunch of loads down this way, guarantee you."

My lead sheet started to fill up, and finding this Danny O'Neal guy was at the top of the list. If he was alive, our task of identifying the body could be arduous, unless fingerprints could help us. Our F.A.A. friend ran the tail number on the airplane and told us that it was registered to a "James William Cooper," with a Redland address. We needed to get the body fingerprinted at the M.E. first to see if perhaps our decedent was Cooper, or O'Neal, or maybe someone else completely. After a hot afternoon on that levee road, we made our long trek—about an hour—back to the Homicide office but took a detour to the address for Cooper. There was nothing there except empty land and a mailbox with the address on it. No house or barn, no vehicles. We thought we would get a hit on the fingerprints, but we got nothing locally. We sent them to the feds, and that would take some time, to see if he showed up in government service of any kind. In the meantime, we took a photo of the belt buckle and prepared a flyer. With his description and the belt buckle, we could post the flyers at Tamiami Airport, a municipal airfield servicing mostly small airplanes, and Homestead General Aviation, an even smaller airfield with no tower.

My dress shoes had dust and some dried marl along the edges as I read over Danny O'Neal criminal history: possession with intent to distribute marijuana some ten years ago. He also had a pilot's license. We called his house in Venice, Florida, a tiny town east of Sarasota. It was Mrs. Danny O'Neal who answered and told us that her husband had just been extradited back from Mexico on a drug smuggling charge. He was in jail and had been in custody for the last two weeks. Maybe we should see him, just to make sure, and there was an off chance he had some intel he would share.

Jerry Crawford and I made the two and a half-hour drive to the Federal penitentiary in Tampa where O'Neal was being held. O'Neal was a redhead alright, and he was more than happy to talk to us about all his smuggling exploits. They had him, and he knew it. Who did he know that piloted stuff down in Miami, deep south? And did he know any other redheads like himself in the business?"

"Robbie. Check him out. I think his name is Robert Robinson. He's not a redhead, but he flies out of Tamiami and is in the business. A lot of these guys don't look like smugglers, you know. They're clean cut, nice houses, wives. They're your neighbors."

O'Neal didn't know any other redheads in the business. He didn't know anyone named James William Cooper, either. But the tip on Robinson might be a passageway to more information. After a week, we still had no ID on our victim. Was this guy brought in from the outside, maybe? As far James William Cooper, the address in Redland was no good, and I was sure by that time that the name was bullshit too. We would have to find the previous owner of the plane and see who they sold it to.

Then, we got the phone call. "I'm calling because I saw the flyer you posted at Tamiami Airport," the caller said. He sounded like an older gentleman. His voice was raspy and had an ever so slight tremor to it.

"I'm concerned," he went on, "that it might be my son. He's an airplane mechanic, and he usually stays in touch with me, or at least answers my calls, but I haven't been able to get a hold of him for three weeks now."

"What's your son's name?" I asked him.

"Harry Rivenbark."

I closed my eyes when I heard it. The image of Harry popped into the front of my brain just then, holding a rifle, talking about the Everglades, hunting, fishing. And airplanes. In that flash of a moment, I saw our old gang: Garry, John Marcus, me, and Harry, drinking Jack Daniels and barbecuing at my house after a day of shooting out by Chekika Hammock.

Harry Rivenbark, Sr. told me his son's address and I met him there with the keys we got off the body. To our dread, the key fit the door to his apartment. We had our positive ID now.

The senior Rivenbark held together pretty well, at least in front of me. He told me he retired from Eastern Airlines as one of their most senior pilots. "I wrote the manual for the DC-9, when we first brought it out," he said without a hint of bragging.

Sad as it was, the search of Harry's apartment was a gold mine: in a dresser drawer I found a bunch of aerial photographs of the very site of our crash scene. They were nearly identical to the shots Crime Scene had taken during our helicopter ride. Someone had gone on a reconnaissance mission to get some landmarks and gain familiarity with the site. We also found an address book full of names and phone numbers that would prove to be very useful to us.

It was odd, investigating a death case, looking through the victim's phone book, and seeing *my* own name and number there.

The first person I would call was John Marcus. John, I was pretty sure, had stayed in touch with Harry way more than I—or anyone else—had. Harry was a bit of a loner, and I always saw him as someone who wanted to fit in, to find some clique he could be popular in. He had loved his time in the military, and when I contacted the Army and some of the people he had served with, I found that his M.O.S. involved setting up airstrips for wilderness aircraft landings. It all made perfect sense now. The United States Army had given Harry the skills he needed to fit in with the right clique, alright, and John confirmed it.

"Yeah, Harry told me he was helping out a friend of ours from high school—Bill Cook, and some other guys," John explained to me over the phone. John, an excellent bass player, had also parlayed his skills to get in with the right people. He was in Nashville playing with country music legend Tanya Tucker. John had hit the big time.

"They were flying in loads of weed from the islands," John went on to tell me. "Harry helped bring the planes in at night and helped them offload it. They paid him $10,000 every load. That's what he told me."

Harry had asked John if he wanted in, but John declined. Besides, John was playing music under the bright lights, making good money for doing things that wouldn't land a person in prison. Or get him dead and headless in the Everglades.

"Poor Harry," John finished the call with. "He fucked up, but he was a good guy. Billy Cook was part of the group," John said, but named no one else.

I flew to Nashville and took a tape-recorded statement from John. He was the only witness we had at this point, and he had named someone involved: Bill Cook, whose name was in the address book I got out of Harry's apartment. John always loved

Grand Marnier, I remembered, so I got a bottle from a liquor store in Nashville a few blocks from his place. We finished the statement, and drank a toast, "To Harry," I said, raising my glass.

"Yep," John said with a sad smile, "To Harry."

****

John King looked at me with a smirk. "You got an investigative trip, on an *accidental?*"

He had been ribbing me for a while about the hours I had put in on the case. I kept telling him that if we could substantiate that there was weed on the plane, then we have felony-murder charges. He enjoyed the banter, and so did I. He would ask, "And did you find any weed on the plane?"

Every time John was near and I made mention of a lead I had to do on Harry's case, he would mutter, with his trademark smirk: "Hardest worked accidental in history."

And he was right, in a way, but the department gave me leeway to work it as "unclassified" until we came to that crossroad when we had to cut it loose and spend time on other things. Harry's case was emblematic of what was happening in south Florida in 1986: cocaine smuggling was still rampant, coming in by freighters, speedboats, and planes. The Colombians and Cubans were in on the fast money game everywhere, and the drug rip-offs and murders that came out of the cartel activity were rampant. While law enforcement was training all its eyes on the Miami coast and the trying to catch the white powder moving north out of south Florida, these local white American guys were literally flying under the radar.

My theory at this point was that the fictitious "James William Cooper" was either Bill Cook or possibly this Robbie Robinson, who Danny O'Neal had told us about. To try to confirm this, I called up FAA to see if they had the bill of sale for the Piper

Navajo, and they did. When the copy of the bill of sale arrived by certified mail, the case took an upward jaunt: Below the signature of "James William Cooper" was a handwritten phone number. It looked vaguely familiar, so I thumbed through Harry's address book, and *bingo*—It was the phone number for Bill Cook.

Now I just had to confirm it with the former owner and see if he could ID Cook from a lineup. The former owner of the airplane was a retired Delta Airlines pilot who had sold the plane to a "James William Cooper" just a year prior. The man lived outside of Atlanta and was happy to meet with me.

"*Two* fellows came up and paid me for the plane," he said. "Mr. Cooper had a friend, I just don't remember his name."

I got driver license photos of both Cook and Robinson and wrote up a trip to Atlanta. John King couldn't resist cranking up the intensity of the tormenting. "*Another* investigative trip," he chuckled, loud enough for everyone in the squad room to hear. "On a fuckin' accidental."

The pilot and his wife met me at a small municipal airfield east of Atlanta. They flew in on their Beechcraft Bonanza, which I learned that day was a fast single-prop plane with a V-shaped tail. I watched them land. I would be lying if I said that, at this point in the investigation, I hadn't developed a desire to fly. Navigation, I thought. A chance to use the modern versions of the RDF and go from one place on the map to the other, without red lights and crazy drivers.

I met the couple at a restaurant inside the tiny airport. She, a Delta pilot, ordered a beer with lunch, and her husband told her, "You go ahead and have a beer, I'm flying us home."

They were extremely nice people and were intrigued by my case. The Piper Navajo he sold them was the "Chieftain" model. It was a workhorse plane, not built for speed like his Bonanza, but instead the ideal aircraft for ferrying a small group of passengers to and from the islands. Or, I suggested, a couple thousand pounds of weed?

"Oh, yes." He smiled and nodded. "Taking those seats out would be no big deal, and then you have yourself a nice big cargo bay."

From photo lineups I had assembled, he identified *both* Robert Robinson and Cook as the ones who showed up to buy the airplane, and now I felt that my "accidental" had taken on new life. He brought the bill of sale with him, and I made a copy of it so we could do a handwriting comparison if we needed to. He chuckled as he recalled the transaction.

"They showed me to their car, and they had a duffle bag with $180,000 in it. Huh! I wasn't about to do that. I told them to meet me at my bank, and we would conduct the sale there."

I took a sworn statement from him and flew back to Miami, eager to start working on Cook. He lived in a secluded part of western Dade, at the northeastern corner of what some would call Redland, others would call "way west." The old, bulky looking house was on a couple of acres and looked old. Cook's stepfather, I learned, was a pilot for Cubana Airlines in the 1950's before it became taken over by the Castro regime. This little crew, Harry, Bill Cook, and who knows who else, had a legacy of flying in their families. Cook didn't show up in any intel we had on narcotics, however. Whatever smuggling he had done, he had done intelligently, or he had been tremendously lucky. Who, then, were the people on the ground who distributed the cargo?

With the help of our Narcotics Bureau, I found the names of Buford "Butch" Pyatt, and another character named James Marcus Williams, both with histories of marijuana smuggling here and in central Florida. Did they know Cook? It was too early to tell, but Pyatt had been snagged in a central Florida case, and flipped, giving up a large group of airplane smugglers being investigated by

FDLE. Pyatt and a group of others were bringing in loads from Jamaica and the Bahamas, and instead of landing in south Florida, they would take it up to a place called Peeples Farm, in Highlands County, south of Orlando. The farm was enormous and had an airstrip on it surrounded by pine trees. No one could see it from any road in the area. I met with the FDLE investigator—another John King—a laid back guy with an easy smile, who had a ton of intel on all of these guys.

This group, of which Pyatt had been a member, had a pretty nifty M.O.: avoid the heavy law enforcement pressure on the Miami area and the expressways heading north out of the city, by landing at Peeples, offloading onto RVs and covered pickup trucks, and drive it back *south,* to avoid unwanted detection. Who gets suspicious seeing an RV coming to South Florida on the Turnpike? Pyatt got caught when one of the pilots got spooked and their crew started dumping product in the woods. When Pyatt went looking for it, he ran right into an FDLE surveillance. King and I traded all the information we had on Florida smugglers, and it was a big help.

"Danny O'Neal. Yeah, I know that guy," King told me.

King had amassed enough statements and evidence to shatter the Peeples group, most of whom he had just gotten indicted the past year. In addition to Pyatt, King said we should talk to a James Marcus Williams too. Williams had been a peripheral player with the Peeples organization, but was based down in Homestead, and was more of a south Florida guy. Though he had never heard or Cook or Robinson, this John King ("Fiddle" John King, as Remmen would call him, to distinguish him as FDLE) had another nugget for us, too.

"Radio John," King told us, "is a guy named John Masters. He lives down your way. He's a radar and radio communications guy. He brings the planes in over the peninsula, at a certain spot and low altitude that the radar misses," Fiddle John explained. "He would monitor F.A.A., DEA, and Customs radio traffic, and tell the pilots the safest place and time to come in. Peeples' gang was paying him $7000 a flight."

John Masters—the name sounded vaguely familiar. Again I consulted Harry's address book again, and thanked my old friend for being so meticulous about recording his associates' names and numbers: there was John Masters' name and phone number, on the same page as Bill Cook's. Masters was a big find, and I wanted to bring him in. Clearly, he was a smart, valued asset of this quietly successful smuggling clique. Masters, too, was a former Palmetto Senior High classmate of Harry, and Bill Cook. Things were coming together.

I decided to talk to James Marcus Williams first. Making contact with Masters right now would certainly cause him to alert Bill Cook to our investigation. That was going to happen eventually, but I didn't need it to happen this early. Jack Remmen and I talked to a long-time Homestead resident and FBI agent, Jack Hexter, who knew some things about Williams and his cohorts. Remmen and I met up with Hexter at his Krome Avenue office and then headed out to find Williams. To say that Williams had that "deer in the headlights" look when we showed up would be putting it mildly. We suggested Williams take a ride with us in Hexter's Bronco, so that he could point out some places—like Cook's house—to firm things up. As we headed west, out of civilization and towards the nurseries and farm fields deep in the Redland, Williams looked nervously out the window.

"Ya'll fixin to kill me? Is that where we're goin'?"

He was serious. He really thought we were going to do him in. Once we calmed his fears, he started talking. We would say a name, and then he would say one, and he sneered when I dropped Butch Pyatt's name.

"I got me a buck knife I'd like to bury in that fucker's back if I ever see him," he muttered darkly.

Our efforts paid off: Williams didn't know Cook, but he knew Robinson. "Worked on his plane at Tamiami a couple of times." He had never flown with either of them, nor had he offloaded with them either. And he didn't know Harry.

"But I did hear about that crash," he said, staring out the window. Now all the eyes inside that truck were on him.

"Yeah, from whom?" I asked him. He glanced at me, then back out the window. "From Robbie," he said.

Unfortunately, all Robbie told him was that a recent load had gone bad "out by Aerojet," and that they had to scrap the airplane. That comment alone strongly indicated that Robbie had been along on the failed operation. He didn't talk about Cook, and he didn't talk about anyone dying, but little by little we were getting somewhere, on this accidental of mine.

John King's friendly jabs about all the time and money being spent on my case were more than just a joke; there's no question that I had a bias in the case. Jack Remmen had asked me if I could investigate it impartially, and I told him I could. I believed that, and I believe that I *did* so. I never shirked my responsibilities and efforts on everything else that came in—and there was plenty—-and I did my part as a team member with our caseload. But what I didn't do was dump Harry's case and write it off as the accidental John King needled me about. I might have done that in short order, if Harry had not been my friend.

John Masters was a clean-cut guy with a nice house in the suburbs, the very profile Fiddle John King had described. He even owned a liquor store in Kendall, and I could only presume that the capital to buy the place was all from this group's smuggling exploits. I drove by the liquor store and when I saw the storefront window,

I laughed out loud: a large ad for a brand of Scotch covered the window: "Old Smuggler".

I contacted Masters, and to my surprise, he came in. Terse and quietly arrogant, his knee hammered nervously through the entire sworn statement. The only reason he came in was to fish for what we had. The little he told me was peripheral and mostly already known. His answers came in short, often one-word bursts. Yes, he knew Bill Cook. How?

"Friend."

"Do you ever provide any services for him, with regards to airplane travel?"

"Specify."

"Ever monitored law enforcement radio transmissions or help him bring airplanes into Florida without detection? Is that specific enough for you?"

"Don't know anything about that. Are you done?" he spat after about a half hour of talking, "because I have an appointment."

I'll bet you do, I thought. To get on the phone with Bill Cook or Robbie Robinson, no doubt. I told him I had more, but he said he had to go. There was not much I could say to keep him there. With that, "Radio John" and his Fifth Amendment privilege bolted out the door.

I spent some time watching Bill Cook. There was a narrow dirt road off that led from 184th street to his house, and I could position myself there without him seeing me. I spotted a large covered shed in the back, and wondered what it was for. There was never any movement, so I would do "spot surveillances"—drive by, sit for fifteen minutes or so to see who might show up and I could get a license plate number. I stopped going for a week or so when the squad got busy with a homicide, then went back when things were calmer. This time I was surprised to see a hornet's nest of activity in the back yard.

The canopy covering the large shed was gone, and there was a large boat in the back. About eight or ten people were there, and a hoist was taking the boat off of its platform and onto a large flatbed truck. I could have used a team of surveillance people at that moment, but it was just me, so I notified the dispatcher what I was doing, and got Remmen on our point-to-point channel to let him know what was going on. This wasn't some pleasure fishing boat. This vessel was at least 34-feet long, with a massive, deep hull, outfitted for ocean travel. And maybe lots of storage.

It wasn't a half hour later that the truck was heading out of Cook's gate, with an entourage of about four cars and pickup trucks. I followed well behind and trailed the caravan east, then south, to a Redland house about six blocks off of U.S.1. There, Cook and his moving crew put the boat into another huge shed, which already housed this boat's identical twin brother with the same enormous hull formation. Cook, and whoever owned this house, was in the process of putting together another smuggling project, one that wouldn't crash in the Everglades.

I excitedly got back to the Homicide Office and researched the address of the house. It was owned by Bob Hoog, the owner of Hoog boats, a popular flats fishing boat manufacturer. The hulking twins in his back yard were a comical contrast to the well-known Hoog line of bay boats: Hoogs were 15-18 footers, sleek, flat bottomed, with stern platforms and trolling motors, so the angler could cruise slowly in water one to two feet deep, stalking highly prized bonefish and other flats fish. Those two behemoths would run aground in anything shallower than eight feet of water.

The prosecutor who was the "on-duty ASA" (assistant state attorney) the day I walked in with the Rivenbark file under my arm was a young woman named Jamie Campbell. We had done a case or two together, so I was glad to see her. The on-duty ASA gets any walk-in cases, warrants, and charging questions from detectives.

When I told her that I had probable cause to get a warrant for two counts of "Unlawful Aircraft Registration," she thought I was playing a joke on her.

"What?" She said with a laugh, "you're kidding me on this, right?"

"No," I told her, "look." I showed her Florida Statute 329.10. "It's a third-degree felony." Then, I showed her my evidence: the bill of sale, signed by "James William Cooper", and Bill Cook's phone number, the identification of Cook made by the nice old retired Delta pilot who sold the Piper Navajo to Cook and Robinson, and John Marcus' statement that Harry had been offloading for them.

"Ok," she sighed heavily. "I'll give you your warrant. This is a first for me, from a Homicide investigator, that's for sure."

"For me too," I said, thanking her.

I walked out of the State Attorney's Office knowing that this might be as far as we ever would take my "accidental." But I had one last task to see if that was the case: arrest Bill Cook and see if we could get him to talk. There was no answer at his door the three times I went there, no cars anywhere. I went by Hoog's place, and the boats were still there, so he hadn't gone on that expedition yet. Maybe another flight was going on.

The rental manager at Tamiami Airport was a very helpful guy whose brother was a cop with us. We found out that Robbie Robinson kept his twin-engine Cessna there. In fact, he even tipped us off one day when Robbie was about to land, and we got there in time to watch him taxi the plane back to the hangar. Robbie was alone and quite surprised to see us.

A bespectacled, forty-ish guy with a well-trimmed dark beard, smiled at us as he climbed out of the airplane.

"I know a guy named Bill Cook, yes," he said, his eyes darting from me to Detective Mike Tabernero. "But I haven't seen him in a while. I'm pretty sure he's out of the country."

"Out of the country, where?" I asked.

Robinson just shrugged.

"How about that plane you guys lost out on Aerojet?" I asked him. "What happened out there?"

Robinson was still smiling, but he was having a hard time preventing the smile from turning into a grimace.

"Aerojet?" He waited, to see if we would give him a little more. This was a dance that we often had with some suspects. They wanted to pump *us* to see just how much we knew. In this case, I didn't see any danger in feeding him additional information. We really had nothing to lose.

"Yes. Aerojet." I paused for a moment, then held up a photo of Harry. "Where Harry Rivenbark died."

The smile had all but crumbled now. "Um," Robbie said, almost stammering. "I'm not sure what this is about. But I'm not comfortable having this conversation anymore."

I gave him my business card. "Let us know when you are, Mr. Robinson. Because we're going to keep working on it." And with that, we left.

I was still trying to piece together just how Harry had been killed. An execution was out of the question, and it just made sense that it somehow was related to the crash. I wondered if someone at the Medical Examiner's Office would mind doing a short study on his decapitation. To my amazement and delight, Dr. Joe Davis himself took an interest. He asked me to send him all the scene photos and said he would review the autopsy file and let me know what he found. Then, he called me to his office one day. This was not something to be taken lightly. Davis was a world-renowned forensic pathologist. He lectured globally, with the finest medico-legal minds in attendance. The man was a legend. The very building we sat in that day, the "new" Medical Examiner's Office, was later named The Dr. Joseph Davis Center for Forensic Pathology.

"It's an interesting case," Doc Davis said to me that afternoon. "I've been looking carefully at the margins of the wound, the decapitation. It's not consistent with any kind of weapon. Let me look at this in a little more detail and we'll talk again."

I gave him a copy of the scene and body portion of the report, and all scene photos. When I came back two days later, Davis explained his theory.

"This decapitation is much more in line with a massive blunt force—and I believe he was struck by the leading edge of one of the wings of the airplane, as it was landing, or in the process of crashing."

"And there's no evidence on the body that would suggest a propeller strike, do you agree?"

"That's right," Doctor Davis nodded. "He would have massive wounds from a moving propeller. This was the wing. Especially what you told me about the plane spinning around after striking that tree. I'm sure this was the wing hitting him."

That was good enough for me and made perfect sense. I had gone as far as going to Miami's National Weather Service station and asking them for the weather records for that spot along the eastern Everglades near Aerojet during the hours we believed the crash occurred. Their report noted a cluster of very powerful thunderstorm cells moving through that area in the early morning hours, between midnight and two a.m., that would have brought wind gusts of forty to fifty miles an hour and possible hail. If the plane had come in during that time, Harry would have had one hell of a time with his reflectors, or whatever he was using to aid in the landing. No doubt, the pilot would have had some difficulties as well, landing on a dimly lit levee road—which took a mild right-hand curve at one point—in a fierce storm.

I imagined a chaotic landing scene, and Davis' assessment fit perfectly. If he had been on that levee road, there would have been very little space for him to dive out of the way. One side would have put him in the canal, and the other into the marshy area where we found the plane and the severed tree.

By poring over Bill Cook's short arrest record—which included a marijuana smuggling arrest at Black Point (before there was a marina there)—we learned of an ex-girlfriend, a brief employment at Hoog Boats, and a couple of other places we might find him, but he wasn't there. One day, we found a car registered to him in a parking lot on U.S. 1. The car looked like it had been sitting there for a while. Inside, on the back seat, was a flight manual for a DC-3 airplane.

After a month of looking for Cook, I was starting to believe that he had gotten wind of the warrant and may well have left the country as Robbie told us. Then one day a very pleasant lawyer named Michael Tarre called me.

"I understand you're looking for my client, William Gordon Cook," he said.

I told him he was correct. "Well," Tarre went on. "He's had some health problems. Some type of digestive, intestinal thing. I think it's from the stress of being wanted on this case of yours."

That's what happens when you leave a good friend's body to rot in the Everglades, Billy. "He wants to turn himself in," Tarre said. "Can we come to your office tomorrow and take care of that?"

We would be glad to host that meeting of course. Michael Tarre was an affable guy, bearded, dark haired and slender, in a neat suit. He wasn't officious or contentious with us at all. Bill Cook looked stoic and quiet, an almost sage-like figure with a large beard and shaggy, salt and pepper hair. He wore a plaid long sleeve shirt and jeans, looking every bit the Redland smuggler whose stomach wanted to stop churning over the death he had caused. Since this was likely the last chance I would ever have to speak with him, I wasn't going to give his innards a rest. We sat in one of the lieutenant's offices and I went over the routine questions. A couple of times, Cook cupped his hear and quietly said, "Can you repeat that please?

"Mr. Cook," I started out, "you're here today charged with two counts of unlawful aircraft registration, and these charges are related to the death of your friend, Harry Rivenbark."

His face went dark, and he dropped his head. As he stared at the floor, I relished the moment. Cook's guilt-ridden face was as close to a confession as I would ever get, and the only justice we would ever get out of this case, the only measure of closure I could go to Harry's father with.

Then I went through the Miranda warnings, though I knew that was a fruitless act, with his attorney right there. Matter-of-factly, Tarre just nodded when I was done and said, "Mr. Cook won't be giving any statements." He asked me if we could talk outside for a moment, so we left Bill in the office and went into the squad room.

Tarre grinned. "You see how he had trouble hearing you sometimes? These smugglers, their hearing goes from flying those prop planes so much." We shared a chuckle over that, and I think our laughter was as much over the fact that everything was so obvious in this case that Tarre himself had no problem acknowledging what his client was.

"Will there be any more charges coming?" Tarre asked me.

"There might. Once we substantiate how much weed was on the airplane, we could be looking at some felony-murder charges, for sure." |

He nodded thoughtfully and stroked his beard. "Ok. Thanks."

And that was that. I booked a quiet, compliant William Gordon Cook into the Dade County Jail, and Tarre bonded him out the same evening.

Robinson and Masters lawyered up, and we never found anyone who could give us an admission statement from Robinson, Cook, or anyone else. Cook pled guilty to the charges and got five-years' probation. The Florida Water Management District salvaged the two undamaged Lycoming engines from the wreckage and put them in their two new airboats.

It was all over. I had pushed this as far as it would go. I would have to hope that someone would emerge and give us the full story of that flight one day. At least now I could tell John King that I had at least gotten *some* criminal charges out this whole thing—out of the hardest worked accidental death in Metro-Dade history.

Chapter Ten

82nd Avenue

It was called "Suniland." Before the 1990's, it wasn't considered an elite place to live as it is now, as the western section of the "Village of Pinecrest. Our little street in Suniland was anything but upper crust, it was just a typical suburban neighborhood where kids like me rode their bikes to Suniland Pizza or the Suniland Twin theatre, barely a 10-minute pedal from my house. The fastest way to get from my house was to take 82nd Avenue, and that brought me to the Suniland Shopping Center, where all that good stuff was. My friend Stan and I biked everywhere. Stan lived well east and south of me, by the Deering estate, and it wasn't unusual for him to ride over to my house, or me to his and hang out together. Things were changing though, even as early as 1971, when Stan and I came out of the Suniland Twin theater to find both of our bikes gone. The idea of people stealing things around there never really occurred to us, and we both ended up getting new bikes. I earned this bike by mowing lawns—it was a decent tradeoff for my parents: if I had not gotten another bike, my dad would have had to drive me the ten miles to school in the Grove. Much better that I ride the two miles to the corner of 136th Street and 72nd Avenue, where Stan and I would meet up, then pump hard the rest of the way to make it in time for the opening bell. I had strong legs when I was 13.

My second bike, however, met its fate on 82nd Avenue, too. I was coming home from another friend's house when a fierce thunderstorm kicked up, and I decided to cross over 128th street, just before the intersection at 82nd, to get some cover from the carport of a nearby house. People didn't mind those things back then. In my haste, I didn't look before I crossed over, and the next thing I knew, brakes were screeching, there was a sickening crunch, and I was on the windshield of the car as it shrieked to a stop. A second later, I was sailing through the air and onto the pavement. Laying there on the shoulder of the street, I looked down at my legs to see if they were still there, and they were. Other than being a little bloodied from hitting the asphalt, I was fine, but my bike was a crumpled ball of metal in the middle of the street.

Not more than a year later, Dad was crossing the same intersection, right at 128th and 82nd. A teenage girl blew the stop sign and totaled our white 1968 Plymouth Satellite station wagon, a car I loved and nicknamed the Great White. Dad was fine, and so was the girl, but the Great White, like the shark in the movie Jaws, was no more.

That stretch of 82nd avenue was accumulating more bad memories than good.

On October 4th, 1985, our squad got a case of a man shot at a rockpit on the edge of the Everglades, where Route 41 meets State Road 27. There was nothing out there except sawgrass and canals, and the only people who went out there were plinkers with their rifles and handguns—much like I had done with John, Harry, and Garry. Someone, it seemed, had plinked our victim. This wasn't the way the cartel killed people. The case made little sense, except that the killer took his car. Even so, car thieves usually don't kill people.

Jay Vas was the lead detective in the Emilio Briel case, and it was a tough one. Briel was someone's target, and his gold '77 Chevy Monte Carlo was missing. Emboldened by their murder of Briel, these unknown killers went back four months later to the same rockpit and shot Jose Collazo, who was also target shooting, and took his black 1979 Monte Carlo.

Just thirteen days later, the police airwaves were abuzz with a BOLO for a gold-colored Monte Carlo and two white males who had just struck a Loomis armored car in Kendall. From November on, this heavily armed duo hit four more times at banks in the south end along Dixie Highway. In all but one case, the gold Monte

Carlo was used, and the last two robberies were at the Barnett Bank on the corner of 136 street and Dixie in Suniland, a two-minute walk from my old house. In one of the heists, a Brinks guard was shot, but survived.

By this time, the FBI had formed a task force to start looking for the two suspects, who had become increasingly brazen and violent. On April 11th, 1986, task force FBI Agents Jerry Dove and Ben Grogan spotted a black Monte Carlo cruising the parking lot near Barnett Bank and alerted the rest of the team. They followed the car north into the residential area, and watched it make three left turns—a classical countersurveillance tactic—before heading north from 128th Street, on 82nd Avenue.

I was a few miles south of that location when I got notified to head to 82nd avenue and 123rd street—all I was told was that there had been a police shooting involving FBI agents. On my way there I got two more calls from the office: multiple law enforcement officers were down, and possibly FBI agents killed. What the hell was going on? When I got to the scene, that quiet little avenue I rode my bike to the movie theater on had been transformed into a maelstrom of activity. A mob of detectives, bystanders, news media, and uniform officers swarmed around a crime scene on 82nd Avenue where a black Monte Carlo was crashed into a small tree, blocked in by two other cars.

Two bodies lay on either side of the car. I walked over to the one on the ground by the driver's door. His eyes stared blankly skyward, and I remember thinking that he looked like David Crosby, the musician. I learned quickly that these were the robbery suspects the feds had been looking for. I also learned that two FBI agents, Benjamin Grogan and Jerry Dove, had been killed in the shootout.

The agents' had already been removed from the scene just before I got there. Five other agents had been wounded and were already at the hospital. Blood was everywhere on and around the cars. Across the street and slightly to the north was a retail center with a rooftop parking garage. It was lined elbow to elbow with news media cameras. The firefight between the agents and the robbers occurred in front of a duplex, in a rectangle of space not much bigger than someone's living room. When the subjects' car hit the tree, they didn't get out and run away, like most wanted subjects would do. They got out and started firing, all the while *advancing* on the FBI agents, who were taking cover behind their cars. The subjects, Michael Platt and William Matix had assault rifles, and the agents had revolvers. With blood literally spurting out of massive wounds in his chest and neck, Platt continued firing with a shotgun and a handgun, while Matix poured round after lethal round out of a Ruger Mini-14 at the team of agents. At one point, Matix, even with his life draining from him, leaned over one of the cars and shot and killed Agent Jerry Dove as he attempted to reload.

As seven agents lay on the ground, the severely wounded subjects crawled to Grogan's car and tried to get it started to flee the scene. Agent Edmundo Mireles, himself wounded and barely able to use one arm, staggered to his feet, put his Remington 870 shotgun between his legs so he could rack a round into the chamber, and blasted 00 buckshot into the back window. Platt and Matix were still alive though, sluggishly trying to start the FBI car, which was peppered with bullet holes and splashed with theirs and the agents' blood. Mireles, with six bullet wounds in him, made his way to the driver's side and emptied his revolver into both Platt and Matix, finally killing both of them.

In a briefing on the side of the road, with an army of news media watching from the rooftop parking area, we were given various leads. The subjects were dead, yes, but there would be hundreds of questions to answer and corroboration needed. This was not a homicide that would be in the papers one day and forgotten the next. The magnitude of this horrible event would make FBI history. Every minute detail would be scrutinized, analyzed and studied by FBI supervisors, the FBI Director, and to the DOJ. Our homicide investigation had to be as thorough and airtight as if we were going to trial.

In the briefing, Sgt. Dave Rivers explained that the two subjects were indeed the bank robbers we and the FBI had been looking for and he quickly gave us details necessary for us to go handle our various leads. Rivers pointed to a lady standing just outside the yellow lines, in the crowd of onlookers.

"Nyberg, that lady lives down the block and says she heard the shooting. She came out with her camera, and took a bunch of pictures. She's your lead. We need those pictures."

The lady was very nice, but, she said, "I gave my film to one of your female detectives." She pointed out a nearby woman with an ID tag on a lanyard around her neck. The lanyard showed her name, and the words "Associated Press." I approached the woman and told her we would need the film. It was evidence.

"Oh," I added, "and...did you tell the lady who gave you the film that you were with the police department?"

"No, no," the reporter said, "I just told her um...that we needed the pictures."

"Well, *we* need the pictures." I took out a property receipt. I asked her to sign the property receipt, indicating she was giving the roll of film to me.

She became visibly nervous. "Ah, well, I'm sorry, I don't have it. I gave it to my editor, and its already on its way to New York."

That fast, on its way to New York? She stuck to her story, and I went back to the woman who had taken the pictures. The AP reporter had never actually said that she was with the police department. Instead she saw the woman as an easy target and used an air of authority to imply that she was law enforcement. The lady bought it, and now I was on a chase to get the film. The witness showed me her house—it was almost at the end of 82nd avenue, and she had a driveway made of oyster shells. Across the street was the Suniland shopping center, where my friend Stan and I had our bikes stolen outside the Suniland theater. She had heard the shooting, stepped out to the street with her camera, and used the zoom lens to see what was going on.

"I saw smoke," she told me, "and men crouching as they moved across the street. It looked like they were holding bullet proof vests out in front of them with one hand and shooting with pistols with the other."

Dove and Grogan's backup team, I thought. *Holding their vests in front of them* like hand-held shields. My god.

The film compartment in her Pentax camera was empty at the time, so she ran back inside, quickly popped in some film, and ran back out. Then she started clicking, but by that time the shooting had ceased, and all she could see was a jumble of police and fire-rescue vehicles. Still, we needed to see what was on that roll of film.

Our department had just purchased an enormous RV and customized it into a mobile command post. It had phones, fax machines, and everything else we needed for something like this. They would have a phone I could use to call the AP. When I got inside the Command Post I had to check in the with the brass and explain my lead. They got me a phone, and I called the Associated Press office in New York. It took me a while to get to someone in charge, but I was told me that the film had already gone to the lab for developing. This, I knew, was well-rehearsed bullshit, but I pressed on, and told them we would get subpoenas if we needed to. Then, I thought of another idea. I went back to the nice lady with the oyster-shell driveway, and told her what I needed from her.

"I'll be listening on the phone," I told her, "and I want you to be the adamant citizen who is demanding your film back, or you'll go to the *Miami Herald* and tell them the whole story."

She was impressed with our Command Post vehicle as she sat down at the desk with me. I got the same New York AP supervisor on the phone and the lady did a fabulous job. I want my film back, *now*, she told them. I don't want to have to go to the news people here and make a big deal about it, and I don't want to have to call my lawyer.

"It's *my* film," she told them, "not yours." I loved that part.

There was a brief silence, and the supervisor on the other end said, "Yes, Ma'am. We'll have a courier deliver it to your house in an hour."

In an hour, all the way from a photo lab New York! Imagine that.

For the next week at least three teams from Homicide were consumed with the scene, the ensuing leads, and preparing reports on the FBI shooting, which had reached international news within an hour. Crime scene and homicide investigators together worked through the night to calculate the ballistics, which came to an astounding count of approximately 144 rounds fired from eleven different firearms. Southwest 82nd Avenue still swarmed with camera crews from all over the globe. It was as sensational a story as anything that had ever happened in south Florida, and was soon dubbed, "The Bloodiest Day in FBI history."

Ten years later, I was amazed that no one had thought to commemorate the street at all. We have streets all over the County and in Miami dedicated to South American Generals, presidents, and Latin American freedom fighters. But what of our own heroes who died protecting us, right here on our soil? I wrote a letter to the Pinecrest City Council and called them. When will you guys honor what happened here?

I was told that I needed to speak to the County, that they were the ones who had a bunch of street signs named after fallen law enforcement officers, sitting in a warehouse somewhere. The signs were made after the Miami-Dade County Commission voted in a resolution that several streets should be named after those officers.

But they never put the signs up.

My next call was to the County Commission. I made enough noise there for someone to make a call to Pinecrest, and next thing we knew, I was attending a street naming dedication ceremony, held at Pinecrest Park—across the street from the shooting scene. It was presided over by Evelyn Greer, the mayor of Pinecrest at the time. Greer went to great lengths to talk about how this all occurred in a different time, when drug dealing was rampant, and how safe Pinecrest was now. It was an embarrassingly defensive stance from a politician who should have been honoring Dove, Grogan and the FBI wounded. The violent confrontation had nothing at all to do with drugs, and the toxicology results from the autopsies of Platt and Matix confirmed it. These were deeply twisted, violent men. They enjoyed the thrill of exacting violence on innocent people, and they were hell bent on going out in a blaze of glory. Their backgrounds—including the suspicious deaths of *both* their wives—are well chronicled in hundreds of news stories, movies, and books—the best of them by Edmundo Mireles (who fired the final, fatal shots into Platt and Matix), entitled *FBI Miami Firefight: Five Minutes that Changed the Bureau.*

I still drive 82nd avenue from time to time. But the memories have all changed. I go past the four-way stop at 128th street, and think of my bike crash, and the "great white" getting t-boned. Four blocks north, the street sign reads, "Agent Jerry Dove Av, Agent Benjamin Grogan Av", and a plaque stands in the swale, across from those duplexes, telling the story.

Though I can still picture me and Stan riding our bikes to the movies, that memory is clouded. Crystal clear are the memories of a chaotic, unforgettable day: crowds of stunned citizens, legions of television cameras, blood covered cars, and the deaths of two men who used to do what I did: carry a badge, work long hours, joke with their squad members, and go home to their families.

When someone in law enforcement is killed, it always hurts. Regardless of where they worked, or what agency they worked for, they are brothers, and sisters. The deaths of Dove and Grogan, though, had a deep, personal ache for me. These things weren't supposed to happen in Suniland.

Chapter Eleven

Tater and Moonberry

My very first pet was a grayish-black mottled little kitten.

"Her coat looks like cinder," my Dad commented. The name stuck. What did not stick, however, was a healthy cat-human relationship. Cinder scratched me on the inside of my forearm one day, and I ended up in the hospital with hives all over the place. Discovery is not always pleasant. The next time I was around a cat, my nose would run, my eyes would itch and water, and I knew I was not a cat person. Cats weren't good for me.

I would never hurt one, though.

It was 1987, but we still had hunters in South Florida. Quail hunters still found empty fields in the Redland. The undeveloped spots around Homestead had dwindled down to almost nothing by the mid 1980's, so the quail hunters would head way west to the edge of the Everglades, where there was still a lot of open space.

James Mixon didn't come out to the east Everglades to hunt. He came out to find a place to live. Mixon had a talent for getting kicked out of just about every place he ever lived; he was an ornery and obnoxious drunk, and even the most tolerant and patient of the Mixon family could no longer harbor him. Mixon ended up at Chekika Park, a remote state park that allowed campers. Chekika nestled up against a shady spot known as Grossman Hammock. To get there, you had to head west as the county's roads would take you and north on 227th avenue (the westernmost paved road in the county) to find the entrance to Chekika. Just north of the park the road deteriorated until it dead ended at the spot where John Marcus, Harry Rivenbark and I used to go shooting.

Jim Mixon couldn't afford a gun, but what little money he did have he spent on beer, gas, and the eight dollars a night it cost be a "camper" at Chekika. We found all this out after we started investigating his death.

Two hunters stalking quail south of Grossman Farm Road found Mixon's body, face down, shirtless, wearing a pair of shorts. He had three bullet wounds to the back of the head.

Finding a murder victim in a remote area was nothing new to us. In the early to mid-1980s it had become positively ho-hum. But this guy didn't look like a victim of the cocaine wars. No jewelry, no expensive clothes—he looked like a bum. Crime scene took the pictures, the wagon came and loaded up the body, and off we went to Hialeah, to find Mixon's next of kin. We spoke to an ex-wife, an ex-girlfriend, and a brother, and I don't recall a tear between the three of them. They all gave a sad shake of their heads and recited the same thing: Jim Mixon left a trail of exasperated, pissed off people in his wake.

Three in the back of the head is very pissed off indeed.

It was the brother who told us that Mixon had been kicked out of his last apartment. He was going to live at Chekika, he told him, far away from civilization, an idea that seemed to sit well with everyone. The rental manager, a 60-ish woman with short hair and a southern accent, pursed her lips when we showed her Mixon's photo.

"He was—'scuse my French—an *asshole*. I got tired of all the complaints from the other campers about him getting' drunk off his ass and startin' shit with everybody."

She had no idea where he had gone. "Drives a black Bronco." She shrugged. "Sorry he's dead, but I ain't gonna miss him." The info on the black Bronco jived with what the family told us, and we needed Chekika's rental list.

"All of 'em?"

"Yep. Everybody. And do me a favor," I told her. "Circle the ones who have checked out in the last couple days. Anyone that might have left in a hurry." I gave her my card. "And please call me if anyone checks out today."

We would have to come back and start talking to residents. There was nothing out by Chekika. The nearest houses sat in a two-block cluster a good five miles south of where the body was found. To the west of us was nothing but sawgrass and oolite rock, eventually giving way to the swamps and hammocks of the Everglades, all the way to Florida's west coast. The surroundings in that area were all faded tan, save for the occasional dark green clump of trees and bushes that grew up around the rock. As we headed south on SW 227th Avenue away from Chekika, I spotted color off in the distance. Sure enough, there was something red in the bushes, just beyond where the skinny roadside canal widened into a pond.

I drove a little further to get a closer look, then stopped and dug my binoculars out of my equipment back in the trunk. With the binos, I could clearly make out a confederate flag, a small campsite, and the part of a vehicle. I couldn't tell what kind of car it was, but it was larger than a sedan, and appeared to have been painted in amateurish camouflage design: wavy stripes of brown, black, and green. There was a narrow, partially flooded dirt path that led from the campsite out to 227th avenue. Just to the east of this spot was another dirt road that led to a small, fenced compound that housed an antenna tower. The site where Mixon's body was found was about three or four hundred yards south of whomever was camping there. If you're out to here to fish and relax, it's a fine campsite, right on the south edge of the pond we were looking across. I wondered if they had heard the shots. Or maybe even fired them.

We talked about going in and paying the campers a visit, then we decided it was wiser to stake the place out and wait for them. If these are our subjects, they're going to see and hear us coming, and that will give them time to get rid of stuff. The element of surprise—and control—is always the more desirable one. We started our surveillance early one morning, and it took no more than a couple of hours before we saw their vehicle bumping along the dirt road, out onto 227th Avenue. It was a Ford Bronco, with the bargain basement camo design. We fell behind the Bronco as it rumbled east on 168th street, and it pulled over almost immediately after we put the lights on the dash and honked our horns. Remmen and I approached the car with Nick Fabregas, the youngest and newest member of our squad.

In the driver's seat was a scruffy, bearded looking guy of about forty. Next to him sat a tanned, brown-haired woman with narrow eyes, wearing a plaid long sleeved flannel shirt. In the back seat was an adorable little girl of about four years, with bright blonde hair. In between the man and woman on the console, plain as day, lay a .357 magnum revolver.

"How about you step out, partner, so we can get that gun out of the way?" I told the driver, who gave me an ID that read, "Jason Brunson." He complied, and I reached in and removed the weapon.

"Your gun?"

"Yessir."

"Your truck?"

"Yessir. It is."

I asked Jason Brunson for the registration of the vehicle, and the female, Ruth Brunson, asked for permission to get it out of the glove box.

"We just bought it," she offered, and handed me a small piece of note paper with some handwriting on it. It read,

I, James Mixon, hereby sell my 1979 Ford Bronco vehicle to Jason Brunson, for the price of $600" It was dated three days ago, which would have been two days before Mixon was found. Below the date was a shaky looking cursive that formed the name "James Mixon."

Neither of them asked why detectives were pulling them over.

"So," I said to them, "where *is* Mr. Mixon?"

Jason Brunson shook his head. "He told me he was heading to North Carolina." Ruth Brunson was nodding.

"Did you know...that he's dead?"

They didn't look at each other, like I expected two shocked people who had just bought a car from the decedent to do. They stared at us instead. "No, I had no idea," Jason said.

I glanced at Remmen and then Nick. "How about we head back to your campsite and have a look around?"

They really couldn't say no. If there was a Fourth Amendment issue here, I hadn't heard of it. Do you have a right to privacy, camping on public land? Maybe, I suppose, inside your tent. That's one for the legal eagles, but either way, just to be safe, we got written consent to search the entire campsite, their tents, and the vehicle. How they came to set up camp there was an interesting story in itself. The land was owned by the state of Florida. The Brunsons set up camp there, and one day they were approached by someone from the State. Vandals had become a nuisance there, breaking into the fenced area and ripping off metal. Jason and Ruth offered to keep out any trespassers in return for the permission to camp there. It turned out to be a nice win-win. The state didn't have to hire security, and the Brunsons had a dandy little campsite on the shores of a wide pond.

Mixon, they told us, drove up one day and told them he had spotted them from the road. He had just gotten kicked out of Chekika, and he asked them if he could fish at the pond. They let him, and he landed a couple of decent sized bass, which they all shared for dinner. Mixon asked them if he could stay at their site until he could find another place, and they agreed. Having a car and a fishing rod met their tenant screening just fine.

As we walked through the campsite, we learned that the only time they would leave was to go buy food. These weren't "survivalists" who lived off the land. They lived off of a convenience store five miles away. They relieved themselves out there in the wild. The little girl, who they called "Muffin", had befriended the local racoons and other critters around the area. While we were there, we saw a small alligator swimming just twenty or so yards from the grassy shore.

"That's Tater!" Muffin said happily. "He's my pet gator." We all got a chuckle out this. We were used to being on crime scenes in the inner city, far from gators and racoons. Our Crime Scene tech snapped a picture of Tater as we continued through the campsite. On a tree near the entrance, we found a wooded sign nailed to a tree. In sharpie-ink, it read: "Per Dog's Campground. Keep out!"

"Who is 'per dog'?" I asked Ruth. She rolled her eyes. "Prairie Dog. That's Muffin's nickname for Jason."

We didn't find anything else that might have belonged to Mixon there.

"We need to talk about Mr. Mixon in more detail. And we'd like to get some handwriting samples from you both. Just to make sure everything's good with this bill of sale."

They went without protest, to Station 4, my old workplace from the brown-gown days. It was a lot closer than the long ride back up to Homicide. Upstairs in the detective bureau of Station 4, Nick and I talked to Ruth, with Muffin by her side, while Jason sat nearby. We decided not to do a full-blown interview until we got the handwriting samples and a set of fingerprints from each of them. Getting confrontational at this point could cause them to change their minds on providing them. Casually, we tossed in a few questions.

"Tell us more about Mixon," I said. "Why did he leave again? What did he say?"

Ruth sat calmly and spoke to us in even tones. She told us that they kind of tolerated Mixon. He would drink, but he would also catch fish, help get firewood, and keep an extra eye out for intruders. She wasn't sure why he had left. But imagining Jim Mixon as a protective figure was a real stretch. It was becoming much more plausible to imagine Mixon, from what we knew of him, being a drunken shithead and making a move on Ruth, or god forbid, Muffin. That motive loomed large as we started to peel away the layers of this strange situation.

Ruth continued talking about Mixon. There were no big problems, she said. Suddenly, Muffin blurted out loudly, "He was mean to Moonberry!"

Ruth's face went dark, and in an instant she exploded on the girl. "You keep your mouth shut!! Don't you interrupt Mommy when I'm talkin' *You hear me*?"

The little girl shrank into herself and pouted sullenly. Ruth's sudden, harsh reaction was striking. Since the moment we had stopped the Bronco until Muffin's outburst, she had been the picture of cool and control.

"Moonberry?" I asked innocently.

Ruth nodded. "She has a kitten—Moonberry." She shot Muffin another glance that seemed to say, "not another word out of you."

We told the Brunsons we would like to get handwriting samples from them. I called up our "Questioned Documents" section and spoke to Tom Quirk, a veteran document examiner who worked the two-person office in the Crime Lab.

"Have each one of them write out the entire bill of sale, word for word, three times." Quirk told me. "Then bring it all in with the original. And see if you can get me some of your victim's handwriting samples too."

To our surprise, both Ruth and Jason acquiesced to our handwriting requests, and sat there like punished schoolkids writing out the note once, twice, three times. There wasn't an utterance of protest or question about it, nor did they didn't blink when we told them we would be sending the .357 to the lab to test fire it and see if it was the weapon that fired the projectiles we dug out of Mixon's skull.

We talked to Jason in another room, and decided we would cut them loose. I had a strong feeling we were going to strike gold on either the bill of sale or the gun, and these two weren't hopping on a plane to Venezuela any time soon. Still, we would try to go by the campsite at least once a day to watch.

Two days later, I got a double-dose of great news—the Brunson's .357 magnum revolver was the murder weapon. And as icing on the cake: Jason Brunson, not James Mixon, wrote the bill of sale and signed Mixon's name. It was time to bring the Brunsons in again. I wanted a confession, or for one of them to turn on the other. We impounded the truck. At least we had proof that it wasn't theirs, so if nothing else, they were going to jail for auto theft.

I sat in one of the Lieutenants' offices with Jason, and Nick took Ruth to an interview room. We put Muffin in Lt. Glen Kay's office, and gave her some juice, some crayons, and a coloring book. After confronting Jason with our findings—that we now knew his gun was the murder weapon and that he falsified the bill of sale—I urged him to come clean.

"We already know you're involved, Jason. Just tell me how it all happened. Start to finish."

Jason was an abysmal liar, changing his story at least three times; once it was "I don't know where he went. He sold us the truck and said he would write up a bill of sale and never did. He never came back, so we just wrote it up." Self-appointed power-of-attorney. Nifty.

"And he went...where?" It's not like you could call a taxi out there.

"He said someone was coming to pick him up," Jason said, his eyes starting to dart around the room.

A few minutes later, it was "he said he was going to North Carolina. I don't know how he was going to get there."

Clearly all this bullshit was being frantically made up on the fly. We went in circles for a while and Jason was starting to disintegrate. I felt the confession coming.

"Jason, you know what happened." I tried to give him a small out, a chance to share the blame. "Did Mixon...try something with Ruth?"

"No...no," he started stuttering. Jason was biting his lip and looking around on the floor like he had dropped something. This was the point in an interview when you couldn't quite see the parade yet, but the drums were getting louder.

Just then, Nick opened the door and stuck his head in. "Ram, I need to talk to you.."

"Nick, give me a minute," I told him—then I leaned close to him. "I'm close!" I whispered.

Nick flashed a little smile. "Ram, Ruth just confessed."

Nick and I spent another half hour with Ruth, then took her into the stenographers' office, where we took her sworn statement. A couple of hours later, after booking Ruth into the Dade County Jail, I sat in Jack's office with Ruth's typed statement in my hands.

"So what was the deal?" Jack said, leaning back. He had that smile, the one a sergeant wore when his squad just closed a case.

"It goes like this, Jack: Mixon came to live with them, just as they told us in the beginning. As the days go on, they come to realize he's a drunken ass. One afternoon, he's bombed, and Muffin is upset about something, crying. Mixon is annoyed at her crying, and he picks up Moonberry, the kitten, and tosses it into the pond. Tater, who is used to being tossed scraps by Muffin—-"

"You gotta be kiddin' me..." Remmen muttered.

"No, this is for real. Mixon tosses the kitten into the pond, and Tater makes a beeline for it. Tater takes Moonberry under the surface and she's never seen again. Needless to say, Muffin is absolutely inconsolable. Shrieking and crying to no end. When Ruth comes to console her and find out what happened, she calmly makes a plan. She invites Mixon to help her go gather firewood. He's three sheets to the wind and doesn't put two and two together. Ruth drives the truck, with Mixon in the passenger seat. When they stop, supposedly for firewood, she points out the window. When he looks, she takes the .357 and puts one in the back of his head. He slumps against the door, and she goes around to the other side, opens it and pulls him out. He flops on the ground, and she gives him a *coup de gras*—two more in the head. Gets back, drives back to camp."

It *was* one hell of a tale. Not your "average" homicide by any means.

We convicted Ruth at trial, and she got life. We charged Jason with auto theft, forgery, and accessory to murder after the fact. He got off easy, agreeing to testify against Ruth, and did five years' probation. Muffin went to live with her grandparents in Naples. Cats, it seems, are nothing but trouble, but Moonberry didn't deserve *that*.

I have told the story to my kids, and to classes full of recruits at the police academy, and students of my Homicide Investigation class.

It has become known as the Legend of Moonberry Pond.

Chapter Twelve

Creatures

Kids get paranoid at night, when they're alone. One night, my parents were gone for a party. They left me some food and told me they would be back by about 11pm. I was nine. It wasn't shocking to leave a nine-year-old at home alone in 1967. Parents weren't as worried about things happening as they are now. Besides, I had my best friend, Don, across the street, and I could go there. I watched some TV but spent most of my time sorting my football cards. That would keep me busy for a long time. Then, the noises.

Our little two-bedroom home in South Miami had jalousie windows, and they had a very distinctive rattle when you opened and closed the door, or even if you tried to pry one off—which was ridiculously easy to do. If you had a screwdriver, you could get enough leverage to just slide one of the panes off at the doorknob level, and you were all but inside the home. Our home also had a dirt alleyway in the back. I used to hop our fence all the time and walk to the U-Totem to buy my football cards. That night, I realized that anyone could hop the fence the other way, too, and be in our yard. What I heard was something like a rattle, a tapping on the jalousies. Was someone trying to break in?

I was scared. My Dad had left some tools around from where he was working on some things in the kitchen. There was a hammer there, and I wasn't exactly sure what I was going to do if someone came through that door, but I sure felt better with it in my hand.

Harold Herndon spent a lot of time in his garage. He had a 1952 Plymouth there that he was lovingly restoring so that one day he could take it out on Sundays ride in style. The Herndon house sat on a quiet street in the northwest sector of Miami Lakes. Harold and Thelma Herndon wanted the serenity of retirement that most folks in their late sixties sought. Harold, though, couldn't stay still. He was an adept handyman and had a side business putting up popcorn ceilings for people, when that type of décor was all the rage. Thelma stayed busy too. She had a big greenhouse in the back yard, and was in heaven tending to her orchids, flowers, and other plants. The Herndons were also lucky enough to have family right next door.

Their daughter, Doris Headberg, lived in the adjacent house with her husband Michael and their two kids. The only glitch in the Herndons' idyllic retirement scenario was their adopted grandson, a troubled young man named James Henry Herndon. "Jimmy" had trouble growing up. In 1987, he was 30 years old and had found his way to several arrests for burglary, drug possession (mostly cocaine). Most notably, he was a suspect in a rape case. Harold and Thelma, though, were good, forgiving people and took him in, time after time. Every time, Jimmy would disappoint their kindness and generosity. They retreated to their garage and greenhouse for their sanity and sanctity—and from the trouble and stress Jimmy brought into their lives.

On December 11th, the plan was for the entire family to get together and wrap presents for Christmas. Harold, Thelma, and Jimmy were supposed to go next door to Doris and Michael Headberg's house for fun and gift-wrapping. It was getting to be late afternoon, and everyone was a little puzzled as to why they hadn't come over yet. Doris went next door to her parents' house and found all the blinds drawn. What the heck was going on? She knocked on the door, and it seemed forever for someone to answer. Jimmy answered, and let Doris in. The place was strangely dark, with binds closed. She looked around, puzzled.

"Where's Mom and Dad?" she asked Jimmy.

"I killed them," he told Doris.

She didn't believe him. He was acting odd, but then, Doris guessed that he was probably high again. Then, she saw her father's

.45 semiautomatic pistol in Jimmy's hand. As soon as she noticed it, Jimmy pointed it at her, grabbed her by the arm, and pushed her down into a chair.

"Sit here," he told her. He tied her hands to the chair with some electric cord and started removing her clothes.

Doris could not believe that her parents were dead, but Jimmy was really getting whacked out, and there were no sounds of her mother and father anywhere in the home. Filled with dread now and wondering if she was going to be next, she complied with Jimmy as he removed her clothes. When he started to fondle her, she said, "Jimmy...no...we're family...stop."

Jimmy mumbled something and stopped, but kept her tied up, naked, to the chair in the living room. An hour or so later, Michael Headberg, Sr. wondered what was taking Doris and all of them so long to come over. He and his 17-year-old son, Michael Jr., went over to investigate.

Father and son went to the back of the house and entered through the sliding glass door that led into the family room. Jimmy went to intercept them there, and the meeting was brief. As soon as the Michael Sr. started asking where everyone was, Jimmy raised the .45 and opened fire. The shocked teenager watched his father fall, then took off running for his house, with Jimmy chasing after him. As the boy was entering the house, Jimmy blazed away with the .45, striking Michael four times. He staggered into the house, got his younger sister, and hid inside a locked bathroom as Jimmy came in looking for them. Jimmy gave up quickly and went back next door, as Michael fought to stay alive, huddled in the bathroom with his little sister. By the time Jimmy returned, Doris had gotten free of her binds and was running out of the house and down the street, naked, to the neighbors. Michael Headberg, Sr. was dead.

Jimmy grabbed the keys to the Harold's white Ford van and fled.

It was my turn to be the lead investigator. What we found at the Herndon house that night was horrific. Harold Herndon lay slumped over a bunch of tools, buckets, and other items in his crowded garage, covered with blood. His head had been smashed repeatedly with a ball peen hammer. It appeared that Thelma may have heard the commotion, came into the garage, and then fled towards the back yard. Jimmy caught up with her in her greenhouse. Her body was in a seated position, folded forward—her forehead down by her knee. She, too, had been pummeled mercilessly in the head with a heavy object. It appeared that Jimmy must have sat on her back as he bludgeoned her. In their favorite places, where Thelma and Harold Herndon had spent countless peaceful and relaxing hours, their lives came to a brutal, frenzied end.

17-year-old Michael was at the hospital with four gunshot wounds, but he was in stable condition, and would probably make it. Doris slowly, tearfully, told us the entire story, and after the scene work was done, we went to the hospital to talk to Michael. The poor kid was in a ton of pain, but was in good enough shape for us to get a sworn statement. After about six hours of processing the scene—which encompassed two houses—we were done, and the three bodies of Jimmy Herndon's victims were carted off to the Medical Examiner's Office for autopsy. One moment, they were cheerfully looking forward to wrapping gifts together. The next, a sudden explosion of violence ended the lives of half the family. Doris Headberg's parents and husband were all dead.

Where would Jimmy have gone? We had put out a BOLO for the van and for Jimmy as soon as Doris told us he had left in the vehicle. She didn't have any ideas, except that Jimmy had grown up on the west coast, around Fort Myers. That was the only place she thought he might go. We had plenty to go get an arrest warrant, so I got to the office and started working on the affidavit. A detective working in our unit shouldn't need more than a couple of years on the job before understanding how to express probable cause in an affidavit for a warrant. Still, we always called the on-call state attorney and ran it all by them. We got the thumbs-up from the duty prosecutor, and now set out to visit the on-call judge. The 11th Judicial Circuit designated a judge to be on call for a week, when urgent needs for warrants came up. This night, it was none other than Judge Ellen Morphonius. "Maximum Morphonious", as she was known, was as tough as they come; an old-fashioned, law-and-order judge who tolerated no nonsense, and gave no compromise to violent criminals. If the statute called for ten years, you were getting ten years. She didn't have much time for excuses, bad childhoods, or any other kind of argument.

It was about 2:30am when we called her, and she said to come on over. Don't mind her dogs, she told us; their barks were way worse than their bite (something you could *not* say about their owner). Ellen Morphonius was in a nightgown and a housecoat as she sat and read through my affidavit. She shook her head as she got to the part about how the defendant used a ball-peen hammer to repeatedly pound her grandparents until they were dead. I handed her a pen.

"Any idea where he might be?" she said, initialing the pages as she leafed through to the last signature page.

"Judge, we have information he may have gone over to the west coast...Naples or Fort Myers area maybe," I told her.

Morphonious put the pen on the signature page and muttered as she signed her name. "Huh...well...maybe some Trooper will pull him over on a dark road, and he'll make a stupid move...save us a lot of trouble."

She handed me the signed warrant. "Hope you get the sonofabitch soon," she said.

"Thank you, your Honor."

And with that, we set out into a dark morning to find a triple-murderer. The whole time, I thought of Judge Morphonius' wishful scenario. It certainly *would* save a lot of trouble.

We all went home around 6am, a few hours after Judge Morphonious signed the warrant. After a few hours' sleep we returned at eleven the next morning. The murders were all over the news by then, and Jimmy Herndon's picture was showing up on every TV news show and in the front page of the *Miami Herald*. Wanted, for the murder of three family members.

There wasn't much we could do except to have the dispatcher keep putting out the BOLO, which they were doing every few hours, so that every shift in every district had it. Then, on the afternoon of December 13th, we got a call from Hendry County, Florida, about two hours away to the northwest, at the seven o'clock mark of Lake Okeechobee.

Deputies in neighboring Lee County had gotten a call of two young women who had been raped at gunpoint. The women took the deputies to a white Ford Van, stuck in the sand, where they said a gangly, dark-haired guy had picked them up hitchhiking, pulled off into a dirt road and raped them at gunpoint. After the assaults, Jimmy couldn't get the van out of the sand. He left them there and fled on foot.

On Highway 50, between Ft. Myers and a tiny agricultural town called LaBelle, a Hendry County deputy spotted the subject fitting the description of their rape subject walking along the roadside. When the Deputy got out and approached him to pat him down, the subject resisted, but the deputy got control of him quickly. A silver .45 pistol was tucked in his waistband. When they got Jimmy Herndon back to their station, he answered their questions, but didn't volunteer anything. The deputies were slow in running him in the system. Finally, he looked at them blankly and said, "I killed three people in Miami."

The deputy processing his paperwork chuckled. "*Sure* you did."

But just in case, his sergeant said, let's run him in NCIC. That's when they found our arrest warrant charging three counts of First-Degree Murder, one count of Attempted First-Degree Murder, and one count of Auto Theft. Within an hour of getting the call, Jack Remmen, a crime scene tech, and I were zooming across the Everglades on I-75 towards LaBelle and the Hendry County Sheriff's Office Headquarters.

I sat down with Jimmy Herndon in an interview room and pushed a Miranda Warning form in front of him. I explained what it was and read it to him as we customarily did. He nodded and signed the waiver, saying he agreed to talk to me without counsel present. Over the next few hours, Jimmy told his tale, though it took some to time to unravel the truth from what sounded like fantasy. He needed money and had been bingeing badly on freebase cocaine. He craved more, but he had run out of money. He went into the garage, where Harold was working on the car, and asked him for fifty dollars, but Harold refused. So far, he was painting a reasonable sounding scenario. Then, however, Harold Herndon turned into a "creature".

"A creature?" I asked.

"Yeah...long nails, and a green face...really scary...huge teeth...so, I grabbed the hammer, and killed it."

"You killed Harold."

"No...it wasn't Harold...it was a...creature." It was clear where this was going, and I was going to have to stick with it for now.

"Ok, you killed the creature that used to be Harold...and then what?"

"Another creature came into the garage, from inside the house. This one had hair sticking up...wild looking hair... I...I had to kill it too."

"Was that the creature you had to chase into the greenhouse?"

Jimmy nodded. "Yes. I had to kill it."

A brief snapshot image of Thelma Herndon's body flashed in my mind...seated, bent over grotesquely, her head matted with blood.

"How did you kill this creature, Jimmy? Same way as the other?"

"Yes. With the hammer."

Next, Jimmy explained, he went back in the house, and locked everything up, and pulled the shades. "I could hear other creatures trying to get in. They were tapping at the windows."

"But what about Doris? You let her in, didn't you?"

"Yes...she wasn't a creature. I knew it was Doris. I wanted to keep her safe from the creatures."

Jimmy was either talking shit to make himself look crazy, or he had hallucinated the creatures. Why hadn't he killed Doris outright? He had already bludgeoned his grandparents to death. I didn't want to distract him from the flow of telling the story. He was talking, and a sudden interjection of his relationship or fondness of Doris could derail the confession—and it *was* a confession, creatures or not. We continued, and Jimmy said he went and stayed at a motel in LaBelle. Something with the word Star in it, he said. He spent the night there, and left for Fort Myers the next morning. He wasn't sure where he was going, but he grew up around there and wanted the familiar surroundings. He said he didn't remember raping the girls, but he said at some point, the van got stuck in the sand. Funny how that happens, I thought. Everyone is turning into horrifying creatures—except for Doris and the two female rape victims. Jimmy said he tried to sleep in the van, but again. "Creatures were tapping at the doors and windows, and I couldn't sleep."

Jimmy's memory, whatever parts were truthful, came in mumbled, fragmented shreds of imagery, sort of the way someone might recall a dream. But the overall storyline was useful, in the event of an insanity defense: Jimmy was fleeing the place he had killed the "creatures. if killing the creatures was acceptable, why would one flee? The legal test for insanity in Florida is whether or not the defendant knew right from wrong at the time of the crime. If you didn't know that what you did was wrong, you wouldn't have to high-tail it for the west coast.

I went over Jimmy's story with him in detail, trying to carefully see if he would depart from the creature theme, but he didn't budge. After I had squeezed everything I could from Jimmy, we left him in the safekeeping of the Hendry County Jail and went to the Starlite Motel, the only one that fit the description Jimmy gave us. Sure enough, the clerk found his registration card.

Our timing was good: The maid had just finished cleaning the room. She had found towels with blood on them, and they hadn't gotten dumped into the laundry bin just yet. Our Crime Scene guy took photos of the room, and then headed out to get photos of the van at the tow yard and process the inside before it got dark. By the time we finished all our interviews and evidence work, it was close to 10:30pm. It had been a long, stressful, but fruitful day. Just the relief of catching Jimmy was immense, and not something that had hit us until we knew were done working for the day.

We were all thirsting for something to take the edge off, but we knew there were no bars open on a weekday at that hour in tiny LaBelle. We found a convenience store near our hotel and got there a couple of minutes past eleven. There was a uniformed police officer in the front of the place, leafing through a newspaper, when we went in and grabbed a six pack of Miller from the cooler.

"Oh, it's after 11," he said. "No alcohol sales in the county."

Are you kidding? We looked at each other, and took the officer aside. Remmen badged him, and explained who we were.

"You heard about that triple-murder suspect from Miami, right?"

"Oh, yeah, I heard about it," the uniform guy said.

"Well, we came up here this morning and we've been working on this thing all day. We could sure use a beer. Anything you can do?" He looked at us and quietly told us to wait outside. We watched him go and talk to the clerk, who appeared to be the store manager. They had a about a two-minute conversation, and the officer came outside to our car.

"Drive around back," he said, tossing his head to the rear of the store. When we got back there, he handed us two six packs of beer. At the officer's request—"give me something to keep the clerk happy, would you?"—we handed over a twenty and were on our way. Now we could decompress back at the hotel with our contraband beer before tomorrow's trip home.

The next morning we picked up Jimmy at the Hendry County Jail and headed back east, skirting the southern border of Lake Okeechobee. As we snaked through the farmlands and sugar cane fields, Jimmy pointed out a few places he remembered he had fished as a child.

"Largemouths?" I asked him. I had just started bass fishing the year before, and had been reading everything I could about it. Bill Schwartz and I had taken to some relaxing Saturday afternoons at different lakes and canals around Kendall with our rods, and a bottle of Canadian Mist. We even caught a fish or two. I really was into bass fishing, however, and was reading everything I could find to become a better angler.

"Oh, yeah. This is the place for 'em. Biggest you'll find anywhere."

We chatted briefly about what bait to use, and what was the best time to fish. He pointed out some other roads and lakes he had, and all the while, I knew I would be repeating parts of these conversations again, at least in my report. Jimmy's future insanity claim was eroding with every story he told about the region, and with every comment about largemouth bass fishing. While none of it was relevant in respect to his state of mind at the time the murders, it was helpful that he could carry on conversations of this sort without any kind of incoherent babbling, disassociated ideas, or claims of being hunted down by green creatures.

When we got to the Headquarters building, an army of news media was waiting for us, shouting questions at Jimmy as we got him out of the car and into the back of the building.

A couple of months later, I gave a deposition to Edith Georgi, one of the esteemed veterans of the Public Defender's Office. About halfway through, she started to dissect the conversations from our ride back to Miami.

"Detective, did Mr. Herndon make any statements on the ride back?"

"He talked about places he recognized along the way, yes. And we talked about fishing. He apparently had done some bass fishing around there."

"We?" Edith probed. "You mean you and he talked about it?"

"Yes. He told me that those areas we were driving through were great bass fishing spots, and so we had a conversation about bass fishing."

"And," she asked me, pursuing her lips suspiciously, "do you in fact, fish?"

I smiled at Edith. "I, in fact, do."

I didn't get a smile back.

The State Attorney's Office at that time had a Major Crimes Division comprised of only their most experienced prosecutors. Most of our homicide cases—especially high-profile murders—were handled by them. Jay Novick was assigned the Headberg-Herndon triple murder, and at my first meeting with him, he told me he would like to have me at the prosecution table. That strategy is rare, but this case had multiple scenes, multiple victims, and a hefty load of physical evidence to sort out. Having the lead investigator at the prosecution table during trial took a lot of pressure off of the prosecutor, and made things smoother during trial. The judge gave the ok, and the defense had no objection, so it was granted. I would be the first witness to testify, and that way, I could remain in the courtroom during all the other witness testimony. The judge could still invoke the rule in the event I had to be called back to the stand for a rebuttal.

My first act as a member of the prosecution team was to attend a meeting with the family. Doris, Michael Jr., and a couple of other relatives who were there to discuss if they wanted to pursue the death penalty. Even as heinous as these murders were, we recognized that this was still a family member, so we were a bit surprised when they all said they wanted him to die in the electric chair. Jay explained the risks of trial, and how, even with overwhelming evidence and the damning testimony of Michael, Jr., there could be forces beyond our control. There was always the specter of the unknown with a jury. There was a small chance that, after sitting through a long trial and reliving the horrors of that night, they could lose the whole thing and Jimmy could walk. Led by Doris, the family conceded that as long as they knew Jimmy would never see the light of day, they would be ok with a life sentence. Jay set up a meeting with the judge and defense counsel.

Next, I was present during *voir dire*. That was a first for me. We never got to see that, and most of us would never serve on a jury because of our law enforcement status. After the jury was picked, it was time for our meeting to discuss the plea offer: Jimmy does life without possibility of parole and avoids the death penalty.

Judge Philip was a short, black, highly energetic man who liked to get things done quickly. Edith Georgi and her co-counsel

Michael Houlihan were there along with me, Jay Novick, and another prosecutor who would be second chair with Jay. They laid out the offer to the defense team.

"In order to avoid trial, during which we would seek the death penalty, Mr. Herndon will have to plead guilty to the three murder charges, the auto theft, the arson case from Miami Lakes, and the two sexual battery cases from Lee County. He serves three *consecutive* life terms, and he will waive his right to appeal on all of those charges."

Edith scoffed and looked at Davis. "Oh, Judge, he can't do that. He's giving everything away. We can't..."

Judge Phil Davis stood up from his chair and walked briskly to the wall. "Edith," he said, smiling at her, "If you're client *doesn't* agree to the terms of this plea, here's what happens."

Then the judge put his hand on the wall and pulled down an imaginary switch while making a loud, buzzing "*ZZHHHZZZZH*" noise.

I looked at Jay and suppressed a laugh. Jay's mouth was hanging open in delighted surprise.

Edith covered her face with her hand. "Judge, please. Please don't do that...."

"Well that's what's going to happen, Edith!" he boomed, walking back behind his desk and sitting down. "If he doesn't take this plea!"

Phil Davis's little electric chair skit was only the beginning of the drama. Edith and Houlihan went and talked to Herndon and came back in a few minutes later.

"He'll take the plea, as long as he gets to eat pizza in here, with you and everyone," she announced.

Novick rolled his eyes. "Oh what bullshit is this Judge...pizza? Are they serious?"

Davis, amused, looked at Edith. "Well, Edith? You're *serious*?"

"Yes, Judge," she said, solemnly. "That's what he wants. We agree to everything the state offered, as long as he gets to eat pizza here, in your chambers."

Davis looked at Jay. "Jay? Pizza? Just pizza in my chambers, and we have a plea. What about it?" This was like a real estate deal. Jimmy wanted one last ride around the cornfield on the tractor before he sold the farm. We all knew it was absurd—and somewhat sickening—but we all knew this was better than rolling the dice at trial. I kept my mouth shut.

"Fine," Jay said, shaking his head in disbelief.

The plea was finalized a couple of days later. Davis gave him three *consecutive* life terms for everything. Back then, a life sentence in Florida carried a "25-minimum/mandatory", meaning the defendant had to serve a minimum of twenty-five years before being even eligible for a parole hearing. A parole guaranteed nothing but that—a hearing. Very few were successful. So three consecutive Life terms meant you would have to do those three times in a row—seventy-five years—and hope that you were successful with the last one.

Jimmy was never getting out.

We were back in Phil Davis's chambers with Jimmy, his defense team, me, Jay, and the Judge. Jimmy was in high spirits. Corrections brought in the pizza, and we all ate some. Herndon acted like someone who had gotten over on everyone, though all we had done was acquiesce to a juvenile and largely irrelevant little ploy. When we were done, he smiled, got up, and let the correctional officer put the cuffs on him.

"Well, Detective Nyberg," he said, turning to me, "I'll see you later."

I might have put up with the pizza, but I wasn't going to let that comment go. I stared at him and smiled. "No you won't. You'll never see me again. You'll never see a lot of things again."

Jimmy Herndon's smile disappeared, and as the door closed, we heard him yelling. The correctional officers, we found out, had to hogtie him to get him back to his holding cell, because he went berserk in the hallway. Good. The only thing better would have been that he choked to death on the pizza.

Chapter Thirteen

Crossroads

Dad pointed toward the bow of the boat on a dark morning as we headed out for our summer Bahamas trip. After a week of preparation and stocking the boat with dry and canned goods, we were on our way, our diesel engine chugging softly as we headed eastward towards Key Biscayne. There, we turn starboard to skirt the southern tip of the island and take the channel through Stiltsville and out into the deeper ocean waters of the Straits of Florida. I was excited. At fourteen, I had never been a part of something this adventurous.

"Keep this heading," he said, fussing with something near the lazarette as he spoke, "until I tell you."

"Ok," I said, happy to be at the helm as I always was. I liked it better than being forward and having to wait for him to yell out when to put up the main, or the jib, though I would be soon doing that once we were out of the channel. I didn't mind putting up the sails, it was just that Dad had a way of whooping out a command with his pipe in his mouth, and part of the words kind of got swept into the breeze into an unintelligible "whuuup!" that I was somehow supposed to decipher into a meaningful directive.

I remember thinking that it looked like time to take our bend starboard, but I kept quiet, remembering that he said to stay on that heading until he told me otherwise. Then, I felt the boat slow and felt the gentle grind that I knew was our bottom plying into the soft marl of turtle grass and mud on the bay's floor. I lowered the throttle just as Dad was saying, "What the....?" and in seconds we were aground, our forward motion halted. He looked towards the dark outline of Key Biscayne and put his hand on his head. "Goddamit, Ramesh! You got too close! Couldn't you see we were supposed to have turned by now?"

I suppressed the anger welling up in me. Being reprimanded in front of Dad's friend, Bob Ross and his son, Richard, who was a year my junior, was humiliating. They all turned their attention on me, the supposedly errant helmsman.

"Dad," I said, "you told me to stay on the heading you pointed out until you told me otherwise."

He scratched his beard. "Yes. Yes, I did tell you that, didn't I?"

Bob Ross smiled at my dad, "You did tell him that, Rolfe. He followed your directions."

"Yeah," Dad sighed. "Ok, it's not your fault. Let's get her off this shoal."

It's not the first time we had run aground—it happens to all sailboaters who spend lots of time in the water—and after about ten minutes of grunting and pushing in the dark waist-high water, we were back on track, and on our starboard tack towards Stiltsville.

Dad was wrong that morning. But I learned that day that at times, you need to trust your instinct, and if I had, we could have saved that bit of time and energy. Let your surroundings give you the signals that it might be time to change, even when the "instructions" you've been given might say otherwise.

Bob Miller was a new member of our squad in 1991, and one of the first cases he was assigned was one of those rare, "golden bb" type shootings, up in Carol City. The case began with a home invasion robbery. A group of Cuban drug dealers went to a house one evening to do a rip-off. They had information that the occupants had a big stash of money. They posed as cops to get the door open, then forced their way in at gunpoint. They tied up the husband and wife, threatened to kill them, and ransacked the house. I don't remember what they got, but they left the couple alive. When they left, as an act of bravado, one of them put his pistol out the window and fired a round at the house. It was a useless, silly, Lone Ranger-type act that served no purpose except to exclaim their jubilation.

But that's where the chaos theory came into play: the wild shot didn't even hit the robbery victims' house. Instead, it went through the front window of their *neighbor's* house, where a woman sat on a hassock, watching TV with her two-year-old son in her lap. The bullet crashed through the glass and slammed into the left side of the woman's head, boring a hole into her brain until it mushroomed against the opposite side of her skull. She toppled onto the living room floor, taking her toddler with her. He got up, and a few moments later a family member in the far corner of the home heard him crying. She came out to find the little tyke standing over his mother's lifeless body, wailing. His distraught and confused sobs continued when we got there, as his mother's body cooled on the living room floor.

We saw all kinds of death. Men, women, young, old—I have more than once carried a dead child in my arms—and we found a way to chug forward, or at least get out and push our way off a dark sandbar after running aground. We joked and drank with each other, and readily embraced the next case, the next grieving family, whatever came our way. Perhaps the onslaught of cases created that ability; we were the rolling stones that gathered no moss, as the saying goes, or the quarterback who was just crushed under the weight of an opposing defender but has no more than a few seconds to shake it off and be able to calmly call the next play in the huddle. The play-clock was always rolling for us. We rarely had time to slow down and let the hit shake us. That night, though, something happened to me.

For some reason this nameless woman, whose face I never even saw and was gone from the earth in an instant, shook me to the core. The helplessness, terror, and confusion of that poor little child seized me in a way I had not felt before. I felt a sob well up in my throat, and I found a dark corner of the yard, outside the yellow tape and away from everyone's view. I retreated there, my heart pounding and my throat dry, and desperately gathered myself. I swallowed the sob down. Down, where it belonged, with all the other prospective sobs, I suppose, that never even made it that far.

*You're a professional…*I told myself… *you're a detective. All your colleagues are around…the neighbors are watching…the Channel 7 LiveEye truck is parked just a short distance away with the cameras on…get your shit together and get back in the game.*

My quick sideline talk worked. I had run aground and pushed myself off. I was back, but the rest of that night, and all the way on the ride home, I knew something had changed. I needed out. I needed to be out of rotation homicide now. As a uniform officer twelve years before, I had watched Jack Remmen and his team work the homicide in North Miami and thought, "I want to do that". Now I thought, "I want to do something else."

But, what?—what would I do after this? Go to GIU somewhere and work burglaries? Go back to the brown-gown? If I stayed on this course, would I run aground again? I had friends at FDLE like John King, and two other guys who had left North Miami PD to go work for the State Division of Insurance as investigators. I remember them talking about how much they liked it. They got to work major cases, but not homicides. They helped the Attorney General's office put together statewide prosecutions on major fraud and political corruption cases, and they investigated state agencies on internal criminal matters. I decided that's what I would do. I made some calls, and found out that even though I was a sworn, active police officer, I would have to attend the state FDLE police academy in Tallahassee. That meant seventeen weeks away from my two young sons, Erik and Greg. They were six and four years old now, and I loved my time with them. To be away seventeen weeks seemed like a long time, and for those two boys, it would be an eternity. The chaotic life of homicide investigation had already caused me to spend many long hours away from home, away from them. But I couldn't stay in Homicide. FDLE seemed the only way out of this dilemma.

I put them to bed one night and sat on the floor after reading them a story. I sat on the floor, listening to their breathing as they fell asleep. I thought of what that would be like, not seeing them more than four months, and with my back against Gregory's bed, I wept quietly in the dark.

The next day at the office, Lt. Glen Kay walked through the office, making a general, kind of "door-to-door" announcement. He walked each aisle of cubicles like a street vendor, calling out, "Anyone interested in Cold Case? They have an opening...anyone? Cold Case?"

I sat bolt upright in my chair. Cold Case! I remembered at that moment that back in 1986, after Greg Smith and I had worked together on the Liberty City prostitute cases, the Cold Case sergeant, Jimmy Ratcliff had said something very flattering to me.

"Ram, if you ever want to work Cold Case, I'd love to have you. You just let me know."

Jimmy was gone from Homicide now, but I was going to play my card. Cold Case meant permanent day shift, weekends off, and very few—if any—late night call-outs. It meant a saner, more family-friendly life. I went to Kay's office immediately and told him about Ratcliff's invitation. Kay wasn't in Homicide when that had happened, so he shrugged, and said, "Let's go talk to Rivers," Kay said.

Sgt. Dave Rivers, who took over Cold Case after Ratcliff left, had been made aware of Ratcliff's invitation to me. "Yep," Rivers said, "Nyberg's got dibs on it, alright."

Kay nodded and looked at me. "Ok then. Looks like you're going to Cold Case."

There aren't many times in life you feel like you're drowning, and someone throws you a lifeline, but this was it. No FDLE. No changing departments and going through all that. No seventeen weeks away from my family. Cold Case, like the cavalry arriving just in time, had saved the day.

As unthinkable as it is, police personnel steal from each other. We had moved into the new headquarters building in 1987. From the old, dilapidated four-story building in the Civic Center next door to the Dade County Jail, our new home was a newly constructed, state-of-the-art complex on 25th street in Doral. We became modernized overnight: electronic access cards, spiffy individual cubicles instead of open desk seating and sharing phones, and an employees' lounge on each floor. We were next door to Robbery. Further down the hall, Sexual Battery and other major crimes units like Arson were on the western wing. In the middle of the second floor sat our new employee lounge, with seating, microwaves, and a nice big refrigerator that didn't smell like the Medical Examiner's office. People brought their lunches there; this included the secretaries and other civilian personnel who stayed in the building all day. We saw a memo one day that lunch bags were disappearing from the refrigerator. Employees were freaking *stealing* each other's lunches, from the goddamn police headquarters building lounge.

Sandy was a reporter for the *Miami Herald*. We all knew her as a sweet, generous woman who loved covering major crime stories for the *Herald*. Sandy was also quite the police "groupie." She would hang outside the yellow tape at crime scenes and was known to bring a box of donuts to us on late night cases. Somehow, she found out it was my birthday, and it was no more than two days after that when I officially left Squad C to join the Cold Case squad. It was the Friday before my Monday start on Rivers' squad. Sandy showed up at HQ with a chocolate mousse cake in a box.

"It has to stay refrigerated," Sandy warned me, "or it will be ruined. Please, keep it in the fridge, ok?"

I thanked her and promised I would. But what of the nefarious 2nd floor refrigerator thieves? I hatched a plan. I took evidence tape and crisscrossed the box with it. This is the same stuff we use to package up evidence on crime scenes. For extra security, I took a black magic marker, and wrote the words, "Homicide- Body parts – Do not touch! Evidence" in three places on top of and around the box. I made it believable with a couple of pink "Biohazard" stickers we were required to use on any biological evidence. That would do the trick. I put it in the fridge with confidence that no one would touch it. A couple of hours later, I got a call from Rivers. "Nyberg—that your cake of yours, in the refrigerator? You wrote all that stuff on it?"

"Yeah, Sarge. I didn't want people stealing it."

"Well, we've got a secretary in the building that went to her Commander, freaking out about the goddamn *body parts* being placed next to her macaroni salad."

"Oh. Oh shit," I said.

"Yeah, now I'm taking heat about it. Take care of this shit *now*."

Thankfully, it was close to the end of the shift, and I could get the cake home, so I got it out of the lounge refrigerator as fast as I could. An hour later I saw Rivers in the hallway at Homicide. He stopped and shook his head at me. He wasn't happy, but he had a hard time masking his amusement.

"You sure know how to make a first impression when you come to a new squad. Welcome to Cold Case."

Chapter Fourteen

Self-Murder

My earliest recollection of learning that people took their own lives was sitting in my living room and watching a movie with my mother. At the end of the movie, one of the characters walks into the ocean to drown herself. Here I was around eight years old thinking, "How do you just let yourself drown?" Was that even possible? I suppose if the lady couldn't swim, that would be another story, but I'm not sure I even considered that. Heck, I had at least a hundred hours of snorkeling under my young belt by this time in my life. The thought of an adult who couldn't swim never crossed my mind.

The whole idea of dying is kind of lost on a person that young. You can't even formulate the concept of becoming older, or what it might be like to be an adult. Ending your own life on purpose just didn't compute in any way, good or bad. There wasn't a hook in my mind to hang that one on. The image and idea of this woman walking slowly into the waves of the ocean's surf and dying flew out of my young mind faster than it had arrived.

Suicide is called "self-murder" in the Florida Statute book—it really is. The lawmakers had to address how to criminalize helping someone commit suicide. This had to have been some drunken legislator from the early 1900's who wanted to leave his mark on the legacy of Florida lawmaking: "We'll call it *'self-murder,'* dammit!". Helping someone commit suicide in Florida is called "assisting self-murder."

I'll admit to being a little bit of a word junkie. The wording of statutes has always amused and intrigued me. Criminal statutes have to have *elements* in a statute. The elements are the criteria, the moving parts, that define an offense. A statute book is a dictionary of crimes. Murder is defined as the unlawful killing of another human being. From there, it's broken down into the different degrees; First Degree Murder has to be with "premeditated design" to effect the death of the person, and so on. Calling suicide "self-murder" is a complete misuse of the language. You can't "murder" yourself, because murder has to be done by *someone else.* The whole discussion—and the statute itself—was moot anyway, because "assisting self-murder" amounted to manslaughter, which had its own statute. It even carried the same penalty. They could have just put a subsection in the Manslaughter statute that said helping someone kill themselves qualified as manslaughter too.

We handled lots of suicides. Sadly, in Greater Miami in the 1980's, there were so many homicides that suicides rarely even made a tiny paragraph in the news, if at all. In 1987, we handled 401 homicides, more than one a day. For a unit with fifty-five detectives, that was a significant workload when you considered that, almost every day, there was also at least one or two suicides, natural deaths (unattended, where no doctor would sign the death certificate), or accidentals. We were responsible for investigating all those, too. Someone dies of a drug overdose, we go out. Someone falls off a building at a construction site, we go out. A 55-year-old man dies at home with no sign of foul play and no lengthy medical history, we go out.

Suicides weren't usually hard to investigate, evidence-wise. They usually have a direct path to piecing together the events. If it's a gun, crime scene would take "hand swabs" for GSR (gunshot residue), and if there were no other signs of foul play and no unusual circumstances, you had a suicide. If the victim left a note, we got handwriting standards from the family and sent the note and the standards to the Questioned Documents office of the Crime Lab to make sure the decedent wrote it, and you had a done deal. In my twenty-one years investigating suicides, I never had a suicide note forgery. When drug overdose was the means, the only struggle you had was suicide vs. accidental. Those types of questions can sometimes never be resolved, *a la* Marilyn Monroe. Did she die of the multi-drug overdose because she was depressed and deliberately took them, or was she depressed and took too many to battle her depression, without the intention of dying? The question remains unresolved.

There were so many, but a few remain in my memory.

There was a guy up in the north end who sat in his car in a closed garage and ran the engine. But again, was he tired, maybe listened to the car radio, and wasn't aware that the carbon monoxide fumes were slowly overcoming him? The family had their doubts, as almost all families do. He was depressed, but this? The answer came after about five minutes of working the scene and searching the car.

While I was walking towards the front of the vehicle to get the VIN# off the dash, I glanced up at the shelf on the back wall of the garage, and saw a line of saint statues—four in all. He would have been looking right at them. Who lines up saints on your garage shelf where the tools and camping equipment are supposed to go? I went inside the house and looked around, and saw a small table full of curios and knick-knacks. There were four dust voids on the table where something had been removed. The family members conceded that the saints had been there and had been moved to the garage. Proof of suicide; case closed.

There was an unforgettable case of a young woman named Helen Klingler. She had been living with her older boyfriend in a house in Homestead. They broke up, presumably because Helen was impossible to live with. The boyfriend, now with a new girl, explained that she had been treated for depression and other disorders all her life. There had been threats of suicide so much that family members and friends got numb to them. Helen, learning that her beau had a new romance, went to the house and knocked on the door. The boyfriend answered the door and Helen brusquely said she had left some things in the bedroom closet she needed to get. The boyfriend shrugged, let her in, and went back to the sofa to watch TV with the new honey. That's when they both heard a loud *BOOM.* It turned out that the one thing she had gone to retrieve from the closet a Colt Python .357 magnum. Helen put it in her mouth and literally blew her head off.

When I entered the bedroom, Helen's body was supine on the floor, and everything above the bridge of her nose was gone. The lower half of her skull was still attached, but the rest of it, and half of her brain, were all over the walls, the bed, and just about everywhere you looked. A large chunk of her brain was on the floor, a few inches from her shoulder. The rest had disintegrated.

I stood there with my clipboard and started taking notes. In any scene I worked, I liked to make a rough sketch of the room, with a crude outline of the body, and then notations "a", "b", etc., to mark major pieces of evidence like the firearm or whatever else was important. As I was standing there, I could hear the faucet in the bathroom, which sounded like it had a slow drip: *Thipp...thiipp.* Then, I realized that there was *no* bathroom there. Where was that dripping noise coming from? A moment later, I found out, when a pea-sized chunk of brain matter hit my legal pad, right next to where I held my pen.

Thipp...thiipp.

The fragments of what used to be Helen Klingler's brain were dripping from just about every corner of the ceiling.

Until that moment in my twenty-seven-year-old life, I really had never appreciated what it meant to "need some air." It's hard to describe what I was feeling, but I would include a tinge of disorientation and even nausea, so I went outside to the driveway and took a few deep breaths. I looked around the neighborhood, enjoyed the fresh air (and lack of macabre precipitation) and decided I would be fine. Now that I knew Helen was still falling from the ceiling, I could deal with it. I would take my notes from just *outside* the room, in the hallway. Jeez, Helen. Couldn't you have...walked into the ocean or something?

The twenty-five-year-old son of an Italian restaurant owner shot himself in their home. He, too, had a history of mental illness and drug abuse. His father was apoplectic that this was going to be ruled a suicide. The shame it would bring on his family was too much for him. But the young man left a note and had said some things to friends that all pointed to him soon ending his life. Understanding victim's behavior in the days preceding the death is essential. It's not uncommon for suicide victims to be suddenly very happy and stress free, in the days before the act. "But he was so happy! He *couldn't* have killed himself!" I heard this dozens of times from family members.

My theory is that these people suffer from extended—and intense—despair and agony from whatever their demons might be. They are morose, depressed, withdrawn. Then, they suddenly realize there's a way out. They make the decision, and it's as if they are anticipating the day their pain is over. The proverbial light at the end of the tunnel has just come on, and it's exhilarating for them. I interviewed so many relatives, friends, and co-workers of suicide victims that I could almost predict it coming before they opened their mouths.

This Italian papa finally accepted what the truth was, but he still wanted to avoid the social stigma he faced from his own family. He called me one day.

"Detective, please...can you just write the report as an accidental death?"

"No, I can't do that. I'm really sorry you've lost your son. But I have to report things the way we found them. It's a suicide. I can't report something that is not true."

There was a short silence. "I can pay you. $1000 is all I can afford, but I can give you that in cash. Just change it to accidental, please."

I couldn't believe what I was hearing. I sighed, relieved that our lines in Homicide weren't recorded. "Mr. Russo, I'm going to pretend that we never had this conversation. My condolences to you and your family, but don't ask me that ever again."

Bribing a police officer is a felony, and had it happened in another set of circumstances, I would have arrested him in a heartbeat. But he was a desperate, shattered man, and it would have served no purpose. He never called again.

Then, there was the suicide to end all suicides.

The scene was a studio apartment in a quiet Kendall neighborhood. Sharon Berkheimer, a forty-seven-year-old American Express employee was found dead on her bed. She had multiple gunshot wounds to the chest—six, in fact. A snub-nosed 6-shot revolver lay on her chest. She wore a light blue denim shirt and matching slacks. The shirt was blackened with soot around her left breast. Next to the bed was a small night table, and an ashtray filled to the brim with ashes. There was no forced entry to the apartment, and nothing in the place suggested any kind of violence or struggle. When we opened up her top we found four gunshot wounds, closely grouped, on the top of her left breast. Two more gunshot wounds, about an inch apart, were found below the breast. This was very odd. How does someone lay still while being shot, unless the very *first* shot completely immobilizes her?

The family members were already proclaiming that this was a murder. After all, Sharon was shot six times. On top of that, Sharon was in the process of bringing a lawsuit against two men in her office she claimed were sexually harassing her. The lawsuit had become her life's obsession. And why shouldn't it? The family members all agreed—these guys were scum. They must have killed her, otherwise they would have lost their jobs, their marriages, and everything else. To Sharon's kin, this was as open-and-shut as the come.

The scene was the first thing we had to go over intricately. There was blood spatter on the wall, next to the bed, that seemed to have been deposited at different heights. One of the new techniques in forensics was blood spatter analysis. The lab sent Toby Wolson, newly trained in blood spatter analysis and one of the most experienced lab people we had, to the scene. Blood spatter analysis is a painstaking process that involves measuring individual bloodstains' length and width. With those numbers, a trigonometric calculation is performed, to determine the *angle* at which the drop of blood struck the wall. Once that angle is determined, the technician pins a string to the middle of the bloodstain, using the wall as the base, and extends the string out into open space, where it secured to a vertical post. After several of these stains are worked, the strings will converge in a spot that indicates where the source of the blood was. It was a fascinating process, one that created a 3-dimensional model of the blood source and its travel. As I watched Toby work, I was glad that I could do the detective work and leave all the measuring and calculating to the scientists.

The blood spatter analysis took hours, but it told a compelling story: It looked like Sharon was kneeling on the bed when the first shots were fired, and that she slumped further and further down as each set of blood stains traveled from her to the wall. The final two rounds were through and through, passing through her back, the mattress, and into the floor just below her. We dug the projectiles out of the carpet. The trajectory showed that those two were almost vertical and fired when she was laying down.

No one who is the target of a violent attack stays so still, without struggling, that these kinds of wounds could produce these patterns. No one goes down without a fight, and when I presented this to the family, they insisted she was "a fighter." If she was such a fighter, then why is there an ashtray, with a mound of ashes, right next to the bed without so much of a speck of ash disturbed or spilled onto the night table? Why wasn't there the chaos we had seen in other homicides? When someone is attacked, they fight as long as their blood keeps pumping. If they can make it to the kitchen to get a weapon to defend themselves with, we often find them there, or near the phone. The typical markers of such violent incidents—items knocked over, blood trailing through other parts of the apartment, forced entry—were absent. Other than six gunshot wounds, things weren't aligning with homicide. Even the .38 caliber revolver, which fired those six rounds, was registered to Sharon.

On the flip side of the argument, how does someone shoot themselves *six* times? With great determination, to be sure. The physical question would be answered by the forensics, and the medical examiner. The other remaining question was *why* she did it, that would involve peeling back more layers of her life. She didn't have a boyfriend. She had been a flight attendant for Eastern Airlines and left to work for American Express. That's when her troubles started.

We found stacks of printouts on a small desk in the apartment. Many of them were emails to and from Amex colleagues, so I took them back to the office to sift through them and try to find some clues. One of the stacks was entirely emails about the lawsuit she was launching against the two harassers. She had been corresponding with a lawyer about bringing suit against the men, and her words reflected her frenzy in going after them.

"I cared about Sharon," one girlfriend told me, "really I did. But honestly after a while the sexual harassment thing was *all* she could talk about. It got pretty tiresome."

Sharon's best friend, Pat, told me the same thing. Pat was a great lady who helped me learn about Sharon's personality. She cared deeply about Sharon and knew her well. Never once did she raise an eyebrow when I told her that this did not look like murder. Pat gave me names and numbers of friends and family members I should talk to. In between picking my way through the mountain of emails, printouts, I talked to Pat and the family members, most of whom were still unwilling to accept suicide. The second week into the case, three significant discoveries emerged.

The GSR tests came back, and both of Sharon's hands tested positive—in large amounts—of gunshot residue. It seemed a certainty that she pulled the trigger with one or both thumbs, as collections from the webbing on both hands hit high numbers in the lab.

"But," her sister argued, "couldn't someone have put the gun in her hands and forced her to shoot it?"

There are rarely things that anyone can say are completely *impossible* when you have no witnesses to an event. Investigation, however, involves putting together known facts with circumstances, means, opportunity, and *motive,* and coming up with the most plausible, workable theory. The family was hanging on for dear life to this theory: Sharon's harassers came to the door, and when she opened it, they barged in. She retreated and got her gun to defend herself. Then the men overpowered her, turned her own gun on herself, and shot her, six times.

But she retreated to her bed? What kind of defensive position can you assume while kneeling on a bed? Her more likely place to retreat is to the kitchen, for a sharp weapon, or the bedroom, to lock herself in. Then, after she is on her back, they stood over her—on the bed—and fired the last two shots, straight down, into her chest, at close range? If these attackers wanted to make it look like a suicide, why not aim the weapon at her head?

The medical examiner tracked each wound for us. The first four were all survivable but would have caused paralysis from the waist down. The last two might have been survivable had she gotten immediate medical attention, but as it was, she went quickly into shock and then bled to death. It *was* medically possible for her to have shot herself six times.

With Pat's help I tracked down Pat's father and aunt; one on the west coast of Florida and the other in southern Alabama. Both visits contained a compelling message. Sharon had traveled to see both of them just a couple of weeks before her death and given away some of her most precious possessions: jewelry, photo albums, clothes. She told them they were early birthday presents. The aunt and dad were perplexed by the sudden generosity. Pat and another family member both said that Sharon was in a much brighter mood during the days preceding the discovery of her body. There it was—that sudden upswing in mood that I had long ago learned was a hallmark of suicide.

Then I found another treasure. At the bottom of a large stack of paperwork were emails and notes written from Sharon to other employees at her office. One of them was to one of the men she was accusing of sexual harassment. It talked about how he had been moved to another department. "Miss seeing your face", she wrote him in an interoffice hard copy memo. Next to those words was a hand-written smiley face. I found other, similar correspondence to her so-called harassers. When I called her attorney, the whole thing became crystal clear.

"She was obsessed," he told me. "She called me about it daily. The problem was her case fell apart. It wasn't going to go anywhere. We couldn't find anything that substantiated her claims."

No doubt that when the lawyer saw those emails with the flirty comments, he saw his ability to win this case go up in smoke. *She* was flirting with *them*, and they didn't reciprocate. An obsession, dashed and destroyed by her own hand. She had lived for this lawsuit. By everyone's accounts it occupied her every waking moment and every conversation she had with the people closest to her. Finally, Pat put the final stamp on it for me. She came back from a trip to Europe and brought me chocolates from Switzerland.

"Just a small thanks," she said, "for working so hard on my friend's case." She also brought something else.

"I had forgotten about this," she said apologetically. "I wish I would have shown this to you earlier. Sharon gave this to me." She handed me a book about friendship. It was one of those small gift books with poems and sentiments; something you would give a close friend on a birthday or Christmas.

"Look at this," she said, turning the pages back to the table of contents. There, on the list of chapters, Sharon had circled the last entry, entitled, "The Final Chapter." When I turned to it, I read a somber, emotional sentiment about how a surviving friend would feel when the other passed away.

"I realize now," Pat said, "she was trying to tell me something with this book."

The last interview I had was with Sharon's younger brother. He was an astute guy in his late thirties, and he listened to me more openly than the other family members had been willing to.

"David," I asked him, "Do you think Sharon was capable of orchestrating this entire thing to make it look like these men murdered her? So that she could get whatever revenge she felt she needed, even in death?"

He rubbed his beard, smiled softly, and said, "She was a smart cookie."

Unless the other family members had anything to say, I would have no more meetings with them. I would refer them to my report and our investigative findings. I had handled homicides that involved less time and work than I had put into this case.

David must have gone back to the other family members and put everything to rest, because I never heard another word from them. Toby Wolson used this case in his presentations when he taught blood spatter analysis courses around the country. And those chocolates Pat gave me were the best I've ever had.

Sharon Berkheimer had pulled off one truly amazing caper, shooting herself six times. She had come closer than anyone else I had ever seen to committing "self-murder".

Chapter Fifteen

APES

Squall is a word most people never use. In south Florida—especially during the winter months—fierce windstorms called squalls whip up on the water and turn a tranquil boating trip bad in no time. I was twelve, and one afternoon, Dad held me by the shoulders and pointed out a line of very dark clouds, low over the water. I saw a thick, dark gray band with almost a greenish tint to it. The space between the band of cloud and the water was gray, and opaque.

"Squall line," Dad said. "Knock down the jib and the mains'l. It's coming this way."

I went forward and started hauling the sails down.

"Whenever you see a squall like that approaching, there's usually some strong wind in it. You have to get the sails down and point the bow directly into the wind, so your hull isn't exposed. You have to do it quickly, because those things move fast."

He was right. No sooner had I lowered and secured both sails than a chilly wind whipped into our faces. It felt like the temperature dropped fifteen degrees. Then, an intense, nearly sideways rain howled around us. We went below to wait it out. In the cabin, Dad grinned. "Well, the deck is getting a nice washdown, at least." The experience is almost exhilarating—as long as you were prepared for it.

"Looks we got us an APE," Dave Rivers said, after we attended the morning Homicide briefing. Sergeant David Rivers was a self-made legend in Homicide and throughout the department. He taught frequently at the Training Bureau and had actually developed a nice side business for himself, teaching Homicide and Cold Case investigations all over the country at various police departments. Dave was born to be in front of people. To say he had the "gift of gab" was an understatement. He had a wealth of war stories on the tip of his tongue, a thousand jokes, comments, and witty phrases ready to add to any conversation. If you happened to say something clever or funny, it was instantly added to his inventory. He was a fantastically entertaining person, and he became well known all over the country. It was almost a given that, when we were on an investigative trip somewhere, the local cops would say, "Miami-Dade, huh? Do you know Dave Rivers?"

Rivers' international fame became an inside joke, and wherever any of us were on an out-of-town trip, someone there would know Dave. One of our Sergeants, John Methvin, used to go on missionary trips to South America, taking clothes, and food too needy families in rural villages. He took a picture of himself and his volunteers, in a jungle in Brazil, with a bunch of the villagers. Methvin—a witty guy himself—had one of the villagers hold a sign that said, "I know Dave Rivers."

If the Miami-Dade Police Department had its own currency, Dave would be on the dollar bill.

One of Dave's favorite phrases was A.P.E.: Acute Political Emergency. It was applied to any case we got that was going to generate a high level of publicity, news media coverage, and hence, pressure from the brass. APEs were always interesting because they stood out from the norm. It was akin to kicking an anthill—you saw people running around and task forces being formed—and everything else we were doing took a backseat. Sometimes an APE would be relegated to just the one squad handling it, but depending on the APE-ness level, it could involve secondary squads or task forces. The Cold Case Squad would almost always play some sort of assisting role.

In the mid-1980s, we got a dandy. I was still on a regular rotation squad when Detective Cliff Nelson got a case of found body parts that had washed up on the shore of Bear Cut, an inlet that connected Biscayne Bay to the Atlantic Ocean between the mainland and Key Biscayne. For the better part of a month, additional parts kept washing up, and it became apparent that they were from two different people, male and female. We didn't have DNA back then, and no hands had shown up, so we couldn't do fingerprints.

A man's head was one of the parts, so work began on mapping the victim's teeth so we could put a "dental BOLO" out to medical professionals, to help us identify the victims. Nothing was coming back, and soon we were calling unidentified victims Hugo and Lolita (after the killer whales at the Seaquarium, just down the street from Bear Cut). Someone else referred to it as the "Bits and Pieces" case, and the male was quickly dubbed Tommy Torso. Our local medical examiner, working with dental experts, soon concluded that the dental work from the male victim was not done in this country, and could have been done in South America. The case became a news media phenomenon. Every local TV channel's lead news story was the new body part washed up on Bear Cut. The case had become a bizarre, perplexing spectacle.

Everyone in Homicide was running down one lead or another. Mike Tabernero was given a lead to contact the Goya spice company, as a soggy packet of Goya basil powder was found in the pocket of the male victim's clothing. Mike was supposed to see if the manufacturing data on the packet could be traced back to a certain location of sale. Many of us, including myself, were given a list of abandoned or towed vehicles from all over the County. Our assignment: track down the vehicles' owners, to make sure they were alive and well. If they weren't, the names were added to a list of possible victims, and we dug further to see where they were. These leads were shots in the dark, but there just wasn't much else to do, and the pressure was on with each day that brought more body parts. There had already been eight occurrences.

It had become the APE of all APES.

Lead investigator Cliff Nelson was a former Air Force SAC Officer, a big guy with a booming voice. In his USAF days Cliff provided security for nuclear missile sites. This was the spit-and-polish elite of military security, and Cliff exuded those principles from every pore. I liked Cliff a lot. He had a good sense of humor which peeked out often from behind his military bearing.

Cliff was under immense pressure and was being hounded by the press on a daily basis. Though you couldn't often tell from the outside, it weighed on him. Straightforward and pragmatic, Cliff also had a towering sense of duty. The case was gnawing at him. Meanwhile the news media had turned the case into a veritable circus.

"One day," Cliff remembered, "I'm driving to work, already feeling the weight of this case going unsolved day after day, and some AM radio station is advertising a contest. I couldn't believe it. A *contest,* to predict what body part will wash up next. If you call it in to the station and you're correct, you win a prize."

Edna Buchanan was the most celebrated crime reporter for the *Miami Herald* at that time. She was by far the most aggressive one we had ever dealt with. Some people hated her because of how brazenly she would go after family members of murder victims and hound them, just to get a good quote for her next article. She, like other reporters, would call our office frequently to try and get information. When we heard her voice on the phone, our defenses immediately went up. You had to be careful what you said to Edna, because it would end up as a quote, or worse, a headline.

After about the fourth arrival of body parts on the beach at Bear Cut, Edna called and asked for Cliff. What would it take to solve this? she asked him. Wouldn't it be great if you get something that could provide the identity of these two people?

"I'd pray for a hand," Cliff told her.

The next morning, Edna's article hit the *Herald* with the headline, "I'd pray for a hand, Metro Detective says." Everyone on the day shift went immediately to work on fulfilling Cliff's request. By the time he walked into the squad room, his desk with festooned with every kind of hand imaginable: inflated surgical gloves, rubber monster hands from Halloween costumes, drawings of severed hands, fingerprint cards, and of course, a plastic pair of hands clasped in prayer. There were easily twenty different kinds of hands taped to Cliff's desk and hanging from the ceiling above his desk. Edna's article was clipped and taped to the wall as well.

Cliff walked into the squad room, looked at the hilarious display on and around his desk and stopped, speechless. Then he broke into a huge grin and the squad room exploded with laughter.

"I needed that," Cliff told me later.

The next day, the woman's torso washed up, severed at the waist and neck, with no arms. At roll call, our commander, Captain Wayne McCarthy stood up and said, "I'd like to commend Detective Cliff Nelson—he's definitely the luckiest person in the world." Everyone looked at each other, wondering if this was to announce Cliff had made an ID.

McCarthy went on: "He's the only man I know who could pray for a hand and get a pair of tits." The room erupted and everyone loosened up for another day of trying solve the mystery of Tommy and Tammy Torso.

They were never identified. More parts washed up, and Cliff finally *did* get the hands that he prayed for. But none of the fingerprints hit anywhere. The teeth and fingerprints made it obvious that these people might never have touched American soil, until they did so in fragments, on the beach. The parts stopped washing up, and so did any hope of taking the case any further. One of the biggest APES of the decade for our department gave way to the regular flow of murder and mayhem. And there was plenty of it.

McCarthy's comment—which today might have gotten *him* on the front page of the *Herald* and result in his firing—was emblematic of the kind of comic relief that pervaded the Homicide Bureau. If you got quoted in the newspaper for anything more than the standard vanilla quotes we usually gave to the media, you had better be prepared for the onslaught of ribbing, jokes, and in this case, plastic hands. We fucked with each other mercilessly. The exchanges were essential to the balance we needed in the workplace. It was easy for a young guy who had just solved a big case or gotten his name in the papers to get a little big for his britches. The glow of notoriety would be short-lived, however. There was no room for star power in the land of GOYAKOD. We were all good at what we did, and we all worked on teams, not as lone rangers. If you started flaunting your success, your team—the ones who should share in the success with you—would be the first to restore your focus. And if you couldn't take the flak? That meant you didn't understand that it was all part of the price of admission, and your acceptance in the unit might still be an undecided issue.

One guy, Frank, who came on around 1988 had a little bit of a chip on his shoulder and it soon became evident that he was less than open to criticism or even instruction. Like many of us, he had been on the department for a while. But when you were new *here,* you were a rookie homicide detective. There were things you did in homicide, like testify in motion to suppress hearings, that you might never do in a thirty-year career if you worked somewhere else. Frank had a way of shrugging and saying, "Yeah, I know." One day, one of the veteran guys was giving him some pointers on how to prepare for such a hearing.

"Yeah, I know," Frank said with his little shrug.

"No—you *don't* know," the senior guy told him.

"Hey," Frank shot back, "I've been on fifteen years."

Someone else in the room who had been watching the exchange piped in now, with the most brilliant response I had ever heard: "Hey Frank—there are some guys who have been on fifteen years, and some who have been on *one* year, *fifteen times.*"

We all got a hearty laugh out of that, and Frank walked away, shrugging, but a few shades redder than before. He eventually learned some humility, and it served him well.

We were handling two curious, compelling cases starting in September of 1994. On November 20th, however, the investigation became one of our biggest APES ever.

It was on that day that a young prostitute named Charity Nava was found strangled to death a block off busy SW 8th street, known as Tamiami Trail. The Trail, which also bears the designation of U.S. 41, runs all the way from downtown into Miami's Little Havana neighborhood, west through the county, across the Everglades, and finally up the west coast into Tampa. The section of the Trail between roughly 45th and 72nd Avenues was known for prostitute activity and was dotted with seedy two-hour rental motels where hookers could take their johns. The discovery of Charity Nava's body was huge news, for two big reasons: One, she was the third prostitute found dead in the area in two months. The first, found September 17th, was a male transvestite named Lazaro Comesana, and the second, found on October 8th, was a girl named Elisa Martinez. The discovery of the first two victims had caused a stir, and the assigned squad was busy seeing what connections there might be, forensically or otherwise. No one was screaming "serial killer" just yet. Like the cases Greg Smith and I handled back in the mid-80's, the victims could be unrelated, result of a risky lifestyle. The nude body of Charity Nava, however, solved the question of whether or not the same killer was responsible. On her back in black magic marker were written the words: *THIRD!*

I will call Dwight Chan 10—below that, were two cartoon like eyes ("*see*") and the words, *if you can catch me.* Dwight Lauderdale was local ABC affiliate Channel 10's news anchor who had been reporting on the first two murders. Not only did we now have a serial killer, we had one that was taunting us and the news media.

This was a fast-moving squall, indeed.

The department was pretty good at handling APEs. We had a Media Relations Unit that responded to homicide scenes whenever we asked them to. They would create a special roped off area just for Media Relations to interact with the news media personnel. We wrote press releases on our cases and sent them to Media Relations so they could go on camera for TV news and radio broadcasts. Lead investigators rarely had to do interviews unless it was something on a scene that a supervisor gave the ok for. It reduced the chance of one of us slipping up and revealing specifics on evidence or suspects.

Within a day or two of the discovery of Charity Nava's body, the office was abuzz with the news of the killer's artwork and taunting message. The FBI had offered the services of their Behavioral Sciences Unit, to do an offender profile. The experts in that unit collected as much information about scene details, evidence, victim details and traits, time of day, day of week—just about every minute piece of data you could find on a case—and came up with a profile of what kind of person we should be looking for. Nationwide, they had a very respectable record. They often got remarkably close to details on age, occupation, and type of neighborhood the offender lived on many of their cases. Miami-Dade Police accepted the FBIs offer. Of course, when you do that, you enter into a package deal: The FBI would be sending people to "assist in the investigation." What that meant was that they would have *their* slick media relations guy doing press releases every evening. When we would finally close the case, there was sure to be a big announcement of how the FBI solved this serial murder investigation. We watched his press releases on the news every evening with amusement. As sudsy as a radio DJ, with coiffed hair and perfect teeth, he could have been a male model. Just the image the feebs wanted, I'm sure.

Five days after Nava's body was found, another girl, Wanda Crawford, turned up dead on a side street of the Trail.

The count was up to four now.

In the Cold Case squad, we were a little miffed. We had been relegated to looking up mundane, almost irrelevant information that had little chance of leading to anything. We had a lot to offer, being four of the most experienced detectives in the unit, but someone high up the chain didn't want us out doing interviews, where we could be most helpful. It was some internal thing between Dave Rivers, our sergeant, and someone in the brass. Rivers was furious about it. Then, things got really complicated. Some of the case facts that detectives were finding on the murder scenes were showing up in the news media, almost daily.

We had a leak.

The integrity of an investigation is paramount. Letting out details to the public serves no purpose except to muddy the waters of your investigation. If the killer left a specific clue on the scene, that's an ace in your sleeve that will help you sift out the truth from the bullshit when you're evaluating incoming tips or witness statements. McCarthy was beside himself, and he urged all of us to come forward if we knew who was responsible for the leak. He went to IR (Internal Review—our name for Internal Affairs) and now a side investigation was underway. Everybody in Homicide was brought in and interviewed. When it was my turn, I remember sitting down in front of the IR Sergeant and thinking, "we do sensitive interviews in Homicide...these guys must be really skilled too."

The investigator-Sergeant took out a piece of paper and sighed. "Ok, Nyberg, right?"

"Yessir."

"Alright," he said, barely looking at me. He was reading from a list of questions.

"Have you had any conversations in the last month with anyone from Channel 7 news about this case?"

I was almost speechless at first. I had been to the country's finest schools in interview techniques and had learned from some of the finest investigators anywhere. This guy was robotically reading from a list of questions with no preamble, warm-up, or rapport-building.

"No," I said.

He pressed on. "Have you received any phone calls from Channel 7 news, or anyone from the news media, regarding the investigation into the Tamiami strangulation cases?"

Really? This was the high-level, intense grilling we were getting to root out the leaker? A bunch of yes or no questions?

"No," I said again.

And on it went, for about six more questions. Gee, Sarge, you're killing me here...I can't take it anymore! I confess!

I answered five or six more "nos" and the laughable "interrogation" was over. What horseshit. No small wonder that the leaker was never discovered through *that* amateurish process.

Our newly formed task force (our department, the FBI, the City of Miami Police, and FDLE) set up surveillances all along Tamiami Trail. A couple dozen or so investigators from Homicide, Sexual Battery, Narcotics, and the FBI were parked on side streets, alleyways, parking lots, and every nook and cranny we could find, to watch hookers and see if we could catch the person who was now nicknamed "The Tamiami Strangler".

In the middle of all this scrutiny, our killer hit again: On December 17, 1994, a young woman named Necole Schneider was found strangled on a side street just off the Trail. Our serial killer—the first we had experienced since a guy called the "Canal Killer" in the early 1970's—was national news, and the pressure to find him (along with the leaker) had reached a fever pitch.

The Tamiami Strangler would kill once more before he was caught, but before that, an interesting side story occurred, one that would never make the news: Mr. spiffy FBI Media Relations guy, who had been giving press releases since the beginning of this ordeal, was caught by another one of our surveillance team people masturbating in his car while watching the prostitutes. I was told we arrested him, but either way, the FBI whisked him out of there without so much as a peep about the incident, and we never heard anything about him ever again.

The New Year arrived without an arrest (other than not-so-Special Agent Happy Hand) but our leak was discovered. Sadly, it was one of our own Lieutenants in Homicide. He was a quiet, well-liked man, and it was a deep disappointment to us all. Like the disgraced FBI Agent, the Lieutenant disappeared from the landscape quickly. He left amongst a backdrop of whispers, likely taking the more appealing of two choices: retire and go quietly into the night, or be prosecuted.

The Tamiami Strangler wasted little time in fulfilling his New Year's resolution to nail another victim, and the body of prostitute Rhonda Dunn was found on January 12th. The count was six, the last one to die before the killer screwed up and got caught.

On June 19th, neighbors called police to report the sounds of a woman's muffled screams and pounding on the wall from the next-door apartment. When officers and Fire-Rescue arrived, they found Gloria Maestre, a 21-year-old prostitute, bound and gagged in the bathroom. Maestre pointed out a photo on the refrigerator of the apartment and told the officers that this was the guy who had abducted her after bringing her there to have sex. Investigators searched the apartment and found a bunch of interesting items, including a beeper belonging to Charity Nava.

The photo was of Rory Enrique Conde, the registered tenant of the apartment. When we brought him in, he gave a full confession to all the murders. The first one, he explained, wasn't planned as a murder. During their sex act, he found out that the "girl" was a male—Lazaro Comesana. That's when he became enraged and strangled him. The rest of the prostitutes, he claimed, were all the reasons his life had gone bad, so they had to die too. In his confession, he said he prayed over Comesana's body. He also stated that he had anal sex with the corpses.

One of my favorite prosecutors, Jerald Bagley, had become a judge by then. He presided over the trial, and determined that each victim's murder would be tried separately. After Conde was convicted of Rhonda Dunn's murder, the jury voted 9-3 for the death penalty, and Bagley sentenced him accordingly. Conde entered into an agreement with the State for the other five murders. This way, everyone was spared the expense and time of five murder trials, and he received five consecutive life sentences.

Over one hundred investigators participated in the case overall, and over 5,000 leads had been generated. As APEs go, this one was hard to beat.

Chapter Sixteen

Every nationality from the Caribbean is found in south Florida. In the 60's and 70's, Cubans were the predominant emigrants in Miami and established their own neighborhoods in the region. Colombians started trickling in after that and by 1982 numbered over 40,000 in Miami-Dade. The next waves from Haiti, Jamaica, Dominican Republic—-and just about every nation in the Caribbean—settled here, mostly in the northwest sections stretching from Carol City east to North Miami and North Miami Beach. Like everyone else, each had their own brand of food, music, culture—and crime.

The Jamaicans also brought their unique political conflicts to south Florida, and the same factions who fought each other on their island continued to be embroiled in ruthless violence against one another on Miami's streets. The political parties in Jamaica had "posses"—-well-armed narcotics-funded groups who controlled neighborhoods in Kingston with fear and drug addiction—to carry out their dirty work, intimidate opponents, and defend territory. The leaders of these posses were like neighborhood "godfathers", working directly under the top political candidates.

Miami's AM station WKAT sold radio time to various Caribbean DJs, and the most popular and flamboyant of the Jamaican community was the sweet-talking Cecil Clarke, better known as "Mighty Viking." Clarke knew how to work his audience, and he had young Jamaican girls at his beck and call when he dressed in his trademark hat and suit in local nightclubs. A big fan of flashy jewelry and expensive clothes, Clarke was Miami's Jamaican celebrity.

One afternoon, a couple of kids riding their bikes through the parking lot of an apartment building in North Miami caught an intensely offensive odor coming from a Toyota Forerunner SUV they were next to. Reluctantly, they got closer and peeked inside. Through the tinted windows, they were able to make out what looked like a dead man, in the back seat, and the stench was even greater. Uniform got there and roped off the scene and ran the tag. I was up, and when I got to the scene the brown-gown handed me a piece of notepad paper.

The owner was Cecil Clarke, and his DOB said he was forty-four years old. His home address wasn't the apartment building, but a house about ten minutes north of there. While we were getting the info and Crime Scene was taking care of the exterior photography, the kids on the bike were joking about something, and I heard one of them say, "He's dead..yeah well, shit happens."

We didn't know Cecil Clarke from the local mango vendor at that point, but we were about to find out a whole lot. The killing took place in the car: out of the four bullets fired into his head, we dug two of the rounds out of the rear passenger side door. Clarke's hands were secured behind his back with duct tape. When we had dead bodies in cars, it was more efficient to tow the car with the body inside, to the Medical Examiner's Office, where both could be worked on without interruption. When the tow truck hooked up the Forerunner, vile liquid, wriggling with maggots, started leaking out of the rear hatch, and formed a puddle on the pavement. One of kids grimaced and said, "Ewww...what's that?"

I happened to be walking by. "That," I said, "is what's left when all the shit has happened."

This was 1988, and there were Jamaican males getting killed right and left. The posses started warring with each other since the middle of the decade, and the slaughter had steadily gotten worse. Just when the Colombians were settling down some (they had learned that brazenly killing with open-air sprays of machine-gun fire was bad for business) the Jamaicans took the murder spotlight. Clarke's murder didn't shake anybody up much—except for the Jamaican community. Everyone had heard of him. Just about every Jamaican with a radio in their store, restaurant, living room, had listened to him at some point. Jamaican Miami was all abuzz about the murder of the Mighty Viking.

I had a ton of people to talk to on my lead sheet. His neighbors, his cohorts at WKAT, and business owners who sponsored his radio show, to name a few. The problem, however, was getting them to talk. People were terrified of the posses, whose operatives had a savage reputation for eliminating anyone who got in their way. Posse hit men didn't bat an eye at opening up on a crowd of people at a soccer game or night club with a MAC-10 or AK-47, just to kill one target. They were still catching up to the lessons the Colombian cartel killers had learned. Posse members carried with them the same type of aura that Italian mafia dons of the 50's and 60's did. Jamaican citizens automatically figured that a murdered Jamaican male was posse-related, and no one dared open their mouths. We had a dozen or so Jamaican murder cases with multiple gunshot victims whose crime was to be at the wrong place at the wrong time. Many Jamaicans had such a thick accent that when they talked fast, falling into their unique *patois,* you could barely catch a word or two. It took practice to understand. In the coming months, however, one phrase would become very familiar to us in law enforcement: *"Me nuh know a ting 'bout dat, man."*

Most of them probably did not know a "ting." Nevertheless, we distributed flyers all over the north end of the county, especially the Jamaican stores and restaurants. In the process, I found a fantastic ice cream store on 27th avenue that had unusual flavors like tamarind. I had stopped by to drop off flyers and talk to the owner and he was nice enough to give me a sample. After that, I made sure to go by once a week for my dose of that tamarind ice cream.

During a meeting with our Narcotics people, we learned that they were working a task force with the feds on Jamaican posses. I told them about Mighty Viking.

"We've got a C.I. that probably knows about that case," one of the Narcotics guys told me. "He's been telling us a lot. We'll introduce you. He's in Jamaica right now. We can't get him here yet. But we'll get him on the phone for you."

Two days later, we talked to the informant, Oscar. "Yeah...yeah I know 'bout Mighty Viking," he said. "He's a gun smuggler."

Gun smuggling. *Finally.* We had a break.

Oscar then proceeded to tell us how Cecil Clarke had a deal going with a group of Jamaicans in Miami who were apparently adept at printing U.S. currency. "Viking brings the guns to Kingston, and flies back with the money and weed," Oscar said.

The barter system was alive and well. Now we had to figure out what had happened during this process to get him killed—*if* that was the situation.

Oscar continued, telling us that he knew this because he himself was supposed to go to Kingston's Norman Manley Airport one day to pick up the guns, which were packed in a wooden crate. Before he got there, he was tipped off by someone that the police were onto the transaction, so he pulled back. Oscar had a newspaper clipping from the *Kingston Gleaner* about the seizure. No one had been arrested for the gun smuggling case yet. Oscar said he could point out people that were involved in the Viking's nifty arms-for-funny money scheme. I made a travel request to Kingston, and after jumping through all the bureaucratic hoops involved for the County to fly us out of the country, we had our authorization. The first order of business was to make contact with the country *attaché,* which was always a federal agent designated as a liaison for American law enforcement visiting for official business. Ours was a DEA guy, and he got me in contact with

Tony Hewitt, Superintendent of Kingston Police's "Flying Squad," so named because they were the only ones with enough political clout to fly to different parts of the island to conduct investigations. They had the stamp of approval, but the Flying Squad, like the rest of law enforcement in Jamaica, didn't have money to do jack shit. Prior to the trip I got on the phone with Hewitt.

"Detective," he asked, "I have a request. Could you please bring some Nestle's chocolate bars? They are hard to find here."

That gave me a chuckle. "Sure, I'll be glad to."

"Oh," he went on. "Another thing too. We are kind of low on equipment here. We could use some holsters."

"Holsters...ok, I think I can get you some holsters." The Training Bureau might have some old ones, I thought. Wow, so their guys went around without holsters?

"And," the Captain went on, "Bullets. Ammo. We need bullets."

Astonishing—they need ammunition too. After hanging up with the Flying Squad guys, I took a trip to the Training Bureau. They were good enough to give me three or four old holsters they had boxed away in an equipment room. They also gave me four boxes of 9mm, 158 grain reloads. A couple of days before the trip, I called Oscar again, and confirmed that we were meeting. He was still on board. He, too, had a favor to ask.

"You know," he asked slowly, "I've never owned a watch. Do you think you could bring me a watch?" I could hear the sheepishness in his voice.

"Sure, Oscar, I'll bring you a watch."

I went out and bought a cheapo $15 Timex, put it in the suitcase with the ammo and holsters, and off we went, Detective Larry Wilkotz and I, to Kingston, feeling like Santa Claus, carrying our sack of chocolate, bullets, holsters, and watches.

We were met at Norman Manley airport by Sgt. Tony Hewitt and his Captain. The first thing they did was ask us for our guns. "You can't carry your guns here. But you'll be with us."

I wasn't crazy about our guns being in police custody, but there was no recourse. It was their country, not ours.

"Did you bring the bullets?" The Captain asked, smiling at me expectantly.

"Sure, I brought them." I patted my suitcase. I figured we'll have gift-giving at their office.

He held his hands out, smiling. "You can give them here now, please."

Right there inside the airport, I opened up my suitcase and handed over the boxes of ammo and the holsters. The Captain beamed like a little kid. He had forgotten all about the chocolate. We walked out into a hot and humid afternoon that felt just like Miami. Larry and I both had our eyes outside, watching and drinking in this place neither of us had ever been, the place where the Mighty Viking—and most likely his killers—grew up. There were no long, straight boulevards. Every street seemed to wind and bend, and our driver honked at every corner. Most everything looked poverty-stricken with the exception of the homes that dotted the foothills of the Blue Mountains, rising up to the north of the city. The road back was Norman Manley Boulevard skirting Cagway Bay. At one point we took a turn and it seemed like we had made a long, circuitous square to get to the hotel, where Oscar would meet us.

Tony smiled at us. "We don't go in there," he said, pointing to the slum we had just avoided. "That's Trenchtown. They know we are police. They will shoot at us."

Larry and I had nothing to shoot back with, so we were grateful for the detour. We stayed at the Wyndham Hotel. It was a pretty nice place, and as soon as we got settled in the room, we went downstairs and met with Oscar. He was a gangly, goofy character who looked like a perfect stooge for some group of badass posse characters. He would never be suspected and could blend easily into a crowd. We had brought pictures of some Miami Jamaicans we had looked up to see if Oscar knew any of them. He gave us a few "maybes" on those, but named a couple of characters who were always in this area of Kingston, working with smugglers who were part of our victim's ventures. We took a bunch of notes and gave Oscar his watch. He grinned widely and thanked us. We set up our next appointment for the next day at 10am, at the hotel. We were going to spend the evening checking out some of the names he gave us with our people back home.

That night after our work was done, Larry and I attended a big barbecue being put on by the hotel out by the pool. They had a live band, steamed fish dinners, and plenty of Red Stripe beer. The place was packed and we had a nice time, knocking back some Red Stripes and listening to a good reggae band.

The next morning, we went down to the lobby at around 9:45 to wait for Oscar. 10:30 rolled around, and he hadn't shown. Jamaicans had this reputation for not worrying or hurrying too much, and they laughed at us Americans and how we obsess about time. The nationwide phrase we kept hearing, whether it was waiting for a government entity to get us a report or for the waiter to bring us a beer was, "It soon come."

But 11:30 came and went, then noon, and still no Oscar. He *no* come. This was worrisome. Was he working both sides? Had someone had gotten wind that he was talking to us, and he got kidnapped or killed? We were not on our home turf and had no way of knowing which way the wind was blowing on questions like this. I tried to get a hold of Tony Hewitt to see if we could help but he was "out". No one had pagers and no one in his office seemed to care much that two detectives from Miami needed to speak with him. Then back at our room, Oscar called.

"Damn, Oscar, what happened to you? We've been waiting!"

"Nuttin man, I didn't know what time it was so I missed reaching up there to see you."

"Oscar—we gave you a damned *watch*! How could you not know?"

There was a brief silence on the other end. I heard Oscar clear his throat then, and say, "Me nuh know how to tell time. I just wanted to have a watch to wear on me wrist. Look nice, for the ladies."

Just my luck, I thought. I buy a watch for a guy that doesn't know how to tell time. This trip had not been quite what we hoped for, but it was a start. We got a taped statement from Oscar and some intel from Hewitt's crew of possible associates of the Viking. We flew back to Miami on Air Jamaica on a Monday morning, and they passed out copies of the *Daily Gleaner* newspaper to all the passengers.

What I saw on the front page was stupefying.

The lead article was about a man who had been shot to death by police on the outskirts of Kingston. As I started to read the article, I damn near spewed my coffee all over the plane: the shooters were none other than Tony Hewitt and his detectives from the Flying Squad. They had been looking for this fugitive—wanted for murder—for over a year. Finally, the article said, the found him, and got into a "gunfight." The wanted subject was shot eleven times. I sat there in utter astonishment as I realized that the ammunition they had used to kill the fugitive had just days before been sitting in a dark storage room at the Miami-Dade Police Training Bureau.

When we got back to Miami, I was contacted by a DEA agent who was working on the task force that got us connected with

Oscar. They were widening their net. Jamaican smuggling and violence were so prolific now that many new players were showing up on the radar screen. American law enforcement in most large cities was getting an extensive crash-course education on Jamaican organized crime, politics, and the people involved.

DEA Agent David Tinsley was a good ol' Georgia boy, complete with a lovable thick accent. A former Atlanta policeman, David enjoyed the hunt and the capture. Putting bad guys in jail was what he was all about, and we got along instantly. His partner in the task force was a soft-spoken Miami-Dade Narcotics Detective named Doug Ayers. Doug was insightful and his laid-back nature was an almost comical foil to Tinsley's country-bred enthusiasm. The three of us made a good team. David and Doug had leads in Kingston on their case, and since we all figured that our dots were going to connect, we went to the island together. We found out one afternoon that David was a big Bob Marley fan, when we drove by a huge statue of Marley in Kingston.

"Oh guys...look at that! I gotta stop...please." We pulled over and it turned out we were at the Bob Marley Museum. David was ecstatic. The place was closed, and from outside a large black iron gate, David gawked at the statue and snapped a couple of photos. Just as we were about to leave, a dude with long dreads and a colorful tam rode up on a bike, holding a fat joint in one hand.

"You want to get inside?" He asked.

"Yeah!" David said. "How? Do you know the security guard?"

The guy grinned and pulled out a key. "I *am* the security guard!"

Doug and I found this hilarious. Oblivious to who we were, the guy happily opened up the gate and walked in with us. Then, we took a picture of DEA Special Agent David Tinsley standing next to Bob Marley's statue next to our host, grinning and holding a big smoldering joint right next to him.

Ayers whispered to David, "Should we tell the guy who we are?"

David grinned and shook his head. "No, leave the poor guy be."

We laughed our asses off about that encounter several times the rest of the trip.

The alliance with Tinsely and Ayers got me introduced me to the AUSA (Assistant U.S. Attorney) Kathryn Moller, who was overseeing their operation. I liked Kathryn, and she liked what we were doing. Federal prosecutors can be highly bureaucratic, even stuffy, but Kathryn was intelligent, easy to talk with, and she liked to laugh. She was currently in the process of indicting a group of Jamaicans, and Oscar was providing information. Oscar, we all agreed, could be a great source of information, but he had his shortcomings. He was a simpleton.

During one meeting at Kathryn's office, two FBI agents attended. They were part of a unit working Jamaican organized crime. We introduced them to Oscar and agreed that we would stay in touch with each other about mutual developments.

The problem was that the word "mutual" is not common in the FBI vocabulary. The Federal Bureau of Investigation is a fine organization, and I will not denigrate their history, their work, or their agents. They have their own agenda, their own system, and their own culture, none of which are necessarily designed to coordinate with anyone else's. They seem to fervently believe that what they are working on takes precedence over *anything* that local law enforcement agencies might be working on, murder or otherwise. In their eyes, their drug case was more important than the homicide of Cecil Clarke. It's hardly deliberate. It's simply upbringing, like two kids brought up in different households.

We had been taking Oscar out on location for several days, and he was showing us houses of people that he knew were deeply involved in the Spangler Posse, the group we believed might be responsible for Clarke's murder. Two things dismayed us: One, Oscar insisted on singing while Larry and I drove him around. This serenade was largely a never-ending medley: popular reggae songs that would suddenly morph into "Swing Low, Sweet Chariot," or any other popular song, from any decade you could imagine. Oscar's singing was positively ghastly, but *he* fancied himself as some sort of Jamaican Frank Sinatra. He sat in the back seat, smiling triumphantly, convinced that he was crooning his way into our good graces.

More disappointing than Oscar's vocal abilities was the quality of his information. None of what he was giving us was panning out. Not yet, anyway. But he knew a lot of detail and had given us *some* data that we could confirm. We had brought him from Jamaica to Miami, so we had to give it our best shot. Hence, we endured his gruesome *a capella*, and worked long hours trying to see what information he was giving us matched up with the known facts of the case, and Cecil Clarke's travels.

One day when we went to pick him up, Oscar disappeared. He had been staying in a little 1-bedroom apartment in Little Haiti that we had helped pay for while he was here. We had given him a beeper so that we could summon him for meetings. Suddenly, he wasn't there, nor was he responding to our pages. I remembered the watch incident in Kingston and gave him a little time. After three days, I was pretty worried. Again, I hoped the posses hadn't figured him out and killed him. It was as plausible as any explanation for his disappearance. I called Kathryn Moller and told her that Oscar was no longer answering our beeps. Had she heard anything?

"Call me back," she said quietly, "I'm going to send a number to your pager."

When we got on a secured line, Kathryn Moller said something I never thought I would hear from a federal prosecutor: "You did *not* hear this from me. Oscar is in witness protection. They have him in a hotel in Miami Beach."

I thought it best to remain quiet at that point. The FBI had hijacked the witness we had shared with them, and if Kathryn didn't tell me where he was, I was going to ask; I just didn't know how. With a sigh, she gave me the address, his undercover name the apartment was rented to, and added, for emphasis:

"We never had this conversation."

"*What* conversation?" I said with a smirk I think she could hear over the phone. "Thanks Kathryn."

The FBI had put Oscar up in a seventh-floor apartment overlooking the Atlantic Ocean. It was extraordinary. As Larry and I walked around the place and enjoyed the stupendous view from the balcony, Oscar told us about his setup.

"They give me nice dinners every night. I'm eatin' real good. They give me spending money too." He showed us a mini-fridge full of Heinekens and said that he's been going out on Miami Beach and having the time of his life.

"But," he said, shaking his head, "Sounds crazy, but they treat me like shit. They demand all kinda stuff I don't know about. They tell me if I don't give them what they want they send me back to Jamaica. I wish I was working with you guys again." Despite all the fancy perks—none of which he had in Jamaica—his FBI handlers didn't know how to talk to him.

"Why didn't you call us?"

Oscar shook his head. "Them FBI guys came here one day and saw your business cards. They tore them up, and said, 'don't talk to these assholes again.' So I didn't have your number."

Since the FBI had decided to put us on their shit list, why not stay on it? Larry and I went ahead and took Oscar out again and had him point out some houses of posse members he thought were instrumental in Viking's scheme. He was happy to be with us and showed us his gratitude by launching into another long and horrendous round of his pop favorites.

When the feebs found out we had taken Oscar out under their noses, they were furious. What we did wasn't exactly illegal, but it sure would have rattled some cages had their higher ups gone whining to ours about us taking a protected witness out on location. We decided that they would get over it. Besides, this is what they got for hauling Oscar away, calling us "assholes" for no good reason, and forbidding him to call us.

After a call to Tony Hewitt to update him about Oscar, I had a list of witnesses—that's what Tony called them—who would help us identify who kidnapped and killed the Mighty Viking. Tony threw in a bonus: information about a private airfield outside Mandeville—about a two-hour drive from Kingston—smugglers were using to fly to south Florida. We had a lot to do on the island, and I was excited. This was the first time anyone on the Jamaican side of the things had anything of substance. I wrote up the trip as quickly as possible, and when I got to the island, I was flabbergasted: Tony Hewitt was not even in the country.

"But," I told another Flying Squad member, "Who's covering for him? Who has the witnesses that Tony told me about? He said they had information on my case."

The detective I spoke to was lost for words. "I got no idea what Tony told you. None of us here no nothing about no witnesses. I'm sorry."

I was going to hear about this when I got back to the States, that was for sure. Nyberg is spending the county's money for two detectives to go out of the country and comes back with nothing? At the least, we went to Mandeville with our now very open schedule. We found the airfield, and I took pictures of it. But what the fuck was that worth? I continued trying to contact Tony in a desperate attempt to interview these "witnesses" (if they even existed) before the trip ended. But no one in his unit knew anything. Not a *ting*.

When I got back, my sergeant, Cliff Nelson (from the Tommy and Teresa Torso case) smirked at me. "You went to Jamaica for three days, and come back with a picture of a dirt airstrip?" He knew what had happened with Tony, but he had to fuck with me, and he never let me hear the end of it.

"I'll tell the Captain," Cliff said, "he'll be thrilled at this monumental discovery of yours. Just look at this airstrip!" Cliff said, holding the photo up and grinning at me.

After this trip, it was clear that Tony and his gang of detectives had used the shit out of us—gotten their ammunition and holsters, killed their fugitive—and now had little time to continue the relationship. And my chances of getting another trip to Jamaica authorized, even if the information was real, were slim indeed. I was the detective who cried "wolf."

To add to the quagmire of misinformation and failed attempts to develop meaningful leads, it was starting to look like Oscar was taking everyone for a ride. As I started to piece together a timeline, I saw that the movements and confirmed activities of our victim, Cecil "Mighty Viking" Clarke, did not come close to coinciding with what Oscar was telling us about the gun seizure, and other details. We were able to put Clarke in *Miami*—not Kingston—when all that shit with the guns at Norman Manley Airport was happening.

"But," one federal agent on the task force said to me, "we don't *want* Oscar to say that."

"Well..." I said, pointing to a calendar we were using to track everyone's movements, "He *did*."

Oscar's story fell apart on several fronts. It had cost us valuable time, two costly trips to Jamaica, and a watch. It had cost the feds about three weeks in a high-rise oceanfront condo, with room service dinners and spending money, but well, but to hell with them. This is what happened with informants sometimes. In the backdrop of all this wasted time, more Jamaican murders were filling up our board at Homicide, and in Broward County, our neighbor to the north. It had now been two years since Clarke's body had been found.

I had to generate some new sources of information, and I asked Kathryn to see who we could talk to. She turned us onto to a guy named Franklin Passley, a co-defendant in Kathryn Moore's indictment of a violent gang of Spangler Posse members. We wasted no time in getting a sit-down with him at the federal lockup in Miami. The place they designated for interviews was nicknamed "the Igloo" because it was always kept so goddamned cold.

We were cautious now about what to believe from these characters, but Passley's help with Kathryn had already checked out, so he had some credibility. He told a story of the Viking's demise that was a bit more believable than Oscar's, and included people we could talk to provide corroboration.

Passley said that as far he knew, Viking had no ties to smuggling, or posses, or anything like that. He was nothing but a flashy celebrity who kept narcotics and a lot of cash with him. A splinter group Passley associated with saw him as easy target for cash. The gang didn't have a sexy name, or any party affiliation he knew of, and was headed up by a guy named Cecil Hart. Hart had the demeanor and reputation of being a stone-cold killer. He preyed on other Jamaicans who might have money, guns, and dope, and he went after them. Hart, Passley told us, got his gang together and put together a scheme to kidnap Viking. They would use a girl named "Candy" to lure him out for a date. Candy would play the part of a starry-eyed admirer, and Viking, true to form, would fall for it. Candy got him to a parking lot, and the rest of the gang descended. They went to his house, took weed, money, and whatever else they could find. When they were done, they made sure he wouldn't go telling anyone.

Hart employed a guy named Carl Lowe to do the shooting. Carl was accompanied by another gang member who took Viking's car, and did the deed while the rest of them divvied up the loot. Passley remembered that when Lowe got back to the house, they were all partying in, Lowe laughed and said, "Viking went hiking."

Kathryn knew Lowe well, having indicted him on a case in the northern district of Florida for possession of cocaine. A host of other Jamaicans were listed in the indictment, including our target, Cecil Hart. A federal judge gave Carl Lowe the maximum at that time for possession with intent to distribute 500 grams of cocaine: an astonishing *life* sentence. I met with Lowe in the federal penitentiary outside Tallahassee, and he gave me Candy's real name.

By this time, I had been working on this case for four years. I was in Cold Case now, so I was getting help from Greg Smith and my other squad mates, John LeClaire and Jerry Crawford. Things were actually falling into place. Carl Lowe's situation couldn't get much worse, and with the small potential of getting his sentence mitigated, he spoke to me. He confirmed most of what Passley said, though stopped short of confessing to be the trigger man. He wanted to know what every inmate wants to know: "What can you all do for me?" If he was the shooter, there wasn't much, though maybe some plan could be hammered out with Kathryn Moller if he testified in federal court. I had to get more corroboration before getting to that table.

I found Sandradee Dudley (Candy) and I'm not sure what she was shit-scared more of: getting prosecuted on Viking's kidnapping and murder or feeling the wrath of Cecil Hart and company. But she talked and filled in some holes in the story. She didn't know who actually pulled the trigger, but now our story was three-dimensional enough for us to get an arrest warrant for Cecil Alexander Hart. It would be the second one he was facing: Broward County had a murder warrant out for him too. He had ripped off and killed a drug dealer in Fort Lauderdale. We still didn't know the exact person in Lowe's gang that had sent the Viking hiking.

As our case was taking shape, so were several cases headed up by Charles "Buck" McCully, one of our Homicide guys who handled a couple of similar cases and had gone on a mission to know every major Jamaican player in both counties. Buck was a wealth of knowledge on Jamaican organized crime, and we shared a lot of info back and forth. Then we got a tip that Cecil Hart was in Kingston, and that the local cops there (*not* Tony Hewitt) had eyes on him. They told us to come down quick, as they felt that any day they were going to put cuffs on him. Of course, we knew that in Jamaica, if they found Hart, it would be more likely that he would die in a hail of bullets. I wondered if they had used up all the Miami-Dade reloads I gave them.

To say we "missed" Hart wouldn't be quite accurate. Again, we met up with the country *attaché* and he took us to a police outpost on the north side of Kingston, a sub-station of sorts. Other than the word "Police" above the front door, the place could have easily passed for a remote gangster headquarters. A small weathered house sat on a shaded lot with chickens and roosters loitering by the front stoop. Two huge guys wearing military gear, berets, and M-16s stood guard outside, eyeing us warily as the attaché's car rolled up. Inside, we were introduced to the local superintendent of the district. He listened carefully while we told him that we had information that some of his people had Hart located. He excused himself, turned away from his desk, and made a quick phone call, talking *sotto voce* to some unknown person. Then he turned back to us.

"We'll call you at your hotel as soon as we have him. We'll let you know."

When we got back in the car, our DEA escort shook his head. "That sonofabitch isn't gonna give you Cecil Hart. He's on the take. I think he just made a phone call to tip him off."

Here we go again, I thought. Another fruitless trip to Jamaica. Cliff was going to delight in this one.

"Why?" I asked. "What makes you think so?"

"All these superintendents out here...they all have their hands out. The local posse leaders pay them off for tips like this. He could be getting half of what he makes all year to alert Hart that you're looking for him."

We went home empty-handed again, but I still felt like we were getting close to Hart. On the plane back, I don't think he was even in Jamaica at all; it would have terribly risky for him to fly, given the two murder warrants. Then again, these guys get their hands on fake IDs and passports all the time. The management of the different players of this case was getting complicated. We struck a deal with Candy and Franklin Passley to lock in their testimony against Hart. Unfortunately, Sandradee Dudley was here on a green card, so her conviction was now going to get her deported. I called INS and talked to the officer in charge of Candy's case. I pleaded with him and told him that she was an important witness in a murder case. Surely, they could delay her deportation for that.

"I'm sorry," he said in the most federally bureaucratic terms, "but there's no relief for this. She's deportable."

Well shit, I have a tree in my yard that's chop-downable, I told him. Does that mean I have to chop it down? But there was no one in the system that was willing to step in and intervene a process that seemed as certain as the setting sun. And so back to Jamaica she went. Candy thought *we* had got her deported. She was furious with us and swore to never help us again. To complicate matters even more, no charging decision was made on Carl Lowe yet. He was still sitting in a federal facility up in the panhandle. This was becoming a problem.

"Constitutional speedies," Greg Smith told me. Greg, who had always wanted to be a lawyer, knew a lot about legal procedures and doctrines most detectives did not.

"If you have someone in custody—like Lowe—and you have probable cause to charge him," Greg explained, "you're violating his rights by not charging him and giving him the right to a speedy trial. You can't just let him sit there indefinitely."

There was no specific time frame on this, but it had to be a *reasonable* time. Another prosecutor explained it like this: "If you have a lengthy delay in charging someone who is sitting there within arm's reach, you had better be able to defend the delay, or you'll lose the opportunity to charge him."

I went to Jay Novick and urged him to do something. Let's charge Lowe *now*.

"No," he said. "I'd rather wait until we have Cecil Hart in custody and charge them both together." When I challenged Novick on the wisdom—and danger of this—he brushed it off. "Don't worry, it will work out. I know what I'm doing." Novick may not have liked the idea of a police investigator warning him about the law, but this was a real risk we were taking.

There was much greater urgency to get Cecil Hart in custody, but it would be six months more before it happened. We had sent his flyer all over the country, to every city where Jamaicans had a stronghold, and one day we got a call from New York PD. The north end of Brooklyn was heavily Jamaican, and some sharp detective in the Brooklyn North Homicide squad spotted Hart walking down the street while they were doing a surveillance on a murder case there. Cecil Hart was in custody.

Finally, we could start mopping up on this case. With Hart off the street, I hoped more people would come forward, and we did get one other subject tell us that Lowe was the shooter. But Novick had dragged his feet so badly on this that we did indeed lose our chance. The constitutional window had closed: we could not charge Carl Lowe.

To avoid the death penalty, Hart took a plea package that included our murder, Broward's murder, and bunch of charges the feds had lined up for him. Because we could never put a gun in his hand, the plea was to second-degree murder, and he was sentenced to 20 years on that charge. He did about a year in state prison until he got transferred into federal custody, where he would serve out the rest of the state time and federal time—eleven years and three months.

Carl Lowe skated on a murder in which he most likely pulled the trigger. He served twelve more years on his federal life sentence for cocaine trafficking charges before appealing it and getting it reduced from life to 26 years, minus the time he had already served. That part of the case was purely and simply botched. As frustrating as that snafu was, I was satisfied that we had closed the case. Everyone involved was identified and behind bars. Jamaican murders were difficult to solve, but teamwork and perseverance got it done on this one.

I have no idea whatever became of Oscar. I'm just glad I never had to hear him sing again.

Chapter Seventeen

Kids don't think about hazards. Kids just charge around with no regard for danger. I was no different. One day, I hopped the fence in my back yard, as I did almost every day, and crossed the dirt alleyway to make the short walk to the U-Totem to get my coveted football cards.

There was a red truck with its emergency red flashing lights on the same side of 62nd Avenue, and EMTs were huddled around a little black boy of about six. I stared in fascination; a white bone stuck grotesquely out of his ankle, and his sock and sneaker were soaked with blood. He was crying and gasping softly—he looked very, very scared. Nearby was a car with its flashers on, and a man was running his hand through his hair, looking at the boy.

"What happened, huh?" one of the paramedics asked the boy, trying to comfort him, "Were you crossing the street to get a sucker?" The boy just looked at the man, sniffling and whimpering.

It dawned on me then—when you have no idea something bad can happen to you, WHAM, it can happen. I thought of how many times I rode my bike all around that area, how many times I had run back and forth across the street, climbed trees, and swam in the ocean, never once imagining that I could get hurt. That's when I heard one of the paramedics say to the other, "Lucky kid. Could have been killed."

Forget getting hurt, I thought, your life can end—by a complete accident, when you're just planning to get a sucker—or a pack of football cards.

Of all the next-of-kin notifications there are to do, accidentals were the worst. When you went on a homicide—*most* of the time—the victim had been in so much trouble all their lives that the dreaded knock on the door was something that family members weren't terribly surprised by. They were grief-stricken and shaken, but not as thunderstruck and completely shattered, as say, the wife of Daniel Gutches.

She came to the door with a smile. A stout woman about fifty-five, she must have wondered, "I wonder what this detective wants?"

Her husband was part of a landscaping crew at a new housing development. One of the new palm trees—big sabal palms they had propped with 2 x 4s—blew over in the gusty wind and fell on him. He was dead. She had been depending on Daniel to support them. She was battling cancer, and he was working two jobs to put bread on the table.

Of all the responsibilities we had, the most overlooked might be the investigation of accidental deaths. Homicides and suicides were what everyone talked about. Accidents though, happen constantly. South Florida is a haven for accidental deaths because of the weather, year-round construction, and water—the greatest death trap of all. Our environment featured the ocean, the Everglades, thousands of miles of canals, and an abundance of swimming pools, all in use 365 days a year.

In 1986, construction began for an exclusive island community called Fisher Island. One sunny day I was up for the next non-homicide and got sent to Fisher Island out there for a construction site death. An electrical worker had gotten crushed by a falling crane. When I got there, none other than Donny Roper, from H & R—my Jack Wilcox homicide—was there. He made a beeline for me when he saw me.

"Hey Nyberg!"

"Hi Donny," I said, "is this your crew out here?"

He made a face. "Aw Nyberg, we're gonna pay through the nose on this one." Then he leaned in towards me with a conspiratorial whisper: "Between you and me—our crane operator didn't have the outriggers out far enough. When the thing tilted, he overcompensated, and over she went."

Between you and me? Donny was dumber than I thought. He just admitted his company's liability to me, and that was going on the first page of my report. The victim had been down inside the foundation where they were putting in concrete "forms", inside of which would run the electrical conduit, plumbing, and other materials. There was probably some yelling going on when that crane was toppling, but I don't think he heard it. Two years later, Roper was surprised to see me in the waiting area of the civil courthouse. He stared at me like I was some kind of traitor.

Both Gutches and the victim on Fisher Island might never have seen what hit them. Others, though, stared it right in the face. Back when I was in uniform, two very memorable train accidents come to mind. In Opa-Locka, four Haitians in a sedan tried to beat the train just west of State Road 9, but they failed. The impact sent the car sailing a good one hundred feet, where it tumbled another fifty feet or so. All four occupants were ejected from the vehicle, one in the back seat with such force that his pants caught on the open window and he was pulled right out of them, with the empty pants left hanging inside the vehicle. They all died, and the when the car came to rest, the front left tire landed right on the driver's head, flattening it like a grape. It was about as horrific scene as I've ever been on, though one in North Miami, a year later, ranked right up there as well.

Though this may have been a suicide, someone was hit on the tracks as a freight train roared through the east side of town between the back of a shopping center on one side, and a residential neighborhood on the other. Chunks of human matter were stuck to the front of several train cars for about five cars down; the victim had been all but obliterated. The next day, I was assigned to work the desk. We all took turns every month manning the station desk, helping citizens walking in, and answering the phone. One man's phone call is unforgettable.

"I was picking mangoes in my back yard...we back up to the train tracks, you know. And I found a human hand in my mango tree."

That's enough to ruin anyone's day, I would think. I told the man it's a good thing he didn't find the hand a week from now.

People die by error, gross negligence, or stupidity. Sometimes, the errors are simple human errors, like "oh crap, did we put an extra 2x4 on those sabal palm trees? Sure is windy today." Sometimes the mistake is by someone else's hand, other times, by the victim's own poor judgement, overconfidence, or ignorance.

Such was the case in the workshop of a U-Haul facility in South Miami. The 29-year-old worker was welding trailer hitch bars together. U-Haul was skimpy on equipment, so there were no proper welding tables to work on. The worker decided to use a 55-gallon drum he found in the shop, placing the pieces on the circular metal top as his welding table. What he didn't know—and what no one told him—was that the drum was used as a waste dump. Over several months, other workers used it to discard dirty oil and fuel-soaked rags. When it was full, someone would take it to the dump. This one was full, but no one had bothered to take it anywhere, and instead they clamped the lid on it.

As the welder guided the point of his torch along the two bars he was connecting, the overflow of the flame gradually cut through the top of the drum, igniting the dense fumes within. The force of the explosion was so powerful that we found a circular mark on the ceiling where the drum lid had rocketed straight up. The blast sent the victim to the floor, and as well severed the hose from the torch head to the tank, bathing him in flames. The flames were still roaring when the fire department truck rolled up. The victim was completely charred from head to toe. As part of our contact with the next-of-kin, it was our responsibility to make sure all valuables were collected from the body. The Medical Examiner wagon was forbidden to transport any jewelry or other personal belongings other than clothing. We customarily took all the clothing off to search for other trauma and to make sure we got all the jewelry from every nook and cranny, so it could be released to the family. In this case, there was no clothing to worry about; it had all been incinerated. All this poor dude had was a gold ring, on his pinky. And it wasn't coming off.

I tried everything to get that ring off, but it wasn't budging past his charred, heat-bloated knuckle. The only option was to take his finger off. I thought of borrowing a hacksaw, but the U-Haul people were suffering enough today from this ordeal and using their hacksaw to take the finger off their dead employee didn't seem like a great option. He was cooked through and through, so I thought that maybe the finger could be twisted off. With my gloved hand, I started twisting. I remember, while performing this procedure, that this just might be the most gruesome thing I had ever done, and maybe ever *will* do, but I forged ahead. After a minute or so, the finger came off, and I slid the ring off the other way.

Twisting a dead man's finger off wasn't how I had planned my day, but this job could put you in some very unusual situations. The alternative was to get an earful from the Medical Examiner's Office—and my supervisor—about missing the ring. A month prior, I had already gotten in a little bit of hot water on a suicide case, in which I missed a ring, and the Medical Examiner had to call me in to come pick it up. It was easy to miss—a labia piercing—I had checked everywhere *but* there.

The wagon was on the way. I laid the dismembered and now ringless finger on the victim's charred torso, threw away my gloves, and started writing up my report.

It was not uncommon for a case to start out looking like a suicide and end up accidental. Or it could start out as somewhat of a mystery, and until that magic piece of evidence or information showed up, we would call it an "unclassified death." The medical examiner carried those types of cases on their books as "pending further studies."

One such case had us thoroughly baffled for a couple of hours. The body was a white male, maybe 30-35 years old, sprawled awkwardly on the front lawn of a house in a residential area near today's Doral. The house was one of five homes on a cul-de-sac, and the body was just a foot or so from the edge of the roadway, close to the mailbox. What was puzzling is that we found blood spatter on the mailbox, blood spatter on the grass and continuing blood spatter in somewhat of a semi-circle, around the body. There were no skid marks in the roadway, the mailbox was intact and undamaged, and no one in the neighborhood heard any screeching of tires, arguments, or anything out of the ordinary. We called the Medical Examiner Dr. Bruce Hyma to the scene, and even he was scratching his head. The blood spatter patterns were not making sense at first. How does a body exhibit 360-degree blood spatter, and no one sees or hears any violent or traumatic event going on? There was no automobile debris (broken headlights, etc.) nearby, no bludgeoning weapons laying around, nothing that would indicate there was any confrontation.

I threw some gloves on and Hyma helped me turn the body over. As we moved the corpse, our curiosity only deepened: the body was laying was in a small crater in the grass. Just as we were processing this new finding, a jet passed overhead. I looked up, and then Dr. Hyma looked up. Then we looked at each other. We were in the flight path of Miami International Airport.

"Are you thinking what I'm thinking?" I asked him.

"It's the only answer right now," Bruce Hyma said. "Maybe a stowaway. He hides up in the landing gear of the airplane, freezes to death on the trip over, and when the pilot puts the landing gear down on final approach, he falls out."

We all agreed that was the only workable theory we had, and the only explanation for the crater, the 360-degree blood spatter, and the lack of other evidence. It took about a day and half to confirm it. A family from Guatemala contacted our department when they had failed to get any call from their loved one. The dots all connected; the victim did indeed stow away on an airliner before it took off from Guatemala City airport, thinking he would be able to stay in the landing gear housing and then sneak off to who knows where once the plane was on the ground. At 40,000 feet he didn't have enough oxygen or enough warmth to survive the trip. I couldn't help but imagine what would have happened if one of the homeowners on that cul-de-sac had walked out to get their mail at the moment this guy came plummeting down out of the clouds and slammed onto their lawn. Or *them*.

40-year-old men aren't found dead at their workplace very often, with no trauma. I was the lead on an unclassified, possible natural death case at an apartment complex. The victim was part of a painting crew and had been transported to Hialeah Hospital after his co-workers found him unresponsive on the ground near a building. He had been pressure cleaning the walls of the two-story building, according to the two workers I spoke with. I looked around and didn't see anything out of the ordinary. Maybe this poor fellow had a heart attack. It had happened to younger people. I remember years ago a Miami Dolphin linebacker, Larry Gordon, 29 years old and in the prime physical condition of his life, dropping dead after a practice.

From the scene, I went to the hospital and viewed the body. He wasn't an overweight man, and he was coated in paint dust from his pressure cleaning. I looked the body over but failed to find anything remarkable. This might be one for the M.E. investigators, who were good at doing historical research and interviewing family members about medical conditions and diseases that ran through the bloodline. I wrote it up as an unclassified and sent the body to the M.E. Then I went back to the scene to talk to co-workers. They were stowing all their equipment away as I talked to the supervisor of the group. I asked him what he saw when he got to the victim. He shrugged.

"Just his equipment, you know? Just normal stuff." I wondered if something could have happened with this gas-powered pressure cleaning machine. Something faulty with it? He dies of the fumes? Didn't make sense—this wasn't an enclosed space. I looked at the building. He must have had a ladder, to reach up to the second floor, right? Maybe the ladder had a problem, he falls off, breaks his neck, something like that.

"Where's his ladder?"

The man nodded towards the maintenance area of the building. "We put it away. It's in the storage room."

"Ok, I'd like to take a look at it. Is it a wood ladder?" I was thinking maybe one of the steps comes loose, who knows?

"No. It's a metal ladder," he told me.

At that moment, as I walked away from the building from where the victim was found, I found myself looking at a power line, about three feet above my head. Now, I could picture it: the victim finishes his work, picks up the ladder, and instead of carrying it horizontally, carries it *vertically*. It makes contact with the power line, and *zap*—game over. The ladder answered the question. I measured it and found that the width of the ladder matched perfectly with two scorch marks we could see on the power lines. After I left the scene, Dr. Wetli called me from the M.E.

"We cleaned off your victim and got all the paint residue off him. Classic electrocution. He's got an entry wound in his hand and one in the bottom of his foot. We have his clothes here too; it blew a hole in his sneaker."

Electrocutions manifest small, bloodless wounds in a human body where the current enters and exits. Our painter victim had a good strong heart, with no family history, we found out later. He just didn't carry that ladder the right way.

Every tourist season we could count on three or four tourists drowning in the ocean. It never failed. Every summer, people lost their lives in swimming pools, canals, at the beach, and in boating accidents. Like all accidentals, they were terribly sad cases, but you never had the time or the luxury to grieve over them, because your next case was coming up, and you had to focus. One case, though, really hit home with me, and stays with me to this day. It was a little boy, about twenty-two months old.

His young parents lived in a townhouse off Flagler Street near the Turnpike. The back patio of their home had the ubiquitous wood slat fence and, as an added feature, a gate, so that one could take a stroll by the canal behind the development, adjacent to the turnpike. The couple lost track of Isaac for only a couple of minutes, and the search turned frantic when they realized he was not in the house. Isaac had found his way out to the back and pushed his way through a gap in the faulty, poorly maintained wooden gate. Outside, along the wide swath of grass, they called his name, over and over.

Our divers found the little boy's body in about four feet of water, near the bank of the canal. At the autopsy, I couldn't shake the fact that his fingernails were caked with green silt, from clawing at the walls of the canal after he had fallen in.

I sat with the mother and father—they couldn't have been more than twenty-five—and as I told them the process, about the body going to the M.E. first, and so on, they nodded, their mouths quivering, their hands clutching tightly to one another. They were fighting hard to keep from collapsing in front of me. My son, Erik, was the same age as Isaac. That was the first time, sitting there in front of that couple, that I had to fight back my own tears on a case. They were such sweet, respectful people. They *thanked* me for being professional. It was excruciating.

When I went for the autopsy, the doctor asked me to go into the cooler and find his number on the tag. Each body had a manila card rubber banded to the great toe, with the M.E. Case number and last name. When I went into the refrigerated room, it was crammed with gurneys, up against one another. It was in our old Medical Examiner's Office, which had become obsolete and couldn't handle the flood of cases that were coming in so fast and furious in the mid-1980's. I searched for the little boy's gurney, but couldn't find it, until I found him: to save space, his little body had been unceremoniously placed between the legs of an adult male victim, heaped on top of the dead man like so much trash. I was overwhelmed at the indignity of it—Isaac should at least have his own space, shouldn't he? His parents could never, ever know about this. It was bad enough that I did.

I know the specific spot where he died; it's visible from the Florida Turnpike. When I drive that northbound stretch, I make sure not to look in that direction, because if I do, I'm back in the morgue's refrigerated room, seeing little Isaac dumped on top of an anonymous corpse.

Chapter Eighteen

The Jewelry Washers

When was nine, my Swedish grandfather gave me two gifts. One was a collection of Buffalo head nickels, thirty or more, some which were minted as early as 1902. I thought they were pretty cool, though I didn't know they would have actual value in the future. I was too young to understand value in the true sense; whether monetary or sentimental.

He also gave me a knife that had a deer's foot handle. It was the most unique knife I have ever seen. Sadly, both of these things got lost when we moved out of our house in South Miami to a bigger place further south. I thought about them both from time to time and would have loved to have either one back. In my teens, I thought the Buffalo head nickels could be worth a few dollars each on the rare coins market. Later though, when I had my own kids, I thought it would be great to have them as a link to my grandfather, and something I could give to my own sons. Imagine, having a deer's foot knife, from your great-grandfather.

Having something—like a knife—is a connection to deceased family member. It means something.

The procedure went like this: you took all the jewelry off the deceased (and hopefully didn't have to twist off a finger). Anything of value that was not going to be used as evidence—wallet, cash, watch, etc.—-was placed in a in a bag. You went to do the next of kin notification and brought the valuables with you. Part One of the notification was the delivery of the bad news. Reactions could range from mild to meltdown, and you never knew just how it was going to go. Part Two of the notification was the return of the victim's personal belongings. Even if the family member had composed themselves during Part One, this act—when their loved ones jewelry was placed on the table—was sure to crumble their defenses.

But that's the procedure. The notification and disposition of valuables should be done as soon as possible, so that things don't get lost and accusations can't be made. Many times, though, we had a decomposed victim. When you took a ring, necklace, or bracelet off a rotting corpse, it was likely going to have pieces of nasty-smelling skin, flesh, and body fluids on it. The items had to be washed.

We didn't have a maid service; Homicide detectives were the ones who washed them.

It was a common sight in the men's room across the hall from our squad room: detectives in ties wearing latex gloves, standing at sinks, scrubbing pieces of jewelry, watches, eyeglasses, and whatever needed cleaning. Only then did we return the items to the families. There was no written policy that told us to do this. It was just what we did. The seasoned detectives taught the new detectives from one generation to the next, when they broke them in. It was about respect. We washed jewelry.

It is nearly impossible to describe the relationship that forms between the lead investigator and the next-of-kin of a deceased person. But there *is* a relationship. I remember when I first got to Homicide, one of the senior guys there was telling another new detective how to handle dealing with murder cases.

"They're case numbers. That's all they are. Don't get wrapped up in who they were and what they meant to their loved ones. It's a case number. Move on to the next one."

He was wrong. Maybe he was fooling himself with that kind of advice and trying to trick himself into believing that kind of emotional Houdini-ism, but the victims were everything. That's not to say that it was ok to get emotionally *involved*. You really shouldn't do that. But where murder cases were concerned, we were working *for* those families. Yes, it was our job to try and find the truth and develop evidence, arrest the offenders, and testify in court. There was great satisfaction in "catching bad guys" and hearing a jury say "guilty." But that satisfaction was infinitely more profound when you saw the tears of relief on the faces of the loved ones, when you heard them thank you. We were the last lifeline—or deathline—to their loved one. They clung to us from funeral to trial, and they never forgot us after that. An emotional investment—albeit small—was nearly inevitable.

In 1989, I was still working for Cliff Nelson, and we got a case up in the northwest section of Miami Lakes that should have ended in a fistfight and a bloody nose for someone. Instead, a young man who had never even gotten as much as a parking ticket was shot and killed.

Ali Zaidi and his best friend, Dinaich Thompson, were looking for a parking space at a strip shopping center. A car passed with a good-looking blonde girl inside. They gawked at her, laughed to each other, and kept going. When they came out of the store they had visited, there was the girl again, with her boyfriend. He was a hothead, and he started cussing them up and down. It was the classic "you lookin' at my girl?" showdown. The two friends brushed him off and got in the car, with the livid boyfriend yelling threats and challenges.

"C'mon! Meet me at the end of the block and I'll fuck you up!" He pointed south on 67th avenue.

Zaidi and Thompson pulled out of the parking lot and onto NW 183rd street, in disbelief that this guy had exploded like he did, and that he wouldn't stop the tirade. Then, while they sat at the red light of 67th avenue, the guy was there again. He had gotten out of his car at the light and was now tugging on the passenger side car door, screaming at them.

"Follow me!" he yelled at them. "We're gonna settle this you motherfuckers!" He again gestured to the road towards the south.

Ali and Dinaich followed him.

The guy's black Honda Civic sped south and then down a smaller road that led to a dead end where some new construction was being planned. There was nothing there but a small cul-de-sac surrounded by woods. Ali grabbed the tire iron from the back seat and the two friends got out.

The subject had a much smaller weapon: a .25 caliber semi-auto handgun. Without a word, he started firing. Ali and Dinaich both hit by gunfire and fled into the woods, bleeding and panting. They stopped running when they heard the subject's tires squealing. Ali had suffered a gunshot wound to the arm, but Dinaich had taken two rounds to the midsection and collapsed in the leaves. Only a couple of minutes later, Dinaich Thompson died in his best friend's arms.

Fire-Rescue got Ali Zaidi to Jackson Memorial Hospital where the triage crew got him stabilized. While one of my squad members went to interview Ali and get all the details, Larry Wilkotz and I went to the home of Dinaich Thompson's mother. They were a very close family and when we got to the house, we found a crowded living room with about six or seven people there for a family gathering. They were wondering why Dinaich had not yet shown up. It was a small but very neat, well-kept house, with trinkets and artwork from Jamaica everywhere. Mrs. Thompson had colorful decorative plates sitting on small shelves along the hallway, depicting scenes from farms and villages. She frowned in utter confusion when we came in and sat down, and then I told her what had happened. Her son was dead, killed by an unknown gunman during an argument.

"No..." she said, shaking her head. She stood up from the table and began to scream. "NO!!" Before family members could grab her, she ran screaming through the house, grabbing the plates off the wall and smashing them, until family members were able to corral her. One of her brothers brought out a bottle of 151 proof Jamaican rum. I thought they were going to pour it down her throat, but instead they soaked a small dishrag in it, and started mopping her head as she panted on the floor. I looked at Larry, and we both were thinking the same thing: we still had the bag of Dinaich's personal effects containing his wallet and a small necklace. Luckily, there were other family members there to release his belongings to her. Family members got assigned Part Two.

Ali got out of the hospital and worked with us as much as he could to put together a description of the subject. The young man was devastated; Dinaich was his closest friend. He was likewise wracked with the guilt from his foolish decision to take up the challenge from our still unidentified shooter. From his description we got a sketch together, made a flyer, and distributed it everywhere in the northwest section. We got nothing—a couple of vague tips that went nowhere. A year passed. Then another.

I fielded many calls from Mrs. Thompson during that time, and she all but begged us to keep trying to find Dinaich's killer. Ali called me too. We revisited his story over and over again. We began to focus on our key to the case: the mystery girlfriend. Clearly, he dropped her off somewhere, or left her when he challenged at the victims at the red light. Ali never saw her in the car when they followed the subject, or when they got out. She could have been laying down in the car, but it made more sense that he left her somewhere. All Ali could remember of her was that she was white, blonde, and pretty.

Whatever slim leads we had dried up. As time marched on, new cases marched in. Dinaich Thompson's case was still in our book as a "O.P." – open pending. In 1992, I went to the Cold Case Squad.

About a year after I got there, Cliff came over to my desk. He had been doing some reviewing of the Dinaich Thompson case since an anonymous tip had come in naming the possible shooter: Jose Badillo. I did some research into Badillo's address history and noticed that he lived at a house in Hialeah for a while, right after the murder. Using this new computer program we had, I was able to see the history of everyone who had ever used that address for their driver's license or vehicle registration. From that, I got the name of a girl about Badillo's age, with a very American, non-Hispanic name. The blonde girlfriend, maybe? They lived at the same address for about a year before Jose Badillo left for Naples to take a job in a machine shop.

When we found the girl, and it turned out that she was the one. She never came forward, she told us, because she was never sure it was him. Badillo hadn't left her at the shopping center, *she* left *him* and made a phone call to a friend to pick her up.

"I tried to tell him to calm down," she told us, "but he lost it. He had this over-possessive, super-jealous temper, and I couldn't deal with it anymore."

She walked to a pay phone and called a friend to pick her up. Badillo came to her later that night, very upset. She never knew, however, that he had killed anyone. Even when she saw our flyers posted around the neighborhood, she could not believe that it was Jose.

With her help, and Ali picking Badillo out of a photo lineup, we were able to get an arrest warrant for Badillo. John LeClaire and I went to Naples and found him at work, handcuffed him, and brought him back to Miami. Ali did a great job on the witness stand, and the jury convicted Badillo of 2nd degree murder and attempted 2nd degree murder, along with use of a firearm during the commission of a felony. On February 16, 2001, Judge David Miller sentenced Badillo to 28 years in state prison.

Mrs. Thompson called me a couple of weeks after the trial.

"I'm having a party at my house," she said, "I want you to come."

It was a nice get together, with many of her family and friends there, lots of good Jamaican food, and a DJ. What I didn't expect was for the DJ to announce my name as the person who solved Dinaich's murder, and for a standing ovation from the other guests. That type of stuff hardly ever happened.

Those simple "thank yous" were the moments that made all the long hours, difficult notifications—-and jewelry washing—-worthwhile.

Chapter Nineteen

We knew a lot of wealthy people when I was a kid. I always wondered why we didn't live in a big house in Coral Gables like most of them did. One family owned a store in Dadeland Mall. The store was called "Arango's" because the owners were Jorge Arango and his wife, Lillian. Dadeland Mall opened in 1962, and it was the first enclosed mall in Florida, possibly one of the first in the nation. Dadeland rapidly gained fame as the greatest place in the region to shop. It was a big attraction. Arango's had unusual furniture, artwork, pottery and unique décor for upscale customers.

Mr. Arango was such a nice man. He had a long face, a warm smile, and was always kind to me. They had a house in Suniland, not far from ours. I remember my parents telling me that the Arangos were from Colombia, and I thought that was quite exotic. I was into geography at an early age, so I knew Colombia was in South America, but I knew nothing else about it. The Arangos were the only people I had every met from Colombia. I remember that the store was on the west end of the mall, and on the north side of the long, east-west hall of shops and restaurants. I thought it was pretty cool—I knew people who were Colombian, and who had their own store in Dadeland.

I had been in the police academy for two weeks when I heard about the big shootout. Crime had been on the rise since the mid-70's, but what happened on July 11, 1979 no one had ever seen in Miami. Two hitmen went hunting for major cocaine importer German Panesso. They found him at a Crown Liquor store with his bodyguard on the west end of the Dadeland Mall. In the broad afternoon daylight, the hitmen opened fire with Uzi submachine guns through the plate glass windows of the liquor store. The drug boss and his bodyguard fired back, and the serenity of Dadeland Mall turned into a blizzard of lead as the four men fired their weapons back and forth at each other. Shoppers screamed and ran for cover and out to the parking lot, and after several chaotic minutes, Panesso and his bodyguard were dead on the floor of the liquor store. Two of the store employees were wounded by the gunfire. The gunmen escaped but left behind an armored truck full of weapons. Miami had never seen such a thing.

The Dadeland Shootout, as it became known, symbolized the kickoff of the Colombian drug wars in south Florida. Miami's murder rate skyrocketed. In 1980, the city had the highest per capita homicide rate in the United States. By the time I got to Homicide in 1985, drug murders were still rampant. Turf wars, retribution killings, and flat-out rip-offs were commonplace, and we were averaging around thirty homicides per month. Add in the accidentals, suicides, and unattended naturals that flowed in, and we fifty-five detectives in the Bureau were always hopping. Cocaine was bringing about $60,000 per kilo; there were hundreds of millions of dollars in cash moving around the streets of Miami. The Colombian cartels based in cities of Medellin and Cali were responsible for the vast majority of the exports, and it was coming in fast and furious. Billy Corben, a now-prominent documentary producer, provides a mean, dead-on accurate picture of what that world was all about in his excellent production, *Cocaine Cowboys.* In that movie, there's a lot of screen time given to a guy named Jorge Ayala, aka "Rivi". Back in 1981, Ayala nearly killed me. A decade later, I brought him a birthday cake.

This tale started when I was a uniformed officer in North Miami. My riding partner and good friend Jim Kolo came over to our house for dinner one night. He was new to south Florida, having transferred down from a police department in eastern Pennsylvania, and he hadn't even bought a car yet. He was getting rides from another officer who lived in his apartment complex in North Miami. I was driving Jim back up to his apartment, and my then-wife Vivian was in the back seat of my 1980 Chevy Malibu. As we were going through the intersection at U.S. 1 and 42nd Avenue northbound, I heard what I thought were multiple gunshots. I immediately looked at Jim, and said, "Is that what I think it is?"

"Sure as shit is," Jim replied, "get down..." and I slid down in my seat as far as I could while still being able to look over the dashboard to drive. The rapid gunfire continued, and as we passed the intersection, it stopped. I slowed down, and we both looked behind to see a black Mercedes in the left turn lane of the southbound side. Smoke was still hanging in the air, and someone was opening the passenger door to get out. I swung a quick U-turn at the next intersection and came back, and we saw a guy running across U.S.1, carrying a small bag. When we got to the car, we saw it was riddled with bullet holes. So was the deceased driver.

Jim chased down the guy across the street. The guy was somehow unhurt; he must have been on the floor, because the driver was peppered with gunshot wounds, and several of the rounds took out his driver's side window. It was a matter of bare seconds that those rounds missed my Malibu as we cruised through the intersection.

We called the City of Miami Police and gave interviews to their uniform and Homicide guys. Next morning's *Miami Herald* had a story that named the victim as a Colombian clothing industry executive of some kind. They all had a cover story, and it was usually something having to do with import-export, like carpeting, furniture, or seafood.

Twenty years later, I was sitting at my desk in the Homicide Office when Sgt. Al Singleton walked over and dropped a printout of a city of Miami police report on my desk.

"Remember this?" He asked.

I started reading the report and recognized the address immediately.

"Yeah! I'll never forget it. It's a wonder I didn't get shot that night."

Al nodded. "Well, the guy who did that shooting is working for us now. He was Griselda Blanco's hitman."

Al introduced me to Jorge Ayala—"Rivi"—and during that first meeting, we took him out of the Dade County Jail to his dentist. There was a lot of babysitting work with Ayala, but that was fairly common when you had an in-custody witness helping you with a case. Rivi was doing what he could to avoid the death penalty. He had done a lot of killing for Griselda Blanco. Ayala's story is well-chronicled in *Cocaine Cowboys,* and Al Singleton is interviewed throughout the documentary. I took Rivi to the dentist at least four times, but the one errand I remember best was when Al came over and said, "I've got a big lead for you."

He took out a piece of paper, and it had an address on it. "Publix grocery store—go to the bakery and pick up a cake. Take it to the State Attorney's Office. They'll handle it from there."

I nodded. "Ok. Whose birthday is it?"

Al smirked. "Rivi's."

What none of us knew about Rivi's "cooperation" (which was substantial) was that, behind the scenes, he was calling the State Attorney's Office major crimes secretarial pool and spending a *lot* of time on the phone with one of the secretaries. Jorge Ayala didn't survive the Colombian cartel wars by being stupid. Besides being a fearless and resourceful hit man, Rivi also had the gift of gab. He was as smooth a talker as you could ever find. He was also patient; after all, he had a quarter of a century to sit in prison before eligibility for a parole hearing. Rivi, it was later discovered, had many whispery, sexual conversations with more than one secretary, and got one so attached to him that there were conversations about her bringing a gun to the jail for him to effect his escape. When this all came out, it severely damaged our case against Blanco, the "Godmother of Cocaine," who was believed to be responsible for upwards of 150 murders, including the Dadeland Shootout and the one on LeJeune and U.S.1, that nearly put holes in my Malibu. Rivi killed people at Griselda's request. Among the trail of victims in those homicides was a 3-year-old boy who happened to be in the car when Rivi tried to kill the boy's father.

There were too many cartel and local drug murders during those years to recount. The Colombians had a virtual monopoly on cocaine importation, using every method they could to bring hundreds of kilos at a time: small airplanes, power boats, tractor-trailers, anchor compartments of freighter ships, and once, a huge haul of cocaine at MIA, hidden in a flower shipment on an Avianca Airlines cargo flight. The murder scenes got so common they started to run together in our memories: a dead body on the living room floor, Heineken beer bottles on the coffee table and a pot of *sancocho*—a traditional Colombian stew—on the stove. We had gotten well versed with the it all: a body in the trunk of a car, rotting in the Florida sun in some shopping center parking lot, tearful widows shrugging and saying "Yo no se," our case files thin from lack of leads, and then that fast, you're off to the next case.

One of my cases was a 40-year-old man named Miguel Veloz, machine-gunned in the driveway of his home just west of popular Tropical Park. We were able to take that case further than most cartel hits, in thanks to the help of a freighter captain by the name of Tirso Barker. He was introduced to us by way of a Customs official who was working closely with our narcotics unit. Barker named several people Veloz was involved with, and the trail went all the way back to a cartel boss named Rodriquez Gacha. Veloz was surmised to have skimmed $13 million dollars from a shipment that Barker had piloted from Colombia to Puerto Cortes,

Honduras, then to Haiti, where it was offloaded and brought to the Florida coast in smaller vessels. Embezzlement in the cocaine trade carried a death penalty and the enforcers in this group carried out Veloz' sentence quickly and efficiently. Barker gave us a thumbnail sketch of how the entire venture went down, enough for us to fly to Panama to interview him in more detail. The best part of the trip was our plane landing in Panama City, when you could see both the Atlantic and Pacific oceans at the same time. It went somewhat downhill from there.

Our country attaché was an FBI agent named Rodney Bell. He was black, 6'7", and very hard to miss. We had to go by his instructions, as we always did when conducting official business in a foreign country. My partner and I got a room at the Ejecutivo Hotel downtown. Panama City was a trashy, unwelcoming place that oozed with criminality. We looked out our 11th story window that day and could see General Manuel Noreiga's compound still surrounded by militia, just days after our government had extradited him to the U.S. Rodney Bell called us at our room and told us to meet Captain Barker at a different hotel, in the café downstairs. He would meet us there, but he was running late.

The café was surreal. Every table was occupied by one or two males, and all eyes were on us as we walked to our table. Many of the men carried black satchels. We weren't carrying weapons—we weren't allowed—and I had no idea who these wary characters were and what they were up to. All we *did* know about Panama was that it was Colombia's umbilical cord to Central America and a hotbed of cartel activity. My partner and I dressed down—polos and jeans—so we didn't look like law enforcement. We spoke in hushed tones with Barker, trying not to look like we were trading secrets. Barker was talking about very dangerous men who would kill him if they knew he was informing. Heads kept turning to look at us, and there was definitely some conversation about us going on a couple of tables away. It was nerve-wracking, like a scene out of a Tom Clancy movie. I expected Harrison Ford to walk in any minute. That would have been better actually, because rather than a discreet Jack Ryan strolling in quietly, here came 6'7 Rodney Bell, looking like a defensive end in a suit. He put his briefcase on the table, and *loudly* remarked, "Sorry I'm late! By the way don't forget to check in at the Embassy before the end of the day." I was sure every head turned to our table now.

My partner looked at me and whispered, "Fuck."

Barker's eyes widened, and I looked up at not-so-special Agent Bell. "Yeah. As a matter of fact," I said, looking at Barker, "we're getting out of here, now."

My partner, who spoke Spanish, quickly said, "I'll get a taxi." He left, and moments later waved us over to the exit and to our waiting ride.

In the taxi, Barker asked, "Who the hell is that idiot?"

We got to our hotel and continued the interview. Later we got Barker a taxi back to his place. He called us that night. "I think there are people following me now. I can't talk to you here anymore. If you can get me to the U.S., I will continue to help. And," he added, "I think the Colombians here in Panama City know who you are. I suggest you leave."

We were slated to leave two days later, but I got on the phone with American Airlines within an hour of Barker's call and got a flight out the next morning. I got to see the two oceans again as we took off, and it was sweeter this time knowing we were in the sky and home bound. We did get Captain Barker to Miami, and he continued to cooperate, falling just short of giving us enough to connect the dots we needed. We never made an arrest in the case, but we shared everything we had with the DEA and our Centac guys. Several of the people involved in the cocaine shipment that got Miguel Veloz killed included a local Panamanian attorney and a popular Cuban real estate broker.

Another Colombian murder case I got was on a Christmas Saturday morning, 1987. The victim was found the trunk of a car at Miller Square in west Kendall. The victim's hands were bound behind his back and he was shot in the head—standard fare for traffickers who screwed up, or screwed someone *over.* My family had planned a Keys getaway that Christmas weekend, but it got cancelled because of Angel Arbelaez' death. I remember being pissed off. The weather was great, and my car trunk at home was already packed and ready to head south. Instead, I had maggots crawling up my arm while we were trying to get Arbelaez' decomposed body out of *his* trunk.

His wife told me he was in the "frozen seafood business."

Who did he work with in the business? *I don't know.*

Who might have killed him? *I don't know.*

Who are his best friends, business associates? *I don't know.*

We found out later from an informant who had heard about the case that she was paid off by the group who had killed her husband. They even paid for his funeral. All she had to do was say "frozen seafood business" and "I don't know," and they would send money for her kids every month.

The same year, I helped Detective Larry Wilkotz with a witness in one of his cases in Tampa. It was like a Barker situation, but local. The guy was an American and had been flying loads for the Colombians in small planes. The FBI was handling him and had him on a long leash. He was able to live at home while he worked a deal with them, and his FBI handler said he was willing to talk to us. We were told not to tell anyone we were coming. We were routinely pretty cautious about that kind of thing, so we assured him that no one but our immediate supervisor, who had to approve the trip, would know.

We could have driven to Tampa, but time was a factor with this guy, so we got an early flight and got there before lunch. We got our rental car at the airport and headed to the hotel. The vehicle was a piece of shit; the windshield wipers didn't work and one of the windows wouldn't go all the way up. On the way, we got paged from the FBI contact who told us our witness would be available in the late afternoon. We decided we would exchange the rental car. Then we would have lunch, relax a bit, go over the case, and head to the witness' house. It was about 4pm when we rolled up to the single-family home and our pilot was watering his plants in front of the house. We got out of the house, and before we could even introduce ourselves, he grinned at us and said, "You changed cars!"

"And, how..." Larry said slowly, "did you know that?"

"The Colombians know you're in town," he said matter-of-factly. He waved us inside. Someone had talked too much about our trip. Who was it? We never found out, but my money is *not* on our sergeant back at Miami-Dade Police Homicide. Just as we had done in Panama, we decided that we would beat feet out of Tampa too. We couldn't get a flight until the next morning, and now I wished we had driven instead. I decided, fuck it, if the Colombians are going to follow us, they are going to end up at *Bern's Steakhouse*. We had been through enough stress, and we were going to spend a little of our overtime money on a good steak and some red wine, with our pistols under our jackets just in case. Dinner at *Bern's*—which is to this day my favorite restaurant—was superb. It's always nice when a great meal ends with a sumptuous dessert rather than gunfire, and the next morning, we were back home.

The cases kept coming: bodies in canals, trunks of cars, dumped in the Everglades, even stuffed in a suitcase. One headless body in a canal wore a t-shirt that said, "Smuggling: It's not just a job, it's an adventure."

It certainly was an adventure—a short-lived one—for 50-year-old Gamaliel Castro. He and a group of three other people, including a pregnant 32-year-old woman, were waiting for the seller of fifteen kilos of cocaine to arrive at their third-floor apartment in Doral. What they didn't know was that their connection, who had introduced the seller, was an undercover DEA agent.. The agent gave the signal on his beeper, and the raid team busted down the door. The occupants fled to the only place they could get away: the balcony.

They jumped.

Amazingly, the pregnant woman limped away. So did another male. Castro, however, went *splat,* and was dead on the scene. You have to know how to hit the deck apparently, and Castro did not. They all eventually got caught, and the DEA called us to handle Castro's death.

The cash profits were immense in the cocaine business. The payment for this deal sat on the floor of the apartment bedroom: a duffel bag stuffed with $800,000 in cash. Seeing that much money was pretty impressive—even unnerving. I was alone for a few moments with the bag, and I called the crime scene tech in to make sure I had some company, and some help

Everyone was getting in on it—pilots, boat owners, doctors, lawyers, and yes, cops. While I looked down from the balcony at Castro's body in the parking lot, I couldn't help but think of the Miami River Cops.

In July of 1985, I had been in Homicide just seven months when I was told about the remarkable case one of the other teams had picked up: three bodies floating in the Miami River. They all had beepers, Rolex watches, guns and plenty of cash on them. Our newly formed Centac-26 squad, part of a national network of high-level narcotics investigators, assumed the lead on the case.

They got nothing from the initial investigation, until they got a phone call from an informant.

To no one's surprise, the three guys were smugglers, and they had a boat they used on the River to conduct their ventures. The informant told our Centac guys that these smugglers went to great lengths to bring in the loads, such as welding hidden below-decks compartments for the kilos into the hulls of the boats to assure that they would be clean if they were stopped and searched. The rest of this guy's tale was a stunner: there were *six* men aboard the boat that night, sitting on the deck and drinking beer when the boat was raided by a bunch of gunmen. The armed intruders wore City of Miami police uniforms.

We had encountered several drug rip-off cases involving suspects posing as law enforcement, so this was not in any way far-fetched. Jorge Plasencia and Alex Alvarez were two of the finest investigators that have ever worked in Homicide. They headed up the investigation, but couldn't dig up any intel on these uniform-wearing subjects in anyone's files, DEA or local agencies. Through their hard work, they got some cooperation from both the City of Miami P.D. and the FBI, and information started to trickle in. It was a gossamer thread of a lead Plasencia and Alvarez were given, but they held onto it and pulled their way up a rocky and often dangerous path to finally realize that the gunmen they were dealing with were *not* imposters, but in fact were City of Miami Police Officers.

During Centac surveillances, they watched these suspected cops driving expensive cars, spending gobs of money in late-night clubs, and buying homes with cash. They learned from informants and hours of observation that the rip-off ventures had started small: a traffic stop and search unveils a kilo of cocaine in the trunk, the officer keeps it, and before you know it, the entire squad of 60 Sector (Little Havana) Miami cops decide to go big: they start squeezing their sources for information on big shipments: who had them, and where?

What resulted was a series of raids on Miami River drug boats. They would force the occupants off the boat and tear up the boat until they found the stashes. They were hauling in cash and coke in big numbers, and they weren't getting caught. One of the informants wore a wire and got one of the cops to talk about the River rip-offs. The ball was rolling.

Six months later, six officers were indicted and put on trial in federal court, but a hung jury resulted. The jurors had been contacted by people who were "friends and family" of the defendants and offered jobs and money. Plasencia and Alvarez, along with their task force of Centac, FBI, and City of Miami Internal Affairs personnel, went back to the grind. They got one of the cops to confess, and that got a lot of the necessary dots connected. All but one of the remaining officers eventually ended up in cuffs. Armando Garcia was still on the loose, and it took a massive effort, spanning several *countries*, before he was tracked and arrested—in Colombia, fittingly.

None of us who worked in Homicide during that era really had time to sit and learn everything that was going on with this case, or anyone else's. We were so busy with our own leads, witnesses, and trials, that everybody else's dramas seemed to course together in a surreal calendar that had no boxes to tell you one day from the next. You got a case, then you got another. Then, when you thought you had a little time off, your team was on call, and your phone rang at 2am with your next project. If it weren't for the stacks of legal pads that we used for each case to keep our notes separated, it would all be heaped together—the bodies, the families, the witnesses, the autopsies, the details, all mixed together like *sancocho.*

Chapter Twenty

My Dad grew up in Minnesota, and he used to tell me stories of himself and his brother playing in the snow. I wondered what it was like. Then my parents told me that I had played in snow, when I was three years old, in Boston. Boston? At eight, I had no memory of this first snow encounter in Boston. Mom and Dad were visiting friends there and I played outside in the snow very briefly, they said.

Why couldn't I remember that? I used to daydream about it when I was little, thinking, "I want to go back to Boston so I can remember it this time." When would I get the chance?

One afternoon in 1986, when Greg Smith and I had been put together to work the hooker murders, we were driving by the Miami Jai-Alai fronton just north of Miami International Airport. We talked about how we had both visited Jai-Alai. As a south end guy, I didn't go to Jai-Alai until I became a cop in North Miami. We used to change shifts every three months at NMPD. Our squad tradition there was to celebrate us getting off of midnights by everyone going to Jai-Alai, drinking beer, and betting. So, right around December of 1981 eight of us went and played though I knew absolutely zero about how to bet.

"Just play your badge number," one of my squad members suggested. They taught me how to play a "$2 box quinella." My badge number at North Miami was 126, so if those three numbers showed up, in any order, I would win. Each bet cost six bucks, and that was all I had in my pocket.

"Don't worry," my sergeant, Phil Sublette assured me. "I can lend you a few bucks so you can play."

But he didn't have to, because my numbers came in on my first bet, and I won around $38. This immediately became fun, and I just kept betting 1-2-6 every time. I won eight times out of fourteen games and walked out of the Jai-Alai fronton that night netting about $150. It was a blast. We would go there a few more times—every time we went off midnights—but I never got that beginner's lucky streak again.

I told Greg the story, and he smiled. "The place is run by the Irish Mafia."

"*Irish* Mafia?" Colombians, Cubans, and Jamaicans I could understand, but I had never heard of any Irish Mafia in Miami.

"Yeah," Greg told me. "They're based in Boston. We had a homicide involving one of their people. Grits was the lead on it." Grits was Shelton Merritt, a big man with a wide face and a gravelly Georgia accent.

Irish Mafia. The absurd side of my imagination imagined leprechauns with Mac-10 submachine guns, trampling over bloodstained 4-leaf clovers.

In 1997 I was on the Cold Case Squad. Lt. Al Harper walked by my desk and dropped a newspaper clipping onto my desk. "Look into this and see what you can find out."

The small article was from the *Miami Herald* and it talked about a group of defendants in a racketeering case in Boston. During a recent evidentiary hearing, lawyers for two of the defendants announced that their clients had been active confidential informants for the FBI. It stunned everyone, particularly the other defendants. The article went on to illuminate the group's involvement in the 1982 murder of John Callahan, the former President of Miami Jai-Alai, in Miami. How would the head of Miami Jai-Alai have to anything to do with Boston? This must have been the "Irish Mafia" involvement Greg had been talking about.

"Grits was so paranoid about that case that he feared for his life," Greg told me. "He was convinced that the FBI was involved, and that they were protecting the two bosses in charge of the whole thing."

I would have to pull the case to get up to speed on it. Then I would call Grits.

Greg added, "Grits was also worried someone was going to go into that case file. He wrapped up the files in a box and put evidence tape all over it."

I had never heard of anyone doing that, but when I got to the second floor of the property room where our old files were kept, I found the box. There was evidence tape alright, but it had been ripped apart. When I looked inside, I was stunned. Our homicide case files have a certain order. You have five separate file folders: one for reports, one for crime scene and evidence reports, one for photos, one called "personal data: Victim", and one for subject or suspect information. "Suspects" were just that: people you suspected. Rather than a neat row of folders, everything was in a pile. It appeared as if someone had removed all the papers from each folder and thrown them in the air. It was a completely disheveled, unorganized mess. Worse than that, report copies were missing. Police report originals were white and the copies, which we kept in the file to use as working files, were pink. That way, if the pinks got lost, you had the originals. Some of the originals *and* some of the pink copies were absent from the box. Grits' suspicions were on target: someone had indeed gotten into the case file and pilfered reams of very sensitive information.

It took me an entire week of going through everything, page by page, to reconstruct the case file as well as I could. Then I called Grits. He was happily retired and living in north Florida.

"I fuckin' knew it," he grumbled. "I tried to tell everyone this was gonna happen. Those fuckin' FBI agents are dirty as shit, I guarantee you," he told me. "You got assigned the case?"

"Yep, some stuff broke open up in Boston and they want Cold Case to work on it."

"Watch yer ass," Grits cautioned. "I mean it."

Grits then explained that early on in his investigation, he discovered that Callahan was a financial wizard of some kind in Boston, a guy who could turn businesses around and had the corporate Midas touch. But, he told me, Callahan got involved with mobsters up there. Grits believed that Callahan was being sought by the FBI as an informant against mob bosses who were running a skimming operation through Miami Jai-Alai, of which Callahan had been the president. Callahan resigned from his post when things started heating up at Jai-Alai, but not before making an important, significant hire: as Vice-President in charge of security, he hired a man named H. Paul Rico, an ex-FBI agent from Boston. Grits figured that both men were in on the murder of a legit billionaire named Roger Wheeler, the owner of World Jai-Alai. Wheeler—revered by the citizens of Oklahoma—was found shot in his car at a Tulsa country club after an afternoon of golf. Why whack *him?* I wanted to know.

"When we worked the scene, we found a dime sittin' on Callahan's chest. Now, whaddaya think that means?"

There was on old saying you never hear any more, because no one uses pay phones: Informing on someone was "diming someone out" or "dropping a dime" on someone. It cost a dime to make a pay phone call in the old days, and so Grits was saying that this was the mob's way of sending a message: "drop a dime" on us, this is how you end up.

Grits left me with a repeat of his warning, "I'm tellin' you, Ram...watch—your—ass."

After the re-assembly of the case file, a couple of more phone calls with Grits, and several hours of reading, I had a fairly good idea of what the Irish Mafia was all about. The mostly Irish collection of gangsters was called the "Winter Hill" gang after their formation in Boston's Winter Hill neighborhood. Their boss was a legend in Boston—James "Whitey" Bulger. His partner was an Italian named Stephen Flemmi. They had a small network of criminals that worked for them, predominantly in south Boston and surrounding neighborhoods. Bulger was a ruthless crime boss, feared by underworld figures and Boston citizens alike. All of this was well laid out in Shelton Merritt's initial investigative report. Grits had met with an FDLE agent who contacted him after the murder and told Grits that the root of Callahan's murder was the Miami Jai-Alai business. Two other murders had preceded Callahan's: Roger Wheeler, the owner of World Jai-Alai who was killed in Tulsa, and a small-time hood named Brian Halloran, shot and killed after coming out of a bar in Boston's seaport district. The FDLE guy was certain these two murders were connected to Callahan's.

Winter Hill was old school: extortion, horse-race fixing, illegal lotteries, and loan sharking. Word around Boston was that Bulger was controlling the waterfront too. He despised drugs, but he would happily exact "rent" money from others who were dealing and smuggling. Bulger and his cohorts had contacts and influence everywhere in the city. Just before the recent RICO indictment of Bulger and the others, Bulger disappeared. Indictments are kept under secret seal in the federal Grand Jury. No one familiar with Bulger and Winter Hill believed that his sudden vanishing was a coincidence.

Our first few interviews with people in Miami and in Boston gave us a profile of our victim. Callahan was extremely well-educated and adept at numbers and finances. He spoke four languages, including Mandarin Chinese. He was, as they would say in Boston, "wicked sm*ah*t." Callahan made a very good living doing business "workouts"—providing consultation with failing companies, especially banks—and getting their financial engines chugging again. But he was anything but a boring, straight-laced accountant. In fact, Callahan had an insatiable thirst for night life. He made it a point to be seen at Boston's most chic and upscale night spots, clubs, including the Playboy club. It seemed that he wanted to be a part of Boston's underworld. The mundane financial world that operated in the daylight wasn't enough. He got his wish. Callahan's late-night lifestyle soon had him rubbing elbows in the clubs with characters like John Martarano, one of the defendants I had read about in the newspaper clipping. Through his friendship with Martarano, Callahan worked his way into the good graces of Winter Hill. Bulger and Flemmi's group already had their talons in World Jai-Alai, a creation of a Connecticut-based group of investors bought by Wheeler. They figured that bringing the fast-paced game for pari-mutuel wagering to the U.S. from the Basque region of Spain would be popular, and they were right. Bulger and Flemmi were likewise correct when they assessed that Jai-Alai could provide some decent skimming opportunities. To effect that, they needed to add some brains to the brawn. That's where Callahan came in.

How and why Callahan ended up shot in the back of the head and decomposed in the trunk of his car at one of MIA's parking lots was still unclear, but Grits and his FDLE contact seemed to be on the right path. Jai-Alai owner Wheeler was murdered on May 27, 1981. Brian Halloran, a close friend of Callahan's, was gunned down on May 11, 1982, and Callahan was found in the trunk of his Cadillac on August 3, 1982. Fifteen months and three murder victims, all of whom were connected back—one way or another—to Jai-Alai and Winter Hill. I learned that Halloran had been working with the FBI, informing on Winter Hill. Callahan, it seemed, may have "dropped a dime" on them too.

The feds tossed a net on the Winter Hill Gang, charging all the racketeering crimes, but Bulger had scurried out from under it just in time. During the preliminary hearings, Bulger and Flemmi's attorneys dropped a bomb: their clients had been FBI informants for the better part of twenty years. The rest of the defendants were stunned. Martarano was so incensed by the news that he called a timeout and announced that he wanted to cooperate against the men he had trusted and worked for, now identified as rats.

Greg Smith and I flew to Boston to meet with the FBI and attend the hearings. We made an appointment and were given the name of an agent who would sit down with us and go over the case. Hopefully we would figure out the tangled relationship between Bulger and Flemmi and their FBI handlers, born some sixteen hence. Since some new developments were happening in federal court, they might not talk about all of it. At the very least, though, they could give us some direction with H. Paul Rico, Jai-Alai, the trio of murder cases, and who they thought was involved in Callahan's murder.

There is unspoken etiquette among law enforcement agencies: You help one another. In fact, when another law enforcement officer comes to visit and ask for help, you find a way—no matter how busy you are—to throw open your doors and assist however you can. We had done it many times for visiting agencies, and we had traveled to many states and enjoyed the same hospitality. Your office is my office, and we'll show you where to whet your whistle at the end of the day as well.

We walked up the steps to the FBI building, a curved edifice just a short walk from Faneuil Hall and the famous Quincy Market. Inside, we were ushered by the receptionist into a waiting room. We sat for a long time there—nearly half an hour—with no one coming out to greet us and no one even offering us as much as a cup of coffee as we waited. I couldn't imagine letting another law enforcement officer sit and wait for an appointment for that long, especially when they knew we were coming. When our contact came out, he smiled pleasantly.

"Tell me how we can help you," he said. It felt like I was meeting the manager of a restaurant after sending back an overcooked steak.

"We just want to find out what H. Paul Rico knew about Callahan's death. Who had come to Jai-Alai to talk either one of them, had there been any threats made to them—that sort of thing. Did Rico know anything about who might have been behind Callahan's murder?"

The agent frowned in thought. "I don't think Rico *knew* Callahan."

Greg Smith and I were stunned. Callahan fucking *hired* him!

"They worked together," I said, "at Jai-Alai. How could that be?" The FBI guy was still doing his dramatic—and not very convincing—chin rubbing.

"Let me let you talk to the SAC," he said.

The Special-Agent-In-Charge of the FBI Boston Office wasn't much more help than his stooge that met us in the waiting area. He told us all this was "old news" and, why were we bothering with it? Old news. What—law enforcement shouldn't attempt to close old cases? We walked out of the FBI office utterly dumbfounded.

"Unbelievable," Greg growled. "They're hiding something for sure."

The next two days in the Federal Courthouse told us a lot. We sat through some enlightening hearings, wherein the FBI was trying desperately to deny that Bulger and Flemmi were actual informants. The mobsters' lawyers, though, had a different take: Bulger and Flemmi fed the Boston FBI Office—Special Agent John Connolly, in particular—significant information about Italian organized crime in the city. In exchange, the FBI ignored a lot of things that Winter Hill was doing. The corrupt nature of the relationship soon turned sordid. Connolly and Ring (Connolly's supervisor) received gifts at Christmas—cases of expensive wine and large checks from Bulger, to name a few. Much of the week-long hearing was a tug-of-war over whether Bulger and Flemmi fit the criteria to be considered confidential informants. During one comical exchange, an FBI supervisor was on the witness stand.

"Agent Wilson," the attorney said, looking through some notes, "would you please explain to the court what the FBI's policy is on how to you handle confidential informants?"

To everyone's amazement, the agent kind of looked around and then said, "I'm not sure how to answer that."

You could have heard the proverbial pin drop in that courtroom. Judge Mark Wolf, himself amazed by the non-answer, broke into a slight grin and said, "How about truthfully and to the best of your ability…?"

The entire courtroom erupted in laughter, including the attorneys and the defendants. The only person who wasn't laughing was the ill-prepared FBI supervisor.

Every time we spoke with someone we got another story, theory, or accusation. This one was doing that one's secretary, so-and-so lied about this and that during an internal investigation; it was a legal soap opera, so convoluted and full of back stabbings and ironies it put most daytime TV dramas to shame. The history of Boston organized crime and the people who pursued them had more sides streets and hidden alleyways than Boston's Italian North End.

One of the most compelling side stories was written about by Ralph Renalli in his excellent book, *Deadly Alliance.* The two opposing forces who brought this all to a head—FBI agent John Connolly and Whitey Bulger—grew up in the same South Boston neighborhood. There was a deep bond between people who lived in South Boston. People who group in "Southie" weren't just neighbors, they were family. They stuck together. The story goes that eleven-year-old John Connolly was starting to get roughed up by some neighborhood bullies, and James Bulger, a few years older, came to his aid. That was the foreshadowing of a relationship that would turn New England's criminal justice world upside down.

We never went on these trips for more than three days at a time as there was always too much to do back home. But the lead sheet was growing, and we had an alliance now with the Department of Justice Task Force in charge of finding and capturing James "Whitey" Bulger, who was now on the Ten Most Wanted List. In the years to come, we became good friends of DEA Special Agent Dan Doherty, State Police Sergeants Steven Johnson and Tom Foley, and Assistant U.S. Attorneys Fred Wyshak and Brian Kelly. Dan was the law enforcement point man, and he was well-suited for the job. About as Irish a guy as I've ever met, Dan had a strong personality, would put anyone and everyone in their place if needed (this included the prosecutors), and he knew his case inside out. When the day's work was put on hold and it was time to quench our thirst, Dan never failed to approach beer drinking with the same focus and diligence. These guys never just took us to "a place" to drink. This crew, with Danny quarterbacking everything, would map out the good places to *start,* and other places better suited to finishing. Sometimes the discussions about our pub visits were as strategically intense as our conversations about the case. Dan and Stevie Johnson also made sure we made it to places like the No-Name Restaurant, the Green Dragon, the Black Rose, and Jimbo's, the seaport joint where Brian Halloran was murdered.

The nightly menu was a happy hour crash course on Winter Hill, Boston law enforcement culture, how city cops got along with the "Staties", how the FBI dealt with the DEA, and how *no one* got along with the FBI—even the FBI themselves. These outings were wall-to-wall entertainment for Greg and me: stories of Boston organized crime, banter-filled trial strategy sessions—that bordered on bristly arguments between Danny and Fred Wyshak—punctuated by deadpan quips from Stevie Johnson. Fred was a more pedantic debater than the fiery Doherty and would usually end up smiling in acquiescence as he sipped his coveted dirty martini. The stories and uproarious sparring between the Boston guys would end only when we were dropped off at our hotel to rest up for the next day. They were delighted when Greg and I would launch into our own debates. One night into our third round of beers, Greg was telling them about the famed Tobacco Road bar in Miami one night.

"Great place, in Little Havana," he said.

"It's not in Little Havana," I corrected him.

"Sure it is. It's south of the Miami River."

"Oh," I said, "So anything south of the Miami River is Little Havana?"

The grins on the faces of Doherty and the rest of the crew were priceless. They could take a break and give *us* a chance to quibble.

"Yes," Greg said. "That's right."

"I suppose that means *I* live in Little Havana," I said. So does everyone who lives in Homestead, huh?"

Greg laughed, knowing he had painted himself into a corner with that one, but we ended up calling another detective back home to settle the issue.

"My money's on Ram!" Dan announced.

Lou Alvarez was surprised and amused to get the phone call, with bar sounds in the background. "Tobacco Road? Nope," Lou said. "I wouldn't call that Little Havana."

And to the whoops and hollers of our Task Force gang, we were off to the next argument.

It didn't take long for us to realize that the FBI was on the opposite sideline. Any inkling of trust that may have existed between Boston local and state law enforcement and the FBI dissolved entirely once the pandora's box about Connolly and Bulger's relationship busted open. "The Boston FBI office was divided," Robert Fitzpatrick told us as we sat and had coffee outside Faneuil Hall. "Fitzy", as he was known in law enforcement circles, was once the Assistant Special Agent in Charge of the FBI Boston office. He couldn't stop telling us how he desperately he tried to go after Bulger and was snubbed because Bulger was working for another agent—John Connolly—and how everything was being shielded by *their* supervisory agent, John Morris.

"One half of the office was working in secrecy with these gangsters, and the other half was trying to do the right thing. I tried to tell the higher-ups that these guys were corrupt, but I got shut down." Fitzy was clearly bitter over his inability to stop what was happening.

All of this, Fitzy's insisted, were brushstrokes on a massive mural depicting an unethical, dysfunctional family. The case, which was still evolving with the new blockbusting disclosures of Bulger and Flemmi's secret informant status, was like an ever-expanding labyrinth of intrigue, conflict, and betrayal. It made it hard to keep up, but spending time with the Boston guys—who had been immersed in it for so long—tamped down the learning curve a bit. At the heart of everything though, was a highly suspect FBI Agent, John Connolly and two of his prize informants, one of whom was now a fugitive.

"You'll never find Whitey," one witness told us. "The FBI's hiding him."

The witness was Patrick "Patty" Perkins, a former bar owner from Boston. He told this to me and Greg in a bar in Fort Lauderdale. Patty lived in south Florida now but refused to meet us at his home. Patty ordered a Bloody Mary. Greg and I were on duty, and it was 1pm, so we both ordered ginger ales. Perkins glanced at us, then turned to his side and looked away.

"I don't talk to anyone who isn't drinkin' with me," he grunted.

Greg and I looked at each other and shrugged. "Make it three Bloody Marys," Greg told her.

Perkins' story was long, involved and mostly about himself. We wanted to know if he knew where Whitey Bulger was hiding. We had already put him on America's Most Wanted, and had run down sightings all over the place, from Seattle to Mexico to Florida. Perkins talked in circles. He told war stories and bitched about being blackballed from Boston by Whitey himself. With some of these guys, you have to be patient and let them vent. We thought we had just wasted our time when, at the end of his second Bloody Mary, he suddenly looked distant and mumbled something about us doing a good job. We asked him to repeat what he said.

"You guys. I said you're doin' a good job. You're...you're on the right track."

"Yeah?" I asked.

"Yeah," Patty said. Then, he looked over our heads to another part of the room, as if talking to himself, and said, "West coast of Florida...not far from here...a house...marina nearby...couple of blocks behind a Coast Guard station..."

We stayed silent for moment, and Patty suddenly stood. "It's been a real pleasure talkin' with you boys. Good luck, huh?" He shook our hands and walked out.

Greg and I stared at each other. "Did you hear what I think I heard?"

"Yep. Sure did," Greg said. "Patty just told us where Whitey is, didn't he?"

It wasn't much to go on, but we searched for Whitey on thinner evidence. Twice now he had been aired on *America's Most*

Wanted and we had received well over a thousand tips. My desk had a stack of them I had to go through and prioritize. One said that Whitey had been seen at an Irish bar in Dania Beach, not far from Fort Lauderdale Airport. We went to the place and set up a surveillance for a couple of days. We probably saw twenty old guys wearing baseball caps coming in and out of there, but no James Bulger. My belief was that we were probably going to find Catherine Grieg before we saw Whitey. There are certain things we humans always need: food, water, maybe medicine. Someone has to go out and buy that stuff (these were the days before Amazon), and it made sense that Grieg would be the one to run such errands while Whitey laid low. None of the leads from *AMW* were worth a shit, but one of them, interestingly, said they saw Whitey playing golf in Naples, Florida. That jibed somewhat with Patty Perkins' enigmatic utterances at the bar.

I started digging into maps of the west coast and researched the locations of Coast Guard stations and put yet another entry on my lead sheet.

The cooperation of John Martarano might well become a reality, but much work had to be done. Martarano was believed to be the go-to guy when people needed to be silenced or taken out for whatever reason. He was, by all rights, Winter Hill's "hit man," and he may even have been responsible for Callahan's death. The problem was that these deaths—which included the murder of Roger Wheeler—spanned seventeen different jurisdictions. If there was to be a plea agreement, the victims of some twenty-plus families, and the powers-that-be in those seventeen jurisdictions, would need to be surveyed one by one to see if they were on board.

With all these things fulminating in the backdrop of an international search for Whitey Bulger, we often felt like we were running alongside a snowball, and each time we thought understood the scope of it, it kept rolling and got bigger. At best, the Boston FBI office was incompetent and reckless. At worst, we were looking one of the worst law enforcement corruption cases in the nation's history.

Florida west coast trip didn't turn up anything. I researched every Coast Guard station in the region and drove some of the neighborhoods to see if anything looked promising. I knew I wasn't going to find a little house flying a Boston Red Sox flag with two FBI agents standing guard or anything that overt. But I hoped to find a spot that might be agreeable to Catherine Greig—a place she could go get their food, their medications. She loved dogs and was into dog grooming; I passed out some wanted flyers at dog grooming shops and headed back east to home.

Bulger and Grieg had been on the lam for thirteen years now. At some point they had to get a *little* comfortable. It was Grieg—not Whitey—I hoped to spot first, though it was ultimately a shot in the dark. I hoped that while pursuing groceries, medicine, or dog care, she would let her guard down enough to be recognized. In the meantime, one of the biggest redaction projects in the annals of criminal justice was underway in Boston's FBI office. Judge Wolf ordered that the FBI make available its 302s (their investigative reports) on any and all matters regarding Winter Hill, James Bulger, and the works. Of course, many of the investigations were still ongoing, and redactions of informants' names, sensitive witnesses, and undercover agents had to be redacted. This caused an uproar between the DOJ Task Force and the feebs, and hours of meetings and legal wranglings went on about what should or should not be redacted.

Trying to retain everything, keep track of all the people we needed to talk to, and attend the seemingly endless meetings about things like redaction was a constant challenge. I flew to Boston so many times it had become my second office. I had other cold cases that needed attention back home, so it was exhausting. My marriage was beginning to slowly unravel. My oldest son was a teenager, and there were eruptions between him and my wife that I often wasn't there for. Several times I was on the phone in futile attempts to referee the volcanic outbursts that were happening with greater frequency. She wasn't coping, to put it mildly. My absence didn't help.

Martarano's plea began to slowly take shape. He wanted a sweetheart deal, and he would likely get it. Without him, twenty-one murders would remain unsolved. With it, we could give closure to all those victims' families and secure his testimony against Bulger and Flemmi. There was now some urgency to try and develop as much information as we could *outside* of Martarano's knowledge so we could have more leverage with him, but with Bulger still at large people weren't terribly willing to talk. One thing had crystallized in all of our minds: Special Agent John Connolly, who was in charge of investigating Winter Hill activities, was compromised. He did more than turn a blind eye to some of criminal behavior Winter Hill was pulling off. He might even be *complicit.*

By this time, another investigator joined our team: Mike Huff, a sergeant with the Tulsa, Oklahoma Police Department. Mike was an affable guy, but an absolute bulldog as an investigator. He was assigned what was arguably the most publicized unsolved murder in Tulsa history: the "gangland-style slaying", as the media loved to call it, of widely admired billionaire and World Jai-Alai owner Roger Wheeler on May 27th, 1981. As our investigation kept rumbling along, it became more apparent that John Martarano was the likeliest person to have shot Wheeler between the eyes in his car after his golf game. With Mike's help, the task force had discovered that Winter Hill members had tried to get Wheeler to sell Jai-Alai to them. Wheeler had done some homework. His auditors found missing money that looked like it was linked to a skimming scheme at Miami Jai-Alai's parking concession. He also got wind of surveillances done by Connecticut's Parimutuel Gaming Commission that connected Winter Hill people to similar unsavory business practices there, and he sold his fronton in Hartford. Wheeler was an honest businessman and he wasted no time in going to the authorities with his concerns about dirty stuff going on in Jai-Alai. Winter Hill could not take the chance on him going to the authorities with his findings and blowing the whole operation. His killer, a white male with a large beard, had not yet been identified, but Martarano was known to use disguises when he carried out his jobs.

Massachusetts had twenty murders on the books that could be traced to Martarano. None of them, however, had that final straw prosecutors needed to file charges. We had just one murder—Callahan. Likewise, Tulsa had just the Wheeler murder. But Mike Huff and I actually loomed large in the future legal proceedings of all the Winter Hill players who might be charged with murder: Massachusetts had no death penalty. Florida and Oklahoma did. They wanted us on board in a big way.

Martarano, who had literally killed for his two bosses, was livid when he heard that they had been informing for the FBI the whole time. After four years of work and some fifteen trips to Boston, we still hadn't found Whitey. To negotiate a plea, both sides need to come to a sort of demilitarized zone: the defendant relates an outline of what their information will be (known in legal circles as a "proffer") so that the prosecution can assess it and structure the plea agreement accordingly. In Martarano's case, the proffer essentially had to be reviewed by the prosecutorial entities in each jurisdiction: indeed, one county in Massachusetts could not speak for the wishes of another, or for that matter, Miami-Dade County in Florida.

This proffer process was arduous, complex, and ugly. It was, in essence, a deal with the devil. Martarano held all the cards. Without him, the government had nothing with which to prosecute him, Bulger, Flemmi, or any other co-conspirators. With him, if he confessed to the murders *and* included Wheeler and Callahan, Bulger and Flemmi could ultimately be sentenced to death. Naturally, part of Martarano's requirement was that he himself avoided the death penalty. Finally, in 1999, the agreement of all prosecutorial entities in all jurisdictions was secured. Our deal with the devil was almost done. The proffer was in, and now we had a long-awaited meeting with Martarano for him to tell his tales. He had but one caveat: "I'm not going on the record about any of this if the FBI is in the room," he said to Danny, Greg, Steve Johnson, and me. "I'll only tell everything to you guys."

The FBI was enraged and they pissed all over themselves trying to wiggle their way into what they felt was their rightful spot at the table with Martarano. I got a call from the SAC of the Boston office one evening. He all but begged: "Nyberg, please get us in that room. It's really important that we be there."

"It's not up to me," I told him, "and you already know that."

In the end, the feds had no choice but to concede. Their arrogance in insisting that they be present for Martarano's debriefing was appalling. I couldn't help but remember the day Greg Smith and I were smugly told that all this was "old history" and that Callahan and H. Paul Rico never knew each other. Now, they were desperate to be in the inner circle. It was likewise not lost on any of us that FBI informants who had given or were about to give damning testimony on Bulger and Flemmi ended up dead. The argument could be made that Martarano needed protection from *them.*

Whitey had a lot of people working for him, though only a few did the real dirty work. And only two did the profoundly *nasty* work. Martarano, it was believed, pulled the trigger when it was needed. Kevin Weeks got rid of the bodies. Weeks was known as Whitey's "right-hand man". He ran errands, carried messages, and performed the occasional intimidation or rent collection when needed. But he also faithfully soldiered the most gruesome tasks needed, at Whitey's behest. Once, when the group realized they had to move out a particular house, Weeks even *dug up* decomposed bodies out of the basement and relocated them. He had buried them there, as ordered by Whitey. *We're moving. Pack up the chandelier carefully...the sofa and dresser go into to the moving van. Oh, and the bodies—Kevin, you find a spot.* The U.S. Attorney's Office had enough to indict Weeks in late 1999, and Weeks, who wisely saw the handwriting on the wall with Martarano, became a government witness. In January of 2000, he led the task force to five bodies he had buried, all Bulger and Flemmi's victims. While all this negotiation and political wrangling was going on between the DOJ and the FBI, Kevin Weeks was called before the Grand Jury and gave devastating testimony of his own. Weeks was present when Brian Halloran was killed. He had seen FBI Supervisory Agent at James Bulger's house. He was also made aware of a meeting in New York between Steve, Whitey, and Martarano, regarding the subject of John Callahan. And that was just scratching the surface. Weeks also added to the case against John Connolly. He knew that Connolly, who they called "Zip", was the one who tipped off Bulger about the pending indictment. How did he know?

"Zip is the one who told *me*. I carried the message to (Whitey)."

On March 19, 2001, we met with John Martarano in the basement of the John Joseph Moakley U.S. Courthouse in Boston. Slowly, methodically, he went through every murder. The first thing I wanted to know was whether he was the trigger man on John Callahan.

He nodded. "Yes," he said quietly.

As everyone had suspected, Callahan was the last of domino to fall in Winter Hill's frantic play to keep their Jai-Alai scheme—indeed their entire operation—afloat. Martarano confirmed it all. Roger Wheeler was not going to sell Jai-Alai to Winter Hill. Instead, he got the authorities involved.

"I wore a beard," Martarano confirmed with us. "Flemmi sent the guns in a truck to Tulsa for me to pick up." The information Martarano needed to stalk Wheeler—his routine, his car, a picture to match the face—was provided by former Boston FBI Agent H. Paul Rico.

"Rico planned it. He was behind it from day one," Martarano said. "He and Callahan knew everything about it."

Then, he explained, Bulger and Flemmi got wind that Brian Halloran was informing on them to the FBI. Now, how on earth had they heard *that?*

So Halloran got taken out, just after he walked out of Jimbo's. John Martarano pulled the trigger on that one too. The last weak link in the Jai-Alai chain was John Callahan. Bulger told Martarano that they were sending Callahan down to Miami to meet with him and handle some business, but that "Callahan had to go."

"If Callahan didn't go," John explained, "we were all going to go down."

It had become commonplace for Martarano to pick up Callahan on his frequent trips to south Florida. They were friends. Martarano had keys to Callahan's condo and his Cadillac. Martarano enlisted the help of a fellow Winter Hill member, Joe McDonald, since some movement of cars—as well as the body—would be necessary. He met Callahan at Fort Lauderdale

Airport and helped him with his bags. As soon as Callahan sat in the passenger seat, Martarano calmly loaded his suitcase in the back of his white Dodge Van, and then shot Callahan in the back of the head with a .22 automatic. He then drove the van to a private garage where he kept his now-dead friend's Cadillac for him. He and McDonald transferred the body to the trunk of the Cadillac.

"Oh," Martarano added, "and when I did, some change fell out of his pocket. I read in the news stories later about the dime on his chest." He scoffed and shook his head. "It was nothing like that. There was no message or nothing like that. The dime meant nothing. It just fell out and landed that way."

Martarano wasted a few hours having coffee, waiting, "to make sure no one was on to me." Then, he took the Caddy to MIA, and left it there.

"Why there?"

"It would take a little longer to be found. It would cross up the story a little bit, make it look like he had come to Miami for something."

With McDonald's help, Martarano took Callahan's wallet and watch and dumped it near Little Havana.

"The cover story we had was to make it look like he got involved with some bad Cubans," he explained.

Martarano's detailed story finalized our four-year effort into the Callhan murder. A month later we were back home, waiting for the U.S. Marshals were going to bring Martarano down soon so we could take him "on location." Doing this with a witness was important in a case like this. "On-location" meant the witness would take you to each spot, show you what happened, and sometimes even be photographed pointing out something significant. It helped corroborate and solidify the story. Because Martarano was WITSEC (Witness Security Program), the U.S. Marshals Service was careful to the point of being secretive.

When I called up to Dan Doherty to ask when the Marshals were coming down with John, he told me they probably won't say—they'll probably just show up. That's just what happened. Before we met with them, they wanted a rundown of every location we were going to, so that they could scope it all out before we arrived. They took no chances. When we met with the Marshals WITSEC team, we got into a Suburban with bullet proof windows and doors so heavy you had to use both hands to close them. I sat next to Martarano in the middle seat, and he had a marshal on his right as we went to the various places, starting with the parking garage at Ft. Lauderdale Airport where the murder took place.

At one point, he pointed out the building where Callahan lived. As we took some quick photos from inside the Suburban, we saw Martarano staring at the floor, suddenly very quiet.

"What's the matter, John?" The marshal next to him asked.

He gave a brief shake of his head and sighed. "I *liked* Callahan," he said quietly.

John Martarano's plea had enormous ripple effects. Stephen Flemmi knew that he had better save his ass too; again, a toss of the dice with Massachusetts would have been fine. But Florida and Oklahoma's death chambers loomed over him too. From somewhere on the planet, we knew James Bulger was watching the dam break on his Winter Hill empire.

231 miles west of Boston, in the rolling farmlands of southern New York state is a tiny town called Otisville. The Federal Correctional Institute—almost as big as the town itself—takes up the northern outskirt. Our team took up almost the entire waiting room on a chilly November 30th, 2004. I, along with Fred Wyshak, Stevie Johnson, and Dan Doherty, had two new team members: Assistant Inspector General Jimmy Marra, and Michael Von Zamft, from our State Attorney's Office in Miami. Michael had been assigned the prosecution of former FBI Agent John Connolly.

Otisville was a WITSEC facility, so it took a while before we were all processed in, searched, fingerprints scanned, and forms filled out.

Pursuant to a recent proffer agreement, Stephen "the Rifleman" Flemmi, a once-feared killer and partner of Whitey Bulger, sat across from us in an Otisville interview room. Flemmi was the complete opposite of the plodding and taciturn Martarano, who answered every question calmly and efficiently, one at a time. Flemmi's demeanor was like one of those guys at the carnival trying desperately to sell you something. He went on a hundred different tangents, down rabbit holes that had nothing to do with what we were asking him. He tried to ingratiate himself to us with stories of this gangster and that, and things that happened back in the 60's. Every answer had an embellishment, a window dressing, a distraction. If he ever had to testify, he would be a handful to control.

It took hours to sift through all his bullshit and theatrics, but we finally got we needed from him too. He corroborated almost everything Martarano said, and he all but put a noose around FBI Special Agent John Connolly.

"Every time we met with Connolly," Flemmi said, "Jimmy (Bulger) was there. Connolly never told us *not* to kill anyone. He never told us to stop doing what we were doing. He would tell us someone was a threat, and the guy would end up dead. He never even asked us about it."

And Callahan?

John Connolly met with Bulger and Flemmi and told them that the FBI was trying to get Callahan on tape, to compromise him and turn him into an informant against them. After that, the two Winter Hill bosses called a meeting with Martarano in New York and told him that Callahan had to be silenced. They also told Connolly about their plan to spread the word that Callahan was "involved with some bad Cubans down in Miami", knowing that Connolly would disseminate the same story to law enforcement networks after the murder.

"He never told us not to take action. He never said you know, 'stay out of this, it's a law enforcement problem.' We killed people based on information he gave us, and he never even batted an eye."

We had a long sit down with Kevin Weeks, too. Kevin was out on probation, and very forthcoming. Weeks, Flemmi, and John Martarano all had some small, insignificant variations on the Winter Hill. They were the type of differentiations that happened when multiple witnesses were interviewed about the same event, and this was a string of multiple events, people, and situations. What was important and even reassuring for us was this: Bulger and Flemmi ran the organized crime world in Boston. FBI agent John Connolly had an alliance with Whitey Bulger. He assisted them, *enabled* them in fact, to carry out their criminal activity. He cautioned them when there was law enforcement action coming against them so they could divert, hide—escape. Connolly *knew* that when he pointed out a threat to Winter Hill, Bulger and Flemmi would likely neutralize that threat by killing someone. Bulger, Flemmi, Martarano, Connolly, and H. Paul Rico conspired to kill our victim, John Callahan.

All those things were consistent.

One night in Boston, Tulsa Homicide Sgt. Mike Huff clinked beer glasses with me.

"We got what need," he said.

And my department did too. Both the Tulsa Police Department and the Miami-Dade Police Department issued First Degree Murder arrest warrants for James Joseph Bulger and H. Paul Rico.

Early one morning cool Miami morning in December 2003, I met with our arrest team of uniform officers and Task Force members in a Miami Shores parking lot a couple of hours before dawn. That was what we called a "staging area"- where we went over all the particulars of the imminent operation, to make sure everyone knew where they were going and what their role was.

H. Paul Rico's house was built in the late sixties, stylish for the time, backing up to Biscayne Bay. A woman in her early 70's answered with a confused smile, until she saw all the badges and IDs.

"Where's your husband?" we asked her. The raid team went in, weapons at the ready, and at least three of our team were in the back, though it was doubtful the aging H. Paul Rico was going to jump into Biscayne Bay and try to swim away.

"I'll get him," she said with a helpful smile.

Moments later, H. Paul Rico looked up at us, his hands cuffed behind his back, as we explained to him that he was under arrest for murder and was going to be booked into the Dade County Jail.

Rico looked at his wife. "Get me a sweater or something."

Trying to lighten the moment, she put a hand on his shoulder, smirking, and said, "Do you want me to get your Miami Jai-Alai jacket?"

He snapped his head at her with a look would have cut glass. I thought I would burst out laughing and several of us looked at each other and smirked. Rico said nothing, but his wife got the message. Now wasn't the time for jokes of any kind, least of all references to Jai-Alai. In Howie Carr's book, *Hitman,* about John Martarano's life of crime, he recounts that Rico came to the door in his Jai-Alai jacket. I don't know where Carr got that from, but that wasn't the case at all. Mrs. Rico answered the door and made the smartass remark about it.

One month later, the state of Oklahoma extradited H. Paul Rico to face murder charges in the death of Roger Wheeler. He fell ill upon his arrival, and at his arraignment entered a plea of "not guilty" while sitting in a wheelchair in the courtroom. On January 16th, at a Tulsa hospital and under guard from Corrections personnel, he died of a heart attack.

Martarano was in custody. Flemmi was already in the federal slam. H. Paul Rico was dead. John Connolly had been indicted on various racketeering charges, and our State Attorney's Office was now drawing up plans to charge him with murder. Only the big boss—James Bulger—remained in the wind.

I already had eyes on retirement when the Miami-Dade County Grand Jury returned a True Bill of indictment on John Connolly, former FBI agent, for 2nd Degree Murder. It was an odd feeling, fingerprinting a former FBI agent, for murder charges. Connolly was polite and showed the quiet respect one law enforcement officer would have for another. Though I despised him for what he did, I didn't let it show. This was business. Just like what he did. He made his choices, I made mine.

"Sorry John," I said, when I mushed up one of the prints. "I haven't done this in a while. Our ID techs usually do this back at HQ."

"That's ok. How long do you have on, Ram?"

One thing I learned about Bostonians—they will learn your first name and use it as soon as they know it. It was their unique, almost quirky way of winning familiarity with you.

"Next September will be 27 years," I told him. "Then I'm out. Retiring."

"Good for you," he said with a gentle nod. "I wish you the best."

I had never set out to arrest an FBI agent in my career, but there it was—I did.

The saga of Winter Hill and Whitey would go on well past my retirement. I left the job in November of 2006, and it wasn't until 2008 that Connolly would be convicted for 2nd degree murder in the death of John Callahan.

Whitey Bulger was still out there, somewhere.

My childhood quest to return to Boston was fulfilled not once, but eighteen times. The next time after that, I went to visit my son Erik and his new wife, Heather. They had just taken a small apartment there after a new job she had landed. I wondered, as I drove my rental car to their place, where their place was in relation to all the work I had done with the DOJ task force there. None of it looked familiar. Then, when my GPS said I was two minutes away, I glanced out the window and saw that the name of every shop, gas station, and liquor store started with the name "Winter Hill."

Chapter Twenty-One

Vanishing Acts

My Mom loved this particular store called Four Winds. It was full of Oriental artifacts; decorations of all kinds, rugs, furniture, jade statutes, and unique artwork. For 1960's Miami it was an exotic place to shop. I remember the scent of incense that drifted throughout the place. I used to groan every time she would drag me there. Then once, I saw something that caught my eye—it was a wooden bow and arrow. It was mostly decorative, I suppose, but it looked like it worked. Indeed, there was a notch for the arrow—which was only about a foot and a half long—to be loaded onto the bowstring, and the tip of the arrow was sharp.

I don't remember whether I nagged her for it or not, but she bought it. It's probably on the "inappropriate" list for a ten-year-old, especially these days. I tried it out in the front yard. I aimed it at this large cactus-like plant we had the front yard, drew back the bow, and let it fly. To my delight, it impaled the stalk of the plant. Then I just had to see how powerful the launch of this thing could be, so I stood in the street and aimed it skyward, Roman warrior-style. I drew the string back as far as it would go, and-—ZIIIINGG!—let it fly. To my utter amazement, the arrow soared swiftly over the trees of my front yard in a beautiful arc, over our house, easily clearing the top of the roof, and disappeared. I trotted into the back yard—surely it was there, somewhere. But it was nowhere in the yard. I looked everywhere. I checked the bushes, sifting carefully through each hibiscus branch, and walked along the chain link fence in the back, to see if it was hanging somewhere there. I hopped the fence into the alleyway, to see if it had landed somewhere back there. I even engaged my best friend, Don, from across the street, to help in the search. We were on our hands and knees at times, crawling through and under heavy bushes, to find the lost arrow. We got scratched up, dirty, and exhausted during the search. I went back and looked two or three different days. But I never found it. How could something like that just disappear?

Isabel and Jesus Rodriguez were having so much trouble in their marriage that during their divorce that they each took out restraining orders on each other. They had a modest house near Tropical Park, south of Bird Road, with a large shed in the back. Jesus moved out of the house during the divorce and took an apartment in Hialeah. Jesus had an older daughter, too, who lived near his new residence.

One morning in November of 2001, no one came to pick up the girls from school. A concerned vice-principal called Isabel several times, as she was there every day on time to get the kids. Finally, she called Jesus. He came and got them, ranting to school officials about his horrible wife, who he called "the devil" to anyone who would listen. He even told the vice-principal that his evil wife has been taking up residence with her new boyfriend and obviously doesn't care about the girls anymore.

But close friends of Isabel were more than puzzled when by nightfall no one had seen or heard from her. One of them called the police and made a missing person report. We have gotten cases from Missing Persons before, where they might take a week or so until they realize that there is something foul going on. They wasted no time at all in calling us in on this one. In fact, we got involved the day after Isabel Rodriguez' disappearance.

Lead investigator Ann Bogen was a sharp and determined investigator. She was also realistic. Her squad, which had been very busy with a slew of their own cases, could definitely use a hand with this case, so she brought the Cold Case Squad into the fold. We got all the info we needed from Ann, including photographs of the victim and of Jesus. We learned from Ann that, while Isabel *may* have a boyfriend, there was no solid evidence of that yet. Jesus, however, had acquired his own companionship, who also went by the name Isabel. By the time we all had our fresh legal pads ready to start working on the case, the consensus was that Jesus' wife was dead. This was a bitter divorce case, and the mother of these two girls, boyfriend or not, was known in her social circles to be a responsible, committed mother. Everyone told us that her silence was wildly out of character. To avoid confusion during our discussions and meetings, we started referring to the two women as "dead Isabel" and "live Isabel."

Ann assigned me and one of the Missing Persons detectives to start an area canvass. The area canvass was one of the first things you learned how to do in Homicide. Area canvasses were vital. You knocked every door on both sides of the street, and often on the next block as well, to see if anyone heard, saw, or knew anything. These weren't Hollywood area canvasses; we got the person's name *and* the names of everyone else who lived in the house.

"Are they here, right now? Can you get them so we can talk to them to? Not home? When will they be back, or how can we contact them right now?"

And if they weren't home, we came back when they were. It was part of the *GOYAKOD* culture. You didn't come back to the lead detective and say, "no one was home at this address." You kept going back. There had been more than one occasion in which the killer lived on the same block, and people in the house were lying about them being, or not being there. It was intrusive. It was nosy. We got under people's skin sometimes, but it came with the territory.

I started my part of the canvass at the north end of the avenue and worked south. The people were all pleasant, and no one had any issues being cooperative. No one knew much, if anything. On the east side of the avenue, there was a house under construction. I saw a guy working there, installing electrical conduit. Interestingly,

Jesus Rodriguez had taken in interest in the house too, and had stopped there almost on a daily basis to talk to the same guy.

"Yes, he would talk to me," the worker said. "Always talking about his wife. Said she was the devil," the man chuckled. "He was obsessed with talking about her."

He remembered seeing Jesus' car driving up and down the street, almost every day. Yesterday, though, he didn't see him.

After several houses, I met with the Missing Persons detective in front of the Rodriguez house, so we could compare notes. It was a quiet street, so we were literally standing in the roadway when a uniformed car pulled up. The patrol officer was relieved when he saw it was us.

"Someone called in two suspicious men in front of their house. Anonymous call," the officer told us. "I guess that's you guys."

Not one minute later, a Toyota SUV pulled up in the roadway. A man and woman got out, walking briskly towards us. I made eye contact with the woman, who looked to be in her mid-thirties.

"Hi," I said, "Are you the one who called the police?"

She looked past me. "I'm not talking to you," she said curtly. Then she approached the uniform officer, "I need to talk to you," she said. She motioned for him to walk to the side where they could talk in private.

"Whatever you need to say," he said to her, "you can say right here in front of these detectives." She was quite put off by this, but by this time the man she was with started talking to me. He was ebullient and high strung, wearing a t-shirt that had the emblem of the Broward Sheriff's Office on it.

"Hello, Detective...you know, it is a shame the way my wife is behaving. I am having to take care of my two young daughters, and they have no idea where she is. She has run away with her boyfriend in New Jersey, and I cannot find the strength to tell them this. How could they understand that their own mother doesn't love them, you know?"

By this point, I had not said a word. I just watched, nodded, and listened. I noticed that the man had about a half inch scratch on his nose.

"You must be Jesus," I said.

He nodded, and, rapid-fire, kept going. "Yes. Isn't what my wife is doing illegal? Abandoning her kids like this? It's incredible. Only an evil person does this to their kids."

I started jotting down some notes, but only briefly. I wanted to continue watching and listening to Jesus Rodriguez and his charged-up soliloquy about his evil wife, there in the middle of the road. I wondered if he was on a gallon of *café Cubano*, or if this was how he was all the time.

"Stop talking to them," I heard the woman say quietly. She had come around and was standing about a foot from his right ear. "Jesus," she said, "shuttup. Stop talking."

Ah, *Live Isabel*, I thought.

Jesus turned halfway to her and shushed her. Then he turned back to me and smiled. "My lawyer has told me not to say anything to the police," he said, "but I feel you need to hear what I have to say. I'm not hiding anything."

Which is just dandy, Jesus, I thought to myself. Do go on.

Live Isabel rolled her eyes, threw up her hands, and walked in a circle, before returning to him. "Don't say anything more, Jesus. "Shut. Up."

I took a step forward and smiled at her. "Isabel, right?"

She gave me a hateful look. "I don't have to say *shit* to you, because—-"

"Isabel, right now, you are about an inch away from going to jail. If you say one more word to this witness," I told her calmly, "while we are attempting to conduct our investigation, I will put handcuffs on you. Do you understand?"

She glared at me and walked away. I watched her get on her cell phone and frantically start talking to someone. I assumed it was Jesus' lawyer.

Jesus, meanwhile, continued his diatribe about Dead Isabel, and who was I to stop him? At one point, I contacted Bill Hellman, Ann Bogen's Sergeant.

"Bill, we've got Jesus here on the scene, and he's talking."

"Oh, nice work. What's he saying?"

"I can't take any credit for it. It took no work at all. He just started jabbering. Same thing over and over, how is wife is off somewhere with the boyfriend."

"Ok," Bill said, "see if you can get a consent to search his car, the Lincoln Town car, and his farm, out west."

We always carried "consent to search" forms with us, for those cooperative souls who were willing to give up their Fourth Amendment rights. Jesus, it seemed, was willing, if not downright cheerful, about tossing both his Fourth *and* Fifth Amendment protections to the wind, and I was just as cheerful to help.

So there, on the hood of my car, with a nearly apoplectic Live Isabel on the sidelines watching, Jesus signed, giving us written consent to search the vehicle and his farm in west Dade, which was way out near Chekika Hammock somewhere. While I was on that roll, I figured I would get Jesus to talk in a more private environment, away from his panicked girlfriend.

"Jesus, how about we go to my office and talk with some coffee, in the air conditioning?"

"Yes, I can come to your office."

"You can follow me there," I said, pointing to his car, which Live Isabel was now in, with the engine running, motioning him over, "or you can ride with me. Your choice."

He clearly didn't want to get an ass-chewing from her all the way to Doral, so he said, "I will ride with you."

Isabel motioned him over, and he stood by the driver's window, talking heatedly with her for a good ten minutes or more. I could see her hand gestures going all over the place, desperately trying to salvage some kind of self-preservation in him, but he would have no part of it. Finally, he strolled back to my car and said, "Let's go." The exasperated girlfriend was shaking her head.

At the Homicide Office, I quickly briefed Ann Bogen on the unexpected visit by our suspect.

"Good. Keep working on him. We're going to pick up the daughter later. By the way, we have cell tower records showing Jesus made some calls around 11am, in close vicinity to the marital house."

I asked Jesus to tell the background of everything first, and I had to stop him a few times to keep him on track.

"We've established that she's an evil, terrible person, Jesus."

"The *devil*," he reminded me.

"Right. Let's stick to what happened. Let's start with your day, from the moment you woke up. Take me through everything."

And, he obliged. The story made absolutely zero sense. He said he picked up his daughter, Michelle, at her place in Hialeah, to help her with her car. It was having some mechanical problem, and he wanted to troubleshoot it. So, they drove from Hialeah to Jesus' farmland out off of 207th avenue, which is about a 45-minute ride, at least, some of it on dirt roads. When they got out there, he decided they should have breakfast, so he sent her to the McDonald's at 92nd avenue and Bird Road. That meant he sent Michelle *another 45 minutes back to the east*, and it is likely that she passed half a dozen McDonalds to get to the one near Tropical Park—and near the marital home. Then, she went back to the farm. Then home. Then, back out to the farm, to bring Jesus' Lincoln

Town Car out there. Then he drove her back to Hialeah, then he went back to the farm. I quickly calculated that they had driven at least one hundred eighty miles that morning and spent three hours or more on the road.

"Why, Jesus?"

"So I could clean the Lincoln."

"That was an emergency of some kind? Getting the car clean?"

"I like to keep my car clean." I shook the lines from the Beatles' *Penny Lane* out of my head and continued. *It's a clean machine...*

"Drive the Lincoln out to the farm to *clean* it, and then drive back out on ten miles of dusty dirt roads?"

It was all just a pitifully silly story, patched together on the fly. I told him as much.

"You're lying to me, Jesus. Stop the lying. Let's get to the truth."

When I confronted Jesus with the information that we had the cell tower "pings" showing he had made calls from the area of his former home, he admitted that he had gone there to pick up the mail.

"There was a restraining order against me. That's why I didn't want to tell you."

God forbid we should violate *that,* Jesus. Better to lie in a murder investigation instead? When I asked him what was in the mail he picked up, the real panic started. He literally looked up at the ceiling for a good five minutes, without looking down or saying a word. After two minutes, I tried to bring him back from the chaos going on his mind.

"Jesus...Jesus. Look at me for a moment." But the gears were whirring too fast in there. I had never been in an interview room with a suspect who detached for that long. Finally, looked down at me.

"Ok..I didn't go there to pick up the mail. I went there to spy on my wife. I think the boyfriend has been visiting her there, so I wanted to catch them."

Now, we were getting a little closer. Michelle, he said, dropped him off on the block behind the house, so he could enter the premises via the back yard. There, he went into the "little house"—the shed—and maintained a surveillance there.

"I never saw them together. I only saw her come and go, when it was time for her to drop off the kids."

And he never went to the front, ever, that day, he said. He left the shed and was picked up by Michelle in the back. There are times in an interview when it's pointless to go over all the convoluted bullshit and the wild variations of stories that the suspect can't keep straight. You could spend more time sitting there, hitting the wall with your sledgehammer and break it down, brick by brick. But sometimes, you just climb over the sonofabitch.

"Jesus—the one person who knows where your wife's body is, is *you*. Think of your two children. They have a right to know where their mother is. They have a right to give her a proper burial."

We were a good four and half hours into the interview by now. Jesus started to hang his head, and I inched closer. This was the time the opponent was on the ropes, exhausted, close to surrender. You moved in here, subtly. You made them feel like there was no way out except to unburden themselves.

"Jesus," I said, "you owe it to your children to have a place they can visit their mother."

Barely, almost imperceptibly, he nodded. Then, he said, "Who will take care of my business? Who would run it for me, if I give you this information?"

Got him, I thought. The fish was all but in the boat.

"Jesus, that can all be taken care of. That's the *easy* part. You have family, you have a grown daughter. Think about the little ones." I figured this was what was going to be the final straw.

He shook his head, crossed his arms, and went silent. I continued pressing, and we went another hour. Ann Bogen came in and sat with me. She put some heat into her questioning and told him this was his chance to come clean. We tried everything. I think we went into Christ and Mother Mary and a few other places to motivate him, but he wouldn't budge. The man who wouldn't shut up all day finally shut down.

People, however, are what they are. Isabel Rodriguez' blood was in the trunk of the Lincoln, and though that was circumstantial, Ann and her team got great statements from workers on the farm. They said they were sent home early that day, because Jesus was going to have a "Santeria cleansing ritual." As they left, they saw smoke billowing up from a large fire on the property.

We also found two neighbors who saw a man fitting Jesus' description, wearing sweat pants and work boots, creeping around strangely--*hiding,* in fact—in the driveway area that same day. Michelle Rodriguez, Jesus' daughter, gave us a sworn statement that her father came to him the day her mother disappeared, and gave him a pair of sweatpants, a pair of boots, and a few other items to launder for him. He asked Michelle to lie for him about the car and their activities that day. It was enough to get the Grand Jury to indict, and once Jesus was in the Dade County Jail, he started running his mouth again. No less than *nine* inmates testified to various admissions the narcissistic Jesus had made to them about the killing and disposal of his wife. He told so many aspects of the murder that it could almost be pieced together with the different accounts. One guy doing time for armed robbery said that Jesus had clobbered Isabel with a baseball bat in the driveway. When he took the car out to the farm and opened the trunk, she jumped up and scratched his face, and he beat her with the bat again.

We dug up just about every inch of that farm. Everything we had at our disposal—ground penetrating radar, backhoes, and teams of detectives with shovels—was put to work, but her remains were never found. It took three trials to convict Jesus—the first one ended in a mistrial when there were allegations of witness tampering during jury selection. The second was stopped when a jailhouse informant told us that Jesus had hired someone to kill Abbe Rifkin, the superb state attorney prosecutor on the case. Finally, on try number three, Abbe got him. The fast-talking Jesus got convicted and sentenced to life in prison.

Isabel Rodriguez was likely turned into bones and ashes. Those remains could have been disposed a hundred different ways, in a thousand different places. Short of doing DNA analysis on a spoonful of dirt at a time, finding any speck of her would have been sheer luck. But for all the work Jesus Rodriguez went through to kill her, burn her, dispose of her remains, ask his daughter to lie for him, and lie to his own children, he was his own undoing.

Ree-Ree

On July 26th, 2002, I took a ride with Sgt. Al Singleton, Cold Case Squad Supervisor, to pick up an important piece of evidence—a dog cage—at a house just north of Opa-Locka. Our target in the investigation was named Geralynn Graham.

Graham had used the dog cage to put imprison her 5-year-old foster daughter as punishment.

"So she wouldn't hurt herself," Graham told people close to her.

That child, Rilya Shenise Wilson, was now missing.

Florida's Department of Children of Families (DCF) is in charge of monitoring foster placements and conducting case visits to homes where children are placed. These monthly visits are mandatory and must be documented by the DCF caseworkers—called Family Service Counselors—on a home visit form. If a child is moved from one foster home to another, other people get involved: the attorney assigned to the case and a guardian *ad litem*. So it was very strange indeed when DCF received a call from Geralynn Graham, asking when Rilya would be brought back to her.

Brought back? DCF asked. We don't have her, they told her. Graham was incredulous.

"Yes you do," she told them.

Geralynn insisted that on January 18, 2001, a "black lady from DCF" took Rilya for some sort of testing. When, she asked, are you going to bring her back? Again, DCF flatly told her that they had no record of Rilya being removed from the home, for testing or otherwise. The ensuing scramble led to Rilya's caseworker, Deborah Muskelly. When administrators started digging into Muskelly's home visit logs, they discovered that most of them were falsified. It became obvious that Muskelly was logging home visits that never occurred, and this was confirmed when investigators from the Florida Department of Law Enforcement (FDLE)—now on the trail because it was DCF was a state agency—discovered that Muskelly was simultaneously working an unauthorized second job as a teacher, all while collecting a salary from DCF. She was double dipping. And foster homes weren't being visited.

By the time Rilya Wilson was officially reported missing in April of 2002, Muskelly resigned. FDLE leveled multiple fraud and theft charges on her, and she was now represented by counsel, so we couldn't talk to her. Her immediate supervisor, a man named Willie Harris, resigned two weeks later. One of the first set of leads our Cold Case Squad was given was to start interviewing Muskelly's colleagues.

"She had the run of the office," the first DCF employee I spoke with told me. "She could come in late, do what she pleased. Everyone else was held to a different standard."

Complaints about Muskelly, both from inside the office and out, came pouring in. They varied from falsification of her mileage log to her secret outside job. The complaints were brought to Harris and largely ignored. While several of us slogged through about three dozen interviews of DCF employees, other team members were learning who Geralynn Graham was, and how Rilya Wilson came to be in her care.

Graham was an intriguing person. The more we found out about her, the more of a fraud she was proven to be. Well before Rilya's disappearance, she started a "church" in Goulds, calling herself "Pastor Cartwright". She distributed free dinners (which she got from the government) to the local elderly. All they had to do was fill out their names and social security numbers on the free dinner voucher sheet.

Geralynn Graham was a massive identify thief, before it became a household phrase. Her partner in crime was a woman named Pamela Kendrick. The congregation all knew her as Pastor Cartwright's "sister." In truth, they were a couple. Pamela Kendrick was good at accounting, making her a valuable asset in Geralynn's various rip-off schemes. Pamela's employment history included a string of accounting jobs, one in the HR department of a company that had no clue their employees' social security numbers were now working capital for the duo of Pamela and Geralynn. Whether it was her racket at the Goulds church or fraudulent tax returns of unknowing employees Pamela smiled at every morning, the two used their wiles to make money off anyone, any way they could. That included being a foster parent.

Gloria Wilson was a miserable, full-blown cocaine addict, and an admittedly unfit mother of her 3-year-old daughter, Rilya. She was also pregnant. Sometime in 1999, Pamela and Geralynn Graham met Gloria and saw her situation. Before long, Rilya was placed in Pamela Graham's foster custody. After Gloria gave birth, DCF placed Rilya's sibling, Rodricka, with another Pamela—Pamela Kendrick. One day, Geralynn and Pamela visited Kendrick's home, so that "Rilya could visit her little sister." DCF was soon afterward notified that Pamela Kendricks' home was in deplorable condition and was a terrible place for a child to live. DCF was a bureaucracy not known for swift action, but suddenly they went into high gear, and *presto*, Rodericka Wilson was in the custody of Pamela and Geralynn Graham.

FDLE's investigation became a task force in no time: the assigned Homicide squad with lead investigator Chris Stroze, our Cold Case team, and an FDLE unit headed up by Agent Ed Royal. Ed was an excellent cop and a fun guy to be around. He never took himself too seriously and loved a good laugh on the job. Ed was also intuitive and persistent, two qualities that are indispensable as an investigator.

The case was a three-lane highway, or a three-ring circus, depending on how you wanted to look at it. We were exploring the lives and potential criminal activity of Geralynn and Pamela Graham. FDLE was dissecting a vastly incompetent—and possibly liable—DCF, Deborah Muskelly, Willie Harris, and possibly others. And *everyone* was trying to find out where Rilya Wilson was.

The news media world swarmed the story from all sides. Did DCF "lose" the child? Did Geralynn and Pamela Graham "murder" her? Was she sold on the child trafficking black market? News anchors and commentators were having a field day with the possibilities and leads were pouring in from the community and soon, internationally. We even had one lead claiming that Rilya had been sold to someone in the Bahamas. Chris Stroze had to abandon his regular cubicle in the office and move into a spare interview room that was now the "Rilya Room", with boxes of records, subpoenas, and incoming leads. From a desk stacked with reports and lead sheets, Chris disseminated leads from a pile that never seemed to go down. We would go in and discuss our lead results with Chris, and there were times the poor guy looked utterly shell-shocked.

While most of the community was confused about what had happened to Rilya, our working theory was that Geralynn Graham—and possibly her lover Pamela—had killed the child and the story of DCF picking her up was an opportunistic misdirection play. They knew Muskelly had shirked her duties, so no one could say with any certainty that DCF had *not* picked her up, but it such an act was simply not part of their protocol. With each passing day, we became convinced she was dead. Her cherubic face was on every newspaper and every news broadcast. By now someone would have raised their hand and said, "She's over here!" But no one had. All we had were "sightings".

Pamela and Geralynn had recently moved out of their modest single-family home in west Kendall, and we got started on the area canvass—the first one—on May 15th, 2002. Only two of the twenty-some door knocks provided anything remotely useful. The family across the street had an 11-year-old boy who told us that two boys showed up there frequently and played with him. They would kick a soccer ball outside and later go inside the home to play video games. This boy remembered seeing two little girls inside the house. He had no recollection of any violent or upsetting events, no temper tantrums, nothing out of the ordinary. The other stop we made was the family of Beatriz and Luis Gomez. They lived next door, to the north of the Graham's house, and their story made the hair on my neck stand up.

The Gomez' had a 10-year-old daughter, and through casual, neighborly conversation the Gomez' learned that the two boys who were frequently at the Graham household were named Frederick and Dominick. Their mother, a woman who drove a small red vehicle, would drop them off there to play. It was unclear what their relationship was to Pam and Geralynn, though the boys called Geralynn "grandma." The Gomez' remembered Rilya well. They saw her being walked down the block frequently by Pamela. Around Thanksgiving, a lot of visitors showed up at the Graham's house. As normal as that should have been, the Gomez' were unnerved.

"They didn't look like...*nice* people," Luis Gomez told me, trying his best to polite. "I got a bad feeling about them."

The couple recognized a photo of Jaabir Muhammad, Geralynn's brother, and said he drove a white Cadillac. Jaabir, we already knew, lived on the west coast near Tampa. Add yet another possibility to add to the long list of Rilya theories. The Gomez' described Geralynn as "standoffish" and not friendly, while Pamela was the much more social of the two. Then the conversation with the Gomez' got way more intriguing. A skinny young man who drove a white Datsun 200ZX seemed to be at Geralynn and Pamela's home a lot. At night, he would lean against the car and smoke cigarettes. One night, they heard a loud argument and looked out the window. The skinny guy was being berated by a heavyset black woman they did not recognize. She was warning him, harshly, "If you don't do what I'm telling you, I'll report you, and you'll go to jail."

The male was deeply affected during the argument, to the point of weeping. "I've got you by the balls," the woman said at the end of the exchange. More intriguing than everything else the Gomez' had to tell me was what they encountered just after Christmas.

"A very strong smell," Beatriz Gomez said. "Very strong."

I looked at them and Beatriz' husband was nodding.

"Like what? Can you be more specific?" I asked. I didn't want to be suggestive, and I definitely did not want to say the word decomposition.

They looked at each other for guidance, and Luis shook his head. "Like urine, and feces. It was hard to define. Like animal urine and feces, but...stronger, different."

"Yes," Beatriz agreed. "Like that. It's hard to say what it actually was." The smell was prominent in the backyard, near the property line, but much more prominent when standing between the two structures. The smell faded when the Gomez' walked away from the house, towards the back property line. Maybe, I thought, it was time to break out the gloves and shovels. The Gomez' wouldn't identify the smell as decomposition, but maybe Rilya's remains had been packed with some other material to attempt to mask the smell. Also, some people aren't familiar with the smell of decomposition. Before I left, Luis Gomez left me with one more odd discovery.

"My wife and I have a computer consulting company. After the Grahams moved out, the owner was going through some items left behind, and found checks made out to Luis and Beatriz' company in a trash can, with the accompanying envelopes torn open nearby. The *only* way that could have happened would be if they were going through my mail," Luis Gomez said.

Our investigation kept circling back to Geralynn, because of Geralynn herself. She made the mistake of not sticking to one story. We had heard at least six different stories Geralynn had told people about the child's disappearance: A Hispanic woman from DCF took her. A black lady from DCF, with an island accent, took her. A Spanish lady from the neighborhood, who she had met at a park, took her New Jersey or New York, to "care for her."

Geralynn was telling anyone who would listen that there were dramatic differences between the two children. Rilya had developmental problems, she would say. She smeared feces on the wall. She had uncontrollable temper tantrums and would break and destroy things in the house. And the stories got bizarre: Rilya would "touch men in their private areas." By contrast, Geralynn described Rodericka as a near-perfect child, a well-behaved princess that never gave her an ounce of trouble. The more people we interviewed, the more we heard this same theme repeated. We interviewed everyone we could find who knew or had come in contact with Geralynn or Pamela in the last two years. Over a dozen investigators were working twelve or more hours a day, interviewing people from California to the Bahamas. Chris Stroze's "Rilya Room" was starting to look like a hoarder's basement.

Parallel with the interviews, we had people serving subpoenas and running down leads from the phone records of both Geralynn Graham and Deborah Muskelly. As is the case with any large-scale investigation, most of these leads end up as dead-ends, or innocent contacts with people who had no involvement in anything. The reason for the meticulous, often monotonous work of tracking and analyzing each call, however, is that every once in a while, you strike gold.

One of my leads was to find a lady named Penny Barrington. Her name showed up on Geralynn's phone number, several times.

"Yes, I know her," Barrington said. "She brought her child to the nursery I work at. Small Fry Nursery in Cutler Ridge."

When I sat down with Penny Barrington in July of 2002 at her apartment, she told us that Rodericka, whom she knew as "Kyla", attended Small Fry. Geralynn never brought Rilya there, but she talked about her frequently. Penny remembered Geralynn saying that Rilya was "a disturbed child" that she couldn't control. Rilya, Penny was told, smeared feces on the wall and once nearly burned the house down. Geralynn spoke glowingly of Rodericka and said that she wanted to adopt her. Penny Barrington then hit me with the real fireworks.

"She told me that she called DCF to come and pick Rilya up because she couldn't deal with her."

I zeroed in. "Are you sure? She said that *she* was the one who called DCF, or did she tell you DCF came on their own and took her for testing?"

"No," Penny said, "she definitely said *she* called DCF to take the child. I wouldn't forget something like that. I was pretty amazed by what she said."

Geralynn had been bringing Rodericka to Small Fry daily. One night, Penny was watching TV at home and saw a news story about Rilya Wilson as a missing child. After the story broke, Geralynn and Rodericka stopped showing up at Small Fry. Concerned, Penny called Geralynn. The woman sounded "lost" Penny said, and at one point said, "What am I going to do?"

"It didn't make sense," Penny went on. "Geralynn said she had contacts with the family court system."

Penny confided with me that she could not have children, and that she shared this fact with Geralynn one day.

"She told me she was going to get a little girl for me. I thought it was the strangest thing to say to someone," Penny said, recalling the conversation. "She said that she had connections with the courts, and that she was going to check the availability of young female children."

After the story broke about Rilya, Geralynn came to Small Fry and gave Penny a bag of Kyla's clothes.

"She wanted to give them to us. A donation, I suppose. She told us Kyla had outgrown them." When Penny looked at the clothes—shirts, tops, and shoes—after Geralynn left, she got a strange feeling.

"Why *then,* you know? Why bring them just at that time?"

Penny invited us to Small Fry and took the clothing out. I laid them out on the floor and took pictures of them. Stroze decided there was no need to impound the clothes just yet. But as I snapped the pictures, I thought that I was probably looking at Rilya's clothes.

Penny referred us to her boss, Tanya Regalado, who had spent way more time talking with Geralynn.

When Tanya first met Geralynn in September of 2001, she told Geralynn and Pamela (who was introduced as her "sister), that her own sister had been in one of the World Trade towers during the September 11th attacks and was in the hospital in New York. Geralynn Graham immediately told her that she was closely affiliated with the Red Cross and could get her sister some help. Tanya thought this was a very odd offer, as the two women hadn't discussed her sister's condition, or what type of help Geralynn could provide. Geralynn also volunteered her own history, saying that her father was a high-ranking member in the Bahamian government.

"She said her father's face was on the Bahamian dollar bill," Regalado told me.

Geralynn carried on with the same replay of the good girl/bad girl story again: Rodericka was the consummate angel, Rilya an incorrigible and destructive terror.

Geralynn's story about Rilya's departure didn't set well at all with Tanya Regalado, who had run children's nurseries and been involved in childcare for twenty years. She had a pretty good working knowledge of DCF and how things worked with foster care.

"She told me a male DCF employee came and picked up the child. Then she said she couldn't remember if that was the case, of whether she might have reported to a male DCF employee that Rilya had been taken."

Tanya shook her head at the memory. "How do you not know that? How do you not have some written record of exactly who was involved in the child's removal, and when?"

Geralynn couldn't even keep her stories straight with two people at Small Fry. Regalado pressed Geralynn for details, but never got any satisfactory answers. In that, Tanya could count herself as part of a very large club, one that was growing by the day.

Geralynn's only real family members were her chronically down-and-out sons, Leo and Kenneth Epson. Leo was holding down a job at an HR place called Teleforce in Lauderhill. He had an open warrant for Grand Theft. FDLE Agent Ed Royal and I went there and arrested him. He went quietly, and back at FDLE Headquarters he went into a detailed history of his mother's previous relationships in Tennessee. Geralynn came out to Leo about a woman she had a romance with while in prison, serving time there for an embezzlement case. Her lover was in for armed robbery. But Leo knew little of Rilya, and nothing of her whereabouts.

Tracking down Kenneth was a more rigorous challenge. Kenneth was in and out of Miami's largest homeless shelter, Camillus House, and we kept missing him. When we finally found him, he told us that a friend of his who had been at the Graham household several times, saw Rilya "tied up" for disciplinary reasons. Though Ken Epson believed his friend, he also believed Geralynn's story that DCF had come to take Rilya away.

"I'll *never* incriminate a member of my family," Kenneth Epson also told us.

We contacted his friend, who had been interviewed once early on and had little to say. But he was done with talking. Terry Goldston, now a member of our Cold Case Squad, teamed up with me and tried to talk to the guy until we were blue in the face. He finally yelled at us on the phone to never contact him again.

The dozens of interviews we were conducting were stirred up similar stories of severe discipline: Rilya had been tied to a bedpost. Rilya had been locked in a small utility room, next to a water heater. Rilya had burns on her face from an unknown source. Geralynn made it a point to tell people that Rilya had been taken to the hospital to have the burn treated. Another time, she swallowed some sort of chemical, the story went, and Rilya had her stomach pumped at the hospital. The girl had "developmental problems," Geralynn told scores of people about Rilya having befallen one calamity after another. One of the stories was about a "small hole above her vagina" that must have occurred before she took custody of her. We heard that—and how Geralynn had taken her to have it examined—from several people.

To confirm the story, I set out with a stack of subpoenas to check every hospital and pediatrician's office in southern Miami-Dade County for records of that visit or any medical examination or treatment of Rilya. Not one single visit, treatment, immunization, or consultation of any kind, at any hospital, or any doctor's office could be found. The absences of medical visits, for a 4-year-old girl with a supposedly long list of injuries and ailments, was profound.

At least now we had Geralynn behind bars, charged with several counts of defrauding the state of Florida. She had been cashing checks from DCF for her foster parenting of Rilya Wilson, long after the girl had disappeared from her house. How long she would spend in jail on these charges was anyone's guess, but it might help to get people talking.

After a team meeting on March 24, 2004, there was a discussion about the Gomez', the couple from the first area canvass who had told me about the smell coming from the Graham's house just after Christmas of 2001.

"We need to talk to them again," Sgt. Singleton said to me. "Let's see if we can get more details."

The Gomez' had moved and were surprised to see me again, though were just as cordial and cooperative as before. Their recollection of the smell changed little, if at all.

"It could have been rotting garbage, or dog feces, but I can't say for sure," Luis said. "I first noticed it when taking out my garbage, which we kept on the south side of our house. The Grahams kept theirs just across the fence, on the north side of their house."

The Grahams had no pets. It was also possible that the Gomez' might never have come across the smell of mammal decomposition and couldn't describe what they smelled other than to call it "rotting garbage."

Two weeks later, we served a search warrant at the former Graham household, 10131 SW 145th Place, where Rilya was last seen alive. The configuration of the rear of the home was such that there was very little grass; only a strip of green on either side, each just 2-3 feet wide. We dug up every inch, and, typically of most south Florida yards, we hit big chunks of limestone rock everywhere. Rilya wasn't buried in the yard. While the rest of the team went through the house looking for "false walls" or any other hidden feature we could find, I went up a ladder and into the attic. There were no false walls, stains, smells, or any kind of anomalies that would raise eyebrows.

The prevailing law enforcement belief had not changed: Rilya was dead. How much she suffered before she died was uncertain, but then we talked to Detra Coakley.

Detra was an unassuming woman who had met Geralynn at the wedding of a mutual friend. Geralynn befriended her and had her over to the house several times. She met Leo Epson, and both girls, Rilya and Kyla. She described Rilya as a quiet, nice little girl who seemed to speak, walk and behave like a normal 4-year-old. She said she never saw any bizarre or troubling behavior from her. Even so, Geralynn told Detra that Rilya was "rebelling", disrupting the household and destroying things.

"Geralynn trusted me, I think," Detra told us. "And ever since the story came out about Rilya missing, she's been trying to get a hold of me."

Chris Stroze and his team got Detra to agree to wear a wire, and we then set up a meeting with Geralynn. Though most of the encounter was uneventful, one startling statement from Rilya got our attention when Geralynn told Detra, "Don't talk about the dog cage."

Our prosecutor was Sally Weintraub, in the twilight of her career but as committed to this case as anyone could ever ask a state attorney to be. It was great to have her in charge of the prosecution. Sally was a focused and insightful attorney with a ton of experience. Very little got by her. I liked her and there was a personal connection: Sally's daughter, Devorah worked with me in uniform in Opa-Locka. Sally wanted to meet Detra herself, so she and I visited Detra at her west Kendall home, barely a two minutes' drive from the Grahams' old place we had just searched.

"It was strange," Detra told us, "hearing Geralynn talk about all these horrible things Rilya was doing, but never seeing any signs of it."

Geralynn told Detra she wanted to "give Rilya back" to DCF. Then, one of the most alarming—and significant—statements we heard during this disturbing case:

"Geralynn asked to borrow my dog cage. She wanted it so she could keep Rilya from hurting herself."

Detra, thinking this must have been a severe situation, acquiesced and brought her the cage. When Rilya wasn't around after Christmas, Detra was told that Rilya went with some of her friends to New York or New Jersey to see a relative. Then Detra was told a confusing twist on the story.

"Geralynn said the car the lady had been driving broke down on the way up north, so the trip was being delayed. The car belonged to a homeless Spanish lady...and that this lady was going to be keeping Rilya." Detra recalled. "None of that made sense to me."

There's an old saying about the truth: you never have to work hard to remember it. We used a tactic in the interview room sometimes to test a story. Ask the suspect to tell it *backwards*. Start from the last thing you did and go back. Psychologists say that when we recall something that we actually experienced, we can tell it chronologically in either direction without a problem. A liar will stumble on the reverse telling because it was never *experienced*. The brain processes truth and fiction differently. Geralynn Graham couldn't tell one event simple event—how Rilya left her care—the same way to two different people, backward *or* forward. This story Geralynn told Detra was piled on to a list we had lost count of.

On August 18, 2004, Sally Weintraub filed charges against Geralynn Graham of Kidnapping, Aggravated Child Abuse, and First Degree Murder. Pamela Graham was charged with only the first two offenses.

Through a proffer from Pamela's attorney, we took custody of her directly from her bond hearing, under the agreement that she cooperate fully with any and all investigations of the disappearance of Rilya Wilson. She was also required to give statements and testify in all matters regarding Geralynn Graham. Pamela was pleasant and engaging, like most con artists are. With us there was no more pretending, however, and there was a likeable side to her. She seemed relieved to be unburdening herself with all the things that she had gone along with under the domineering thumb of Geralynn. She was terrified of the older woman, so much that she begged us to get her a place under a fake name. She was certain Geralynn had the resources and wiles to reach out and get someone to find her and hurt her. Pamela Graham became a protected witness of the Miami-Dade Police Department, and it was my job to find her a place the County was willing to pay for. Pamela was used to being in the south end, and so was I, so I got her an apartment at Briar Bay, just south of the Falls Shopping Center. It was the same complex my old friend Chuck Markman—my late-night shooting buddy—used to live in. I met with the manager and explained the situation so that they understood that Miami-Dade Police was technically their tenant.

Just two days after we formally charged the two women, our receptionist in Homicide transferred a call to me. It was from the women's annex of the Dade County Jail.

"Hey," the woman on the other end said, "I'm in a cell block with this lady Geralynn Graham. And, she's kind of coming apart. She's talking about the baby...the little girl."

To say I sat up straight would be an understatement. There was a time back in North Miami when I went to a call, a domestic disturbance, of a wife being beaten. When I got to the front door, I heard the woman call out from the back, "he's coming to the door, and he's got a gun!" I backed away from the door, looking for cover, and heard the door swing open. I don't remember reaching for my gun or unholstering it. All I remember is that there it was: the two-handed cup-and-saucer grip they taught us in the academy, trained on the husband's chest when his form appeared in the doorway. There must have been scorch marks on the inside of my holster that night.

When this inmate called and started rambling about Geralynn talking about "the baby", my pen appeared in my hand just as automatically.

"And you are...?" I asked, jotting the date and time on my pad.

"My name is Robin Lunceford."

Robin told me quickly that Geralynn was confessing to her. "I'll give you details, but I can't now. I have to go. There are people constantly watching me. The lieutenant here has already called me a snitch. I need to get outta here. Can you guys move me?"

I would see what I could do. I notified Singleton about what we had, and communication with the women's annex staff was handled at the supervisory level. But it was taking all day, and Robin Lunceford called me three more times.

"Nyberg, *please* get me moved so I can tell you guys what's going on," she pleaded.

Finally, we got her out and in front of Sally Weintraub, and Robin gave us what we had spent the last two years in search of: someone who could give us a solid confession statement to shore up the murder charge.

"She told me she killed the baby, smothered it with a pillow," Robin told us. "She told me that the little girl was evil and mentally troubled."

Unfortunately, Geralynn never went into detail with Robin about where the body was. She told her she hid it "near water" which in south Florida could literally be anywhere.

Robin couldn't narrow it down any further than that. Maybe we could work a deal with Geralynn: avoid the death penalty and take a life sentence in return for the whereabouts of Rilya's remains. But Geralynn was already sixty-five years old and the state didn't have much leverage there. Robin's statement was a big moment, but it wasn't a nail in the coffin, either. She was a career criminal and had been an informant on other cases. She came with a lot of baggage. Before too long though, another woman at the Annex—this one a familiar name from another murder case of ours—-came forward with to tell us of Geralynn's suddenly talkative mood. Her name was Maggie Carr.

Maggie of course was no saint either; we knew that all too well. She was charged with murder in a previous murder of ours. Her statement was different than Robin's. Geralynn sought her out because Maggie had a reputation in the jail for being knowledgeable about the law. Geralynn wanted advice, asking Maggie if they could charge her with murder without the body. Magaly Carr knew this situation quite well. It was exactly the reason she was serving time.

"She told me, 'If there's no body, there's no murder,'" Maggie told us. Geralynn also told Maggie that no one was going to care about Rilya because she was a crack addict baby. Besides, Geralynn told Maggie, they wouldn't find Rilya, because "the critters would take care of the body."

The trial started just before Christmas of 2012. After a break for the holidays, the trial picked right back up after the New Year. Maggie Carr's credibility took the same type of pinata-type bludgeoning that Robin's did. She was a convicted murderer, after all. The defense team did their best to convince the jury that Carr's only appearance was to gain favor from the State to get her sentence reduced. But she stood firm.

"I'm here because it's a child," she said calmly.

I was brought back—six years after my retirement—to testify on two points only: my retrieval of the dog cage, and my conversations with Robin. Geralynn's lawyers asked me over and over if I had ever met Robin prior to her phone call, if the Miami-Dade Police Department had used her as an informant, and a dozen other questions to try and paint her as a serial informant/opportunist, to soften the edges of her testimony.

In the end, the jury found Geralynn guilty of Kidnapping and Aggravated Child Abuse. One lone juror couldn't convict on the murder charge, so that was hung, 11-1. Geralynn Graham, one of the most demonic creatures I have ever encountered, was sentenced to 55 years in prison on the charges. At 66-years old, this was as close to a death penalty the state of Florida was going to get.

Rilya was never found. I have lived and driven all over southern Dade County, and it is very likely that I have driven past her remains more than once, and maybe thousands of us unwittingly still do. We can only hope that the suffering she endured in her short life, at the hands of Geralynn Graham, ended quickly.

You don't want to know

Lynne and Clifford Friend were married in 1988. Like half the marriages in America, the relationship disintegrated and they split in 1991. During a bitter divorce, Lynne won custody of their son, Christian. Lynne was a well-liked hospital administrator and had an apartment in Hallandale. Clifford had a place in Pembroke Pines, a short drive away.

Life was moving on for Lynne. She met and fell in love with Ed O'Dell, a Tennessean. They got engaged and the plan was made: Lynne would move to Tennessee and they would raise 5-year-old Christian together. Clifford was livid and filed for an emergency injunction. It was unfair, he claimed, for his son to be moved so far away. The judge, though, would have none of it. Lynne had custody, as well as the right to move wherever she wanted. If you want to see your son, you'll travel to Tennessee.

On August 28, 1994, Lynne got a call from Clifford, who asked if she wouldn't mind swinging by to pick up her child support check. She would leave Christian with the babysitter and go drop off the check. That was what Ed remembered from the last phone call he got from her, the last time he would ever hear her voice.

Since the wild drug wars of the 1980's, U.S. Customs and Coast Guard vessels regularly patrolled the ocean near major inlets of Florida's southeast coast, looking for smugglers of both narcotics and people. On the humid night of August 28th, 1994, they spotted a powerboat at rest, ten miles off Haulover Inlet. It was an unusual place for someone to stop and fish in the pitch of night, so they approached. As they did, they saw the vessel's occupants toss some large object overboard. A Customs agent would later write that it looked like a dark duffel bag. They activated their lights and got closer, and the boat took off. These *must* be smugglers, the agents thought as they pursued. The boat was trying to lose them, but the Customs vessel had superior power and caught up. The two men aboard stood and watched as the Customs officials boarded.

"What did you throw overboard back there?" they asked.

Clifford Friend answered: "You don't want to know."

That prompted a thorough search of the vessel, but nothing of any significance was found. The Customs officers had the lat-longs recorded and went back to search, but found nothing there either. The other man on the boat was Clifford's best friend, Alan Gold. It was Alan's boat, and there no fishing gear on board.

Ed O'Dell tried frantically to find Lynn after receiving a call from the babysitter, telling him that Lynne never came back to pick up Christian. This was beyond unusual for Lynne, a responsible, if not doting mother.

"I will not," Ed said to a Nashville TV reporter, his voice choking on a sob, when asked if he was considering that Lynne had been a victim of foul play. "I will not believe that."

Hallandale police began the investigation, and soon, FDLE was involved. The immediate—and very plausible theory—-was that Clifford had killed Lynne at his home when she came to meet him. Then, he had met Alan Gold at Gold's condo in Sunny Isles, loaded the body onto Gold's boat at the condo's marina, and headed out of Haulover to the dark ocean. Because Miami-Dade County was now involved, so were we.

Greg Smith and I met with FDLE agent Ed Royal and put together a lead list of what was done, not yet done, and what needed to be done *again*. The area canvass around Clifford's place would certainly need to be repeated, and so would an area canvass at Gold's condo, which was some twenty stories tall.

"Do you know this person?" We asked every resident, showing them pictures of both Gold and Clifford. "Have you ever seen them board a boat at the marina? Did you see them on August 28th? Ever seen them carrying something onto the boat?" One door after another.

No one had seen anything.

Lynne's car was found on the roadside a few miles from Clifford's house, with a slashed tire. We canvassed what we could there too; Lynn's killer had chosen a lonely stretch of road with the only a few houses some distance away.

We discussed at length approaching Alan Gold. That had already been done by Hallandale PD and FDLE, and he had declined to talk. In deciding whether this was worth revisiting we had a nagging dilemma, one that investigators struggle with in many cases. What if Alan Gold is culpable? In serving Gold with a subpoena, and *compelling* him to speak to us, the risk was huge. The Fifth Amendment to the Constitution of the United States clearly states that everyone has a cherished protection: "...nor shall anyone be compelled in any criminal case to be a witness against himself..." Once the government compels someone to speak (as a subpoena does), any confession they make is rendered impotent—they can spill their guts about anything from Jimmy Hoffa to JFK's murders, and none of it can be used against them. If Alan Gold was just there to provide the boat and grudgingly agreed to his best friend to help dump the body, the very least we had was an accessory after the fact to First Degree Murder. That might be worth sacrificing to get Clifford as the actual killer.

But what if Alan Gold had been there from the beginning, at Clifford's home? What if he had *helped kill* Lynne Friend? Compelling Alan Gold to talk, without having some idea of his role in Lynne's disappearance, could backfire horribly.

During all our investigative chalk talk, a massive search for Lynne's body was underway. We secured an expert from the National Oceanographic and Atmospheric Administration (NOAA) to estimate the general location of where a weighted body might be based on tides, currents, and time. We went as far as to employ the United States Navy to help search for the body using the most modern, high-tech search equipment they had aboard one of their research ships. Greg and Detective Archie Moore went on the ship for three days, watching video sent from tethered deep-sea cameras surveying the ocean floor thousands of feet down. The effort was even less promising than looking for than a needle in a haystack.

Another expert told us that if Lynne was weighted down sufficiently, she would never surface. "Once the object descended to a certain depth, the weight of the water above would be great enough to keep it from rising, even with the bloating of decomposition. She would just sort of tumble slowly along with the Gulf Stream current, northward somewhere."

In backgrounding every detail of Clifford Friend's life, we found another close buddy of his: an oily, despicable 42-year-old man on probation for child pornography. As unpalatable as it was to work with the guy, we had to try something, and we arranged for him to meet up with Cliff at a coffee shop in North Miami Beach to "catch up." We wired the guy up and listened in while watching through the window of a surveillance van as they met. It was clear from the outset that Cliff smelled it out; when they met, Cliff hugged him, patting him with extra, extended affection, all over his back and hips. They talked for about a half hour, but Cliff never went anywhere near the subject of his ex-wife.

We worked every lead, revisited every potential witness, and re-canvassed every location. We brainstormed at the office and over happy hour beers with just me, Greg, and Ed. I even proposed the admittedly radical idea of faking Lynne's discovery.

"We could work with a TV station from up north, coast of North Carolina, or maybe Maine, some little town on the ocean. They find a body in a duffel bag—we stage the entire thing, leak it to the local media here, and Clifford sees it. Maybe he cooperates, or Alan does."

As fun as that would have been to put together, we didn't have enough information. To do something like that, we would need to know what Lynne had been wearing, and what had been used to weigh down the bag. If we guessed at any of those things and were wrong, Clifford would know we were bullshitting. I still wanted to try it without the details, but it got voted down.

We were unable to dredge up anything new, and concluded that the one remaining door to be opened was Alan Gold. At some point, if nothing else in the case could be discovered, someone would have to make the decision to immunize Alan and solve the case, but Gold wasn't budging quite yet. I retired in November of 2006, not long after Greg did, leaving Ed Royal to work with the new Cold Case squad members.

Ultimately, in 2012, Alan Gold and the Miami-Dade State Attorney's Office struck a deal. He would testify with immunity. His statement got a murder indictment on Clifford. It was just as we had expected. Clifford strangled her in his house and called Alan for help. Alan came over, helped him secure the body, and helped him get the duffel bag onto the boat, and out to the ocean.

"An anchor," Alan Gold testified, when asked what was used to weigh down Lynne's remains. "He held one side, and I took the other, and over the side it went."

Isabel Rodriguez' ashes are part of the landscape of western Dade County. With the hurricanes we have had since her death, her particles could be spread far into the Everglades. Rilya? Who knows. Her tiny body is long skeletonized, crumbling slowly, perhaps near a body of water as Geralynn implied. Someday, a steam shovel might unearth part of her during the excavation for a new building project. And Lynne Friend's slow drift near the ocean bottom might have ended anywhere from here to Nova Scotia or Greenland. She is the ocean's secret.

We never said it out loud, but I think most of us in law enforcement hoped some karmic law existed, one that allowed innocent victims to haunt and torment the people who denied them the life, dreams, and chances they should have had.

Chapter Twenty-Two

Black Tape

When we kids played "army" in the neighborhood, there were no teams that I remember; it was more like every man for himself. Sneaking through the bushes and ambushing each other was the thrill, and if you got killed you owed it to your opponent to go into some theatrics as you "died"—clutch your heart, stagger, tumble, whatever. It was kind of an unspoken rule.

I was watching a movie with Mom and Dad, and I think it was "Lawrence of Arabia"- it was my earliest memory of watching a battle scene where there clearly were good and bad guys, or at least some characters I could identify as the ones I liked. In one scene, someone threw a dagger or something, and it nailed one of these "good guys" right in the chest. He lurched, twitched, and finally pitched over, dead. I was incensed, and very upset—the good guys aren't supposed to die (although I had seen my friends do a better job of it along the hedge in our neighbors' back yard).

"It's just a movie," my parents scoffed.

But I was not happy. The good guys aren't supposed to die.

In May of 1979 I had just gotten word from the Opa-Locka Police Department that I was accepted—I would start the academy in June. That same month, the Miami Herald lead story was the startling news of three Metro police officers shot on a call in Central District. They had all responded to a "shooting in progress." A maniacally angry man with a gun had opened fire on his ex-wife and family members, at one point taking the woman hostage in his car. When Officer Keith DiGenova got there, he struggled with the gunman, who shot DiGenova in the face. He collapsed and his weapon fell from his hand. The other two responding officers, Bill Cook and William Edgerton, arrived seconds later; Edgerton shot the gunman. He was still alive, however, enough to grab DiGenova's weapon and shoot them both. Bill Cook died on the scene. Edgerton survived, and DiGenova lived but suffered permanent brain damage. He was unable to work in law enforcement—or most anywhere else—again.

I was a month away from starting my training and I swallowed hard when I read the story. But it didn't stop me.

In the police academy, during "officer survival" training sessions, the instructors discussed many police shootings, the case of Cook, DiGenova and Edgerton included. They showed us films like "Officer Down, Code 3." That film and book stressed the danger of complacency. In Opa-Locka, you never had to worry about getting complacent. There was too much going on. While I was there, I never heard of an Opa-Locka Police Officer being killed in the line of duty. It seemed to happen in places where things were quiet most of the time. When I went to North Miami, a much quieter community, I drove to work one morning and heard on the radio that a North Miami Police Officer had been shot. I had only been on the department for three months. I went to the dispatcher and asked if he was ok. She looked at me and said, "No...he was shot and *killed*."

That was the first time I had experienced it up close. We had ninety officers on that department at the time, so everyone knew everyone, and most of the cops we had were friends who had worked there together for many years. I had met Carl Mertes briefly when he was working the desk. Other than that I really knew nothing about the guy, because he had been on another platoon. We saw each other at shift change. But that didn't matter. He was another officer. He was a brother.

Mertes stopped a car on Biscayne Boulevard just north of 135th street. The car turned out to be stolen and the driver took off running into the heavily wooded area on the west side of Biscayne.

Mertes ran after him, and the dispatcher lost contact with him after that. A canine officer had to go in and search the dense thicket to find Carl's body. The wooded area was part of Arch Creek Park, which was renamed by the city as "Arch Creek Memorial Park for Carl Mertes." The specter of death was something that hung silently with all of us, though it was a hidden worry. No one brooded about it, save for the couple of weeks after Carl's death. After that, it was back to business as usual: we laughed, joked, ate pizza on the hood of our police cars on the midnight shift, and played grab-ass pranks on each other.

We chose the profession. What we did take seriously was that we adhered to extreme precautions on traffic stops, domestic cases, and arrest situations—the three most dangerous situations an officer can face. To not disrespect our comrade, we didn't talk much about what Carl might have "done wrong." But deep down, we all knew he had left us a lesson: *do not* run after subjects into the woods at night. We put a piece of electrician's tape across our badge, to show our mourning and kept it on until after the funeral. Then, you hoped you didn't have to take any more tape out. But the grim reality was that police supply stores sold elastic black bands for your badge—you kept it in your drawer, just like the black suit you kept hanging in your closet. Regardless of the undercurrents of danger, most of us were happy to be there—jacked up, in fact—to be going out and doing something so few people got a chance to do. Yes, it was dangerous, and it could be tiring, frustrating, as well as physically and emotionally stressful. But because of all those things, the good stuff—protecting the public and catching bad guys—was all the more satisfying. You grew close to the ones who did it with you.

In North Miami one afternoon, we got a burglary in progress call in the residential section on the north side of town. It was an extremely hot afternoon and several of us who heard the call headed to the neighborhood. One of us spotted the subject, and he took off running. There were probably four of us after him on foot, and he was jumping fences, ducking through hedges, and doing his best to avoid us. We were in dark blue uniforms with our protective vests on, and this foot chase was going in a bunch of different directions for at least fifteen minutes. Some of the neighbors had come out on their porches to watch. Finally, it was just me and Clint Shannon, tearing after the guy in an open area between a bunch of houses. The guy was getting tired too, and he stumbled, giving Clint just enough time to catch up. Clint tackled him, and I was right on Clint's heels. The guy was panting, and Clint was panting, trying to tell the guy to put his hands behind his back as he sat on him.

"Ram..." Clint wheezed, managing a smile, "help me cuff this guy..." I was soaked in sweat, and we got the guy up and walked him back to Clint's car. As we got to the edge of the road, residents stood on their front porches, clapping and cheering. Moments like that were nice. We all knew as well how quickly those things can end the wrong way—as it did with Carl.

When I went to Homicide, line-of-duty deaths took on an entirely different complexion. Now I was part of the entity that had to investigate them. The Homicide Bureau was responsible for any "police-involved shooting," but what that really included was any case in which an officer was severely injured by a citizen, or a citizen was injured by an officer. Even if someone was wounded with a knife, it was a "police-involved" case and Homicide was in charge of the investigation.

One night, Larry Wilkotz, Sergeant, Cliff Nelson and I had just finished an area canvass at an apartment building. We were standing out in the parking lot discussing the contacts we had made when Cliff's phone rang. He started to pace slowly as he spoke, and we all knew that it was serious. We were getting another case. We were all staring at Cliff as he jotted down details.

"Police shooting," he whispered to us while he listened to whomever was feeding him the information where we would be going.

"Up in Northeast...two of our guys are down and in critical condition," Cliff went on.

Larry stiffened. He had just recently worked Northeast District in uniform before he came to Homicide. "Do we know who?" he asked Cliff.

Cliff motioned for us to wait, then jotted some more. He looked up at Larry. "Richard Boles..."

Larry threw up his hands.

"...and David Strzalkowski."

Larry threw up his hands again, and walked in a slow circle, looking down.

I looked at him but didn't want to ask. "I worked with both of them," Larry said. "We were on the same squad."

Cliff stared at Larry for a moment. "Are you gonna be ok to work this?" He asked him.

"Yeah," Larry said. "I'm ok."

But he didn't look it.

Cliff didn't have much—both officers were on a call of a disturbed man who refused to be treated by Fire-Rescue. The paramedics let him go. Half an hour later, residents heard someone screaming, and the two were called back to the same area and encountered the disturbed individual. Minutes later, the officers were found dead. They were shot with their own weapons. The shooter, Charlie Street, was a huge man, and though he might have been "mentally disturbed," he wasn't crazy. To kill two police officers, you must possess the strategical savvy to disarm one and then shoot the armed one *first*. That takes some fast thinking and planning.

I got sent to Jackson to see what the story was with Strzalkowski, who apparently was in very grave condition. The rest of the squad went to the scene, off of Biscayne Boulevard in North Miami Beach. As I got there, I saw a familiar face—it was Marty Brenner, one of our Psych Services counselors. He had his arm around a young woman, whose head was down, extremely tense. Strzalkowski's wife, I assumed, and I was right. They walked briskly to a waiting room. My beeper went off just then and I called Cliff.

"Ram, Marty Brenner will be arriving there with Strzalkowski's wife. Just be aware they are there. Boles is a forty-five." 45 was our radio signal for a deceased person. "When you're done finding out about Strzalkowski, find out where Boles is. You've got the body."

Being assigned the body means that you search the entire corpse for wounds. You note the location of each one. To determine body warmth and the level of rigor mortis, you feel the body—limbs and the neck area—and note the conditions on your Medical Examiner preliminary report. We called that an "M.E. sheet". You looked carefully for trauma and documented each wound as well. Finally, you listed and collected whatever clothing and personal property was with the victim.

I spoke briefly to Brenner and asked if he had any updates on Strzalkowski's condition.

"I have," Marty said. "Not good at all."

I nodded and headed off to find Boles. He had been pronounced dead on arrival, and his body was on a gurney in one of the triage shower rooms. I counted seven bullet wounds altogether, two of which were in the face. I tried not to think of him as a fellow police officer. This was just another dead body. Then, before I left, I looked into a large paper bag on the floor by the gurney.

Inside was his uniform. His brown gown.

Somehow, going through his uniform, documenting the damage to the fabric from the bullet holes, and inventorying every pen and coin in his pockets, was a harsher task than examining his corpse. My beeper went off again. Strzalkowski was dead, too.

The trial went four months, with various psychiatrists testifying back and forth on Street's mental capacity. You find out all kinds of things about people during investigations, and trials, and sometimes you wish you didn't know. The night of the shooting was Richard Boles' last night in uniform. The next day, he was supposed to hang that brown gown in the closet and start as a detective in Robbery, right down the hall from our Homicide office.

Street's attorneys tried desperately to keep him out of the electric chair, but after his conviction on two counts of First-Degree Murder and several other related crimes, the jury recommended death with a 12-0 vote.

Five years later, a fight broke out in the exercise yard of Florida State Prison in Starke, where Death Row is. Charlie Street and another death row inmate were stabbed to death.

On the night of April 27th, 1990, my phone rang, and it was the midnight shift detective at the Homicide Office. That detective was assigned suicides and accidentals only during midnights. If a homicide came in, his job was to call out the on-call team, and that was us. The information was brief, and delivered quickly.

"Nyberg, you guys have a police shooting." That could mean anything. Before I could ask for details, he gave me the Northeast District address, and said, "County officer shot. I don't know his condition." I dressed quickly and got there to see Cliff pacing nervously just inside the yellow tape. Several marked units were on the scene, and one had several officers standing around it.

Cliff looked at me intensely.

"Ram, the officer is Joseph Martin. Larry Martin's kid. He's a 45."

He gave me a second to let that sink in. Lieutenant Larry Martin was one of our Homicide lieutenants. Cliff pointed at the green-and-white with all the brown gowns standing around it.

"The subject is in that car. You're my only one here. We need a confession. That's your lead."

I swallowed hard and nodded. God, I thought. I saw Larry Martin every morning at the office. I wasn't even aware that he had a son on the department. Now, he's dead. I walked over to the police cruiser. Several of Joseph Martin's squad members had the car surrounded, and inside, handcuffed in the back seat, was a dirty, miserable looking white male with blood trickling down his face.

"We found him hiding under a car a few blocks away," one of the officers told me. "K-9 had to get him out."

It was clear from the looks on their faces that they had gotten the news—their squad mate was dead. I knew what a squad mate was, and it wasn't just a "co-worker." You depend on each other for your very survival. You have experiences together that do not occur in any other profession. Your squad mate is your brother or sister.

I looked at the guy and opened the door to the cruiser. He saw me, in my dress shirt and tie. Clearly, the arrest had not gone well for him. He had encountered several enraged officers, who were felt in danger once they found him, and he had encountered a pretty excited German Shepherd during his capture, too. Step one was getting a waiver of Miranda. This confession statement, if I could get it, was crucial.

"What's your name?"

"Michael Griffin." He looked up at me with begging eyes. "Will you be my friend?"

I looked at him and resisted the urge to just walk away and let the squad have him. And while that would have been satisfying,

I knew what was coming. Griffin's bloodied face turned briefly into a crystal ball in which the immediate future was reflected: A suppression hearing, then a trial, with me testifying in both. How I handled this, at that very moment, could make or break the case we would have against him.

"Sure, I told him. I'll be your friend." My stomach churned as I nodded reassuringly to him.

"Ok," he mumbled.

"But you'll need to work with me on that. I need you to talk to me. This might be the last time you get an opportunity to tell your side of the story. Do you understand?" He stared at me intensely.

"Everyone from here on in will tell you to shut up. But I'm here to listen. Ok?"

He nodded. "Ok."

His cuffs had to come off, so he could check off the boxes on the Miranda form and sign it.

I turned to Officer Michael Malone, who was standing behind me. "We need to get him out and uncuff him."

"Sure, no problem."

Malone and another of Joseph Martin's squad mates grabbed Griffin and all but threw him out of the cruiser. After he landed with a thud on the grass, they uncuffed him quickly and shoved him back in the back seat. This was going to be a challenge. Griffin stayed quiet for a few moments, not looking at me. I reminded him that I was his friend, and that I was going to listen to every word he said.

We went through the Miranda form line by line while Malone kept the flashlight trained on the paper for him to see. Finally, he checked the "yes" next to the question, "Are you now willing to answer my questions without having an attorney present?" Another "yes" and then a signature.

Griffin told me the story. He and two other guys in the car were stopped after they did a burglary. Griffin was on probation, and he told one of them, "I can't go back to prison." As Joseph Martin approached the car, Griffin opened fire. Martin was wearing a vest, but a bullet struck him barely an inch above the top of it, and entered his throat. He was able to return fire and wound one of Griffin's companions. Lieutenant Larry Martin's son died on the scene.

We won the suppression hearing and won the trial. The other two subjects were sentenced to thirty years, and Griffin was sentenced to death. What I remember most, though, was seeing little nine-year-old Joey Martin, Jr., Joseph's son, all dressed up in a suit every day at the courthouse, bravely watching the whole thing. I couldn't get the little boy's face out of my mind for a very long time.

You never forget where you were at certain times—JFK, September 11th, the Challenger explosion... we connect sudden, dramatic news with the moment we were in.

I vividly remember where I was on January 3rd, 1992. I was at my parents' house in Saga Bay, down in old South District. My boys, who were six and four years old, were spending time with Grandma. We were all casually talking as the kids played, and paying limited attention to the TV. Then the news came on with the newscaster's words, "Police officer killed".

My attention turned to the TV then, and there was a photo of Steve Bauer, my friend from the North Miami Police Department. Mom and Dad knew him too. Steve had been over at the house several times for the annual flag football game we had; my friends and I played the "Birthday Bowl" for some twenty years. Steve a few other North Miami guys loved it. Steve was voted MVP two years in a row. This couldn't be. Steve was the eternal prankster, full of piss and vinegar and positive energy. But there he was, and now the female newscaster was saying his name: "Officer Steven Bauer, shot and killed during an off-duty security detail at Kislak National Bank..." and then, shots of the bank, the yellow tape. I stood there in disbelief. The subjects were still at large.

Later, at the Homicide Office, *everyone* was called in to work with North Miami. In fact, several departments offered their help, and we had a task force that amounted to a small army to hunt down Steve's killers. Just as with Richie Boles, I found out things I wish I hadn't known. The briefing went through the shooting step by step, so we understood what we were dealing with. Steve was working the opening of Kislak bank that morning. Part of his job was to escort the tellers, with their trays of cash, out to the drive-through booths. Four subjects came out and ambushed him, opening up with two different weapons. The subjects took the cash trays and fled. One of the tellers held Steve in her arms while the others rushed to call 9-1-1. Steve asked them if *they* were ok. Then he said, "It's getting dark."

Steve was probably dead before he got to Parkway but they waited until he got to the ER to pronounce him.

Dozens of us worked night and day without days off. Towards the end of what seemed like an endless fifteen days, we teamed up with the North Miami detectives, most of whom were working so much they weren't able to attend Steve's funeral. It was an odd way for me to be reunited with my friends Don Slovonic and Bill Craig. We were all working double shifts, but I felt bad for these guys. They were very close to Steve, and they hadn't even been given time to grieve. Donny was the more outgoing of the pair, and Craig, the quieter, more reserved type. Donny also had a reputation for being clumsy—breaking or dropping things—and in police work you never live this type of reputation down.

There were so many leads being disseminated that we were starting to cross over each other and duplicate our work. A lot of information had come in on the cars that were used, and who one of the subjects might be. The manhunt was the fiercest, most intense I have ever been involved with. Donny, Bill, and I went on about five leads that night, and the last was a very nice lady who lived on the west side of North Miami. We knocked on her door at about 9pm, and it was dark in front of her house, so Donny had his big Kel-lite flashlight with him.

"You know, this is the third time the police have come to my house for the same thing." We apologized, but we needed to hear it again, whatever it was she saw that day outside the bank. She was happy to tell it again and sat us down at a coffee table. In the center of the table was this beautiful glass swan sculpture. Donny sat with the flashlight down, between his legs. As we wrapped up the conversation, we thanked the lady, and Donny brought the flashlight up as he stood—it hit the sculpture and smashed one of the swan's wings into splinters.

All four of us froze, and Donny covered his mouth. Then he scrambled to pick up some of the shards of glass.

"Oh—I am *so sorry*!" Donny said.

The woman tried not to look distraught. She just pursed her lips, and said, "Um, well, it's alright. It's just an object."

We excused ourselves with Donny issuing baleful apologies on the way out. Once she closed the door and we were back out by the street, Bill Craig, who barely ever cracked a smile, broke into hysterics, literally rolling on the hood of their car. All three of us were laughing, but I thought Bill might need oxygen, he was so stricken with hysterics. I think Donny and I laughed more at Bill's laughing than at the Donny's destruction of the poor woman's swan. In the dark mood following Steve's murder, it was as if Steve had reached out with one more prank, and it was just what we needed.

Less than a week later, we had all four subjects in custody. The investigation had been so intense, with so many twists and turns—including a visit by one of the shooters to a Santeria priest—that it would take another book to cover it all. My partner, Greg Smith, did a masterful job in the interview room—he was so damned good at getting people to talk—and got a confession from Leonardo Franqui, the point man of the group of Steve's killers. One of the group, Pablo Abreu, entered a guilty plea and accepted a life sentence. The rest of the crew, Franqui, Fernando Fernandez, Pablo San Martin, and Ricardo Gonzalez, were tried, convicted, and sent to Death Row.

Getting past Steve's death was hard. At the funeral, they played his favorite song, Rod Stewart's *Forever Young,* and we all watched his three kids and his widow, Caroline, walk out down the aisle behind his casket as it played.

Like so many things that change with a profound experience. That song isn't just a song anymore- it is, and will always be, the smiling, mischievous face of my friend Steven Bauer.

Chapter Twenty-Three

The Squad
My "gang" growing up consisted mainly of five people. One was my friend Don Wells, who was two years older than me and lived across the street. The other was Jon Glatstein, whose parents were good friends with mine. We were together a lot, back and forth at each other's homes, and of course, out on the boat, which, at one time, Jon's dad and mine owned together. The other three were the Ross brothers: Robert, Jon, and Richard, in descending order of age. Richard was a year younger than me, so I was kind of the in-between occasional sibling. I spent a lot of time at their house. All told, we were all familial enough for our parents to scold any of us, individually or together, and this happened frequently. Pre-teen boys, left on their own to find things to do on summer afternoons, can wreak all kinds of havoc. Though we were pretty good at violating various parental rules and boundaries, we mostly played endless games of touch football, army, hide and seek, and variations of all three. We sometimes fought, like brothers, but I knew one thing: If I ever was really in trouble, any one of these guys would come to my aid, and I would do the same for them.

1992 was a momentous year, for two major reasons. One was Hurricane Andrew, which struck Miami-Dade County on August 24th. The first, however, was my leaving rotational homicide and going to the Cold Case Squad.

That was not the squad's original name. Back in 1982, one of the rotational squads got a case of an 11-year-old girl, Stacey Weinstein. The little girl was found by her father, raped and shot in his townhouse, after he had gone out to do some errands. It was a horrendously busy time for our Homicide office at the time. The Colombian drug wars were in full swing, and crime in general was rampant in south Florida. The squad needed time to work this high-profile case, one in which the Department's higher ups were constantly clamoring for information to feed to politicians and the media. Drug dealers got killed every day. 11-year-old girls did not.

The problem was, Homicide could ill afford to take a squad out of rotation. The other squads were swamped enough as it was. The command staff came up with another idea: put together a special squad, comprised of one senior investigator each from five different squads, to exclusively work the Stacey Weinstein case. Five squads would simply have to tolerate being one man short. It worked out better than losing an entire squad, during the seemingly endless blitzkrieg of murders coming through the door. Those five guys were given the time to focus on the Weinstein case without interruption. The strategy worked: Stacy Weinstein's killers were identified and arrested; two Stanley Steemer employees who had seen the girl alone in the home and posed as having an appointment there. Marvin Weinstein, her father, had been the prime suspect before that, and was now able to grieve his daughter without the added burden of being suspected of killing her.

The cases were still coming in hot and heavy, so the powers-that-be came to a revelation: Why not keep the Stacy Weinstein squad together, to work cases that have been denied attention due to the heavy workload? They would call it the "Pending Case Squad." The closure of Stacey's case made big news, and the follow-up stories in local media thought the Pending Case Squad found the squad's creation to be newsworthy as well. Someone at the *Miami Herald* nicknamed it the "Cold Case Squad," and the name stuck.

I was happy to get my promised slot on the team in 1992. With seven years in rotation under my belt, my sons were seven and four years old. Cub Scouts and little league were already a part of their lives, and while I was a pretty decent detective, I was doing a bang-up job as an absent father. Cold Case meant the 7a-3p shift, with Saturdays and Sundays off. We were focused on our cases, and we worked them hard. Rather than chaotic trips down frothing rapids, we could afford to paddle in calm, flat waters to do our jobs. We had more time to spend with family.

David Rivers was our squad Sergeant, and there were three other detectives: Greg Smith, Jerry Crawford, and John LeClaire. They all knew me, but other than Greg—who had been assigned with me on the Liberty City prostitute murders—we had never worked closely together. Rivers made no bones about telling me that one of the reasons I had been accepted in Cold Case was predicated on good reports from Greg during our time together. I don't know anyone who didn't love Greg. He loved his work, because for him, it was never work. He loved talking to people more than any human being I've ever known. He would talk to anyone, a bum on the street, a multimillionaire, and he would talk to them the same way. No one got special treatment, no one got talked down to either. Most of us had nicknames in police work, and Greg was no different; he—much like Don Slovonic—seemed to attract calamity and peril all the time. Things broke in his hands, even sometimes when he was only in close proximity. There were dozens of stories of electrical failures, fax machines that ground to a halt, and a camera flash unit that sparked and fizzled to its death when he was doing nothing more than holding it for a crime scene tech. Like the cartoon character, "Ziggy", mechanical things were in great peril when Greg was nearby. Once, one of Greg's cases was featured on a true crime detective TV show, and it was being filmed in Canada. They had to truck in palm trees, to make the set look like a Miami street, and as they were getting things ready, one of the trees fell and hit him in the head. It was only a partial blow, but when he told us the story, we were in hysterics—ol' Ziggy had to be the only person in history to be struck by a falling palm tree in fucking *Canada*.

Jerry "Crawdad" Crawford was a Maryland-bred country boy who had spent another lifetime in law enforcement up that way in Prince George County and other agencies before moving to Florida. He loved a glass of Jack Daniels and a Creedence Clearwater song, and—like the rest of the group—was easy to work with. John LeClaire was a former Marine who had lost his dad at the age of 17. He wound up in Viet Nam as a supply clerk, but, as he told it, got involved in a firefight in Da Nang, during a VC attack on their base. Nothing John said was ever delivered without a smile or a laugh. He was as easygoing and positive as anyone I've ever known, and he would jump in and help with any lead any time you asked. John's wife Linda was several years younger than him and a graduating classmate of mine at Palmetto Senior High. Our school was so big that I never knew her then. It was during the ten-year reunion of Palmetto's class of '75 that I spotted John and came up to him.

"What the hell are *you* doing here, John?" I asked him.

He was as surprised as I was. Then he pointed at Linda. "It's her reunion!"

Who the hell would have known?

There are case file boxes in the police department's records storage warehouse that say "Mookie" on them, because they have my old cold case files within. I got that nickname when Larry Wilkotz and I went up to New Jersey to interview a woman in one of his cases. She was an older black lady, and she stared at me when we sat in her living room.

"What are you?" She asked, "where you from?"

"I'm part Indian, ma'am. From India, on my mom's side."

"Oh, you're a *mookie!* That's what we call 'em up here. Uh-huh. You a mookie."

I glanced over at Larry, who was smiling and nodding, and that's when I knew that nickname would be following me around for a long time.

Any two of us, during a given case, could be "partners." Most often, it would depend on the case, and who was working what leads. The criteria that made an investigation a "cold case" was simple: If the original lead investigator was no longer in Homicide (transferred out, promoted, retired), and there was work to be done on the case, it fell under the Cold Case Squad's domain. Rivers would then assign it to one of us at the "lead." We would all review the case, and work would be doled out at the lead's discretion.

When I got to the squad in early 1992, the Bureau had just finished up on Steve Bauer's murder. My new squad was now immersed in Jerry Crawford's case of a missing British businessman.

Our work on the murder of Howard Bates was non-stop, until August 24th. Work came to an abrupt halt for *everyone,* law enforcement or not, early that morning when a Category Five hurricane named Andrew came ashore just a couple of miles south of my home in Suniland, with 165-mph winds that shattered the county into a state of paralysis. I had been in several hurricanes as a kid, but it had been twenty-five years since a storm of any significance had hit south Florida. Andrew made up for the absence.

There was no water or electricity for a month—longer in some neighborhoods—and some neighborhoods were so badly shredded by Andrew's ferocity they were unrecognizable. Everyone's cases were put on hold, and the entire department was on Alpha-Bravo, cleaning up, patrolling for looters, and trying to re-assemble our own houses and lives. It was an unforgettable experience, and the damage took well over two years to fully repair. In a few months, the roads got cleared, the electricity came back on and we were able to function enough to get back to our jobs—and to the perplexing murder of Howard Bates.

Alex Lucio had a great business idea. The United States had just launched Operation Desert Shield after Iraq's invasion of Kuwait. A Middle Eastern conflict and eventual war with Iraq was imminent and Lucio, along with his business partner Magaly ("Maggie") Carr, decided that disposable surgical and medical equipment would be an excellent business. He formed Disposamed, Inc. and its parent company Bolden Products, with Carr as the comptroller. Lucio bubbled positivity and Maggie Carr was attractive. Together, they got people interested in the products. They rented a warehouse in west Dade and showed interested parties the stacks upon stacks of boxes that were ready to be shipped to Saudi Arabia. Unbeknownst to the eager investors opening their checkbooks, however, the boxes were empty.

Whether Lucio and Carr started the venture out to rip people off is debatable. Either way, they realized that they could fatten their wallets without having a viable product to sell. They met a computer chip entrepreneur, Howard Bates, who was so enamored with Disposamed that he pumped over a million and a half dollars into it. Then, he got suspicious. Things weren't working out. Where were the profits? Where, in fact, were the *shipments?* He decided an audit was due.

Then, Howard Bates disappeared.

The last that Bates' wife and three children in Kent, England remembered, Bates boarded a plane for Miami to fire Carr and see what was going on with a company in which had once held so much promise. Missing Persons gave it to us after a few weeks of trying to find him.

Jerry Crawford had already contacted several executives from half a dozen companies that had provided another $1.5 million dollars to Lucio and Carr. They hadn't gone to the authorities because, as they put it, running into unscrupulous people was part of the cost of doing business in south Florida. They just wrote it off and never bothered to tell anyone that they had been defrauded. We had boxes of records from their communications and transactions with Bolden Products, so much that Jerry commandeered one of the interview rooms; we called it The Bates Room.

I accompanied Jerry and everyone else on various leads and a few out-of-town trips for the same purpose. Jerry and everyone on our squad was certain of one thing: Howard Bates wasn't alive. His profile as an honest businessman and devoted husband and father pretty much ruled out that he had met some hot looking *Latina* and took off for South America. Bates had correctly smelled a rat and was poised to expose Bolden for the massive fraud that it was. Lucio and Carr, we surmised, decided he had to go. We knew the *why*. The rest—who, what, when, how—were still unanswered. Did they hire a hitman, or do it themselves? And where was the body?

Part of our task was to rule out as much of these theories as we could—as we had done with Lynne Friend and Rilya Wilson—to have Howard Bates declared legally deceased.

In the process, Bates' wife told us all she knew about his Miami trip: Howard was to check into the LaQuinta hotel and have a serious meeting with Lucio about Maggie Carr and the troubling lack of progress with Bolden. She gave us his reservation data, and we went to the hotel. There, the manager showed us the security video footage of that day—February 6th, 1991. The video showed Howard Bates strolling into the lobby. Accordingly, there was Alex Lucio, greeting him and shaking his hand. No one at the hotel saw Howard Bates after that. No one in England heard from him, either. Background investigations on both Lucio and Carr didn't uncover much except for the fact that Maggie Carr was a CPA and had an ex-boyfriend named Jim Luge. Jim talked to us openly and told us that she recently had dated a guy named Wayne Merced. She dumped Wayne when he couldn't keep up with her "life-in-the-fast-lane" taste for night clubs and expensive clothes.

"Wayne was *obsessed* with Maggie," Luge told us. "Worshipped the ground she walked on. She dumped him about a year ago, but I think he would do anything to get her back."

An important part of declaring Bates' legally deceased was finding proof that he wasn't using his credit cards. We had to show that he wasn't charging up a bill in a Colorado ski resort or at a beach in Punta Cana, buying margaritas with some mid-life crisis *chiqadita*. We were stunned: we *did* find charges on his credit card well after his February 6th arrival in Miami. Someone had gone on quite a shopping spree at the Pembroke Mall in Broward, one that included the purchases of some high-end lingerie at Victoria's Secret. The midlife fling theory was suddenly resuscitated, but the Bates family wasn't buying it. Sheila Bates knew Howard to be the model husband and father, and while other men who have fallen off the log have been described the same way, the circumstances shouted "murder." Howard, Sheila told us, had a very important business meeting in London the Friday of that same week.

"He would not dream of missing that meeting," she said. Jerry and Greg paid a visit to Victoria's Secret and several other stores. The sales clerks at three stores remembered the buyer who had used Bates' green American Express card, a strikingly attractive brunette who said that the card belonged to "my British boyfriend," and that he was taking her on a vacation soon.

We used "photo lineups" in those days. This consisted of a manila folder with six cutout rectangles. You put your subject's picture in there with five others who bear as much resemblance as possible to the subject. If it's a young brunette, your other five photos need to be young brunettes, with similar hair length and style.

All three clerks, without hesitation, picked out Maggie Carr's photo. It was time to bring her in.

The mountain of circumstantial evidence that Jerry and our team were able to amass in the year and two months since Howard Bates' disappearance was convincing enough to declare him legally deceased. Then, the discovery of Maggie Carr's shopping spree was on the verge of pushing it over any remaining hump that might have existed. Maggie had an explanation. "I found the credit card on the floor of the warehouse," she told us. "I figured he had so much money, he wouldn't miss a thousand dollars or so."

We that we all knew this was bullshit. But it was enough to be a sliver of a possibility, just enough for us to hold off on charging her. Then, all the sifting through Bolden's corporate papers paid off—Jerry found a warehouse in North Carolina. It was supposed to be where all of Bolden's freshly manufactured products were stored and shipped to various buyers. A woman named Tanya Hartman had been hired to run things there. But there was nothing to run.

When Greg and Jerry went to North Carolina to talk to her, she confirmed that Bolden was a gargantuan fraud. Tanya admitted to being nothing but a paper manager, but she was hiding something else, and wouldn't come through with it. Finally, Tanya—a married woman—admitted that she was having an affair with Alex Lucio. During pillow talk, Lucio told her incredible news: the British guy who had invested so much money in Bolden was dead. They—Alex, Maggie, and Wayne Merced—-had killed him and gotten rid of the body. All the arduous, meticulous work had struck gold.

On December 11th, 1992, Jerry called a squad meeting to talk about arrest strategies. He was going to go in front of the Grand Jury the next morning during their 9am session. Once the Grand Jury came back with the indictment, our prosecutor, Kris

Rundle—a Brit himself—would go in front of a judge and have the indictment sealed.

We had to move quickly. Maggie and Alex had to be arrested at the same time and we would simultaneously pick up Wayne Merced. The phone calls to and from Wayne were frequent and prominent in the days before the murder but were absent in Maggie's phone records for months before and after the murder. We felt strongly that he knew something, if he wasn't involved directly. If any of them got word we had arrest warrants, we would risk one of them flying off to a place like Venezuela, a country that didn't have an extradition treaty with the United States. They certainly had the funds to do it.

We got some help from other squads and broke into teams. Jerry called from the courthouse: the indictment was in and sealed. He and Greg went to pick up Alex Lucio, John LeClaire and someone from another squad went to Maggie Carr's apartment, and I went with Detective Bill Saladrigas to pick up Wayne Merced. Merced was employed by a local natural gas company. When we found him, he was literally in a ditch installing a gas line in Miami Beach. It didn't take long to see that Wayne was a slow-witted individual with a sense of duty. We didn't talk much on the way back, but in general terms we told him we were investigating something pretty serious and that his name had come up. The way he looked out the window and swallowed from time to time told me that his insides were churning on that ride to the office.

In the interview room, Bill and I started explaining why he was there. Most detectives prefer to do their interviews alone. I know I did. We very rarely used the infamous "good cop, bad cop" routine that so many outsiders believe is the normal way for us to "interrogate." In truth, it's usually more effective when one person can establish rapport, read body language, and gain enough trust to get someone talking. Two detectives can certainly work a suspect, but most of the time, it was one. Bill and I were told to work on him, and we quickly agreed to do it together.

Getting a confession involves some important steps, starting with knowing your subject. Details about the person's background, education, culture, religion—anything and everything we can find out—gives us the footing we need in the interview room to progress towards a confession. Wayne Merced had a clean record: not so much as a traffic ticket. Murdering someone had to be something he had never dreamed of doing. By the time we got Wayne settled in an interview room and got him a Coke to drink, Greg and Jerry had already started talking to Alex, and had learned some important information about Wayne. Our three-pronged offensive was missing Maggie, but we launched into action.

Jerry gave Bill and me a quick but very useful briefing. Bill and I agreed on a basic approach. We would do the majority of the talking first; establish how well we knew our case, and how confident we were of his involvement. We would make sure we understood how much he loved Maggie, and how much she could influence him. We wouldn't give him a whole lot of opportunity to protest. It was right out of the *Reid School* and Kinesics Interview training I had been to years before; classic criminal interview tactics. Wear down the subject with your knowledge. Calmly deflect any protests or claims of "it's not me"—no yelling, no anger, no intimidation. After some time, when you notice a slight change in body language, move in closer, physically and literally. The subject starts to feel that there is little hope of his lies having any effect on the calm, confident professional in front of him. Create an atmosphere of hopelessness; it's fruitless to lie. Invite the confession, don't demand it. Watch body language some more. When they start to hang their head, swallow, tear up—the "buy" signs—you're close. Move in closer. Tell them it's the right thing to do. Tell them you understand. Tell them you know they are trying to make a difficult decision—tell them you know they are deciding whether or not to tell the truth.

From the outset, Bill Saladrigas and I flowed well together, and both silently felt that Wayne would crumble. We took turns telling Wayne how we found out about him. Bill would talk about one aspect of the case, and then I would describe another, about Maggie and Alex. At times, Wayne looked like he was at a tennis match, his gaze going from one side to the other. He offered up some weak protests:

"I don't know this British guy. I don't know who you are talking about."

We brushed it all aside and continued. "Wayne," I said, "You know better than that. And so do we."

"Do you know how much work we have done on this case, Wayne?" Bill asked. "For almost a year and a half, five of the most experienced detectives in the police department did nothing but work on this investigation, night and day."

Wayne stared.

"We have a whole room dedicated to this case. We have boxes of financial reports and records we've gotten from people who have done business with Maggie's company."

Bill and I looked at each other. "C'mon," I said. "We'll show you."

We walked Wayne over to the Bates Room and showed him the stacks of boxes. Most of them had "Bolden" or "Bates" written in magic marker on the side. Wayne's eyes widened when he looked around the Bates Room. We took him back to our interview room again and resumed.

"Wayne, you've never been in trouble in your life," we told him. "Maggie got you into this, we know that. Just tell us exactly how it happened."

Wayne looked down, then back up at us. Then he nodded. "It wasn't my idea. I didn't want to do it at first."

An hour later, Wayne had told us everything. Maggie called him and told him she needed him to do something for her. That's all he needed to hear. He met her. She told him the problem—a British man who might cause her and Alex to lose their fortune and go to prison.

"She told me that if I loved her," Wayne said morosely, "I would do this, and take care of the problem."

Wayne explained that Maggie pushed a bag across to the table to him. Inside the bag was a .357 magnum revolver. She told him when Howard Bates would be coming to the warehouse, and that Wayne should wait in the room for him to come in.

"I wasn't sure. She asked me if I was going to do it, or if she needed to."

Bill and I looked at Wayne intensely, all the while trying to hide our disbelief. Killing an innocent man, to win the approval of the girl he loved. It was as twisted a fairy tale as anything either of us had ever heard. But it was real.

"I agreed to do it."

Wayne told us how they were going to bring Bates in, and where he should hide.

"I waited behind the door. And when he came in, I did it. I shot him."

"Where?"

"In the head. Back of the head."

"How many times?"

"Once," Wayne said.

"I tried to leave. But Maggie told me that he was..." Wayne squirmed in his chair, looking down. Speaking softly, he said, "He was still alive. He was making noises. Maggie told me I couldn't leave without...um, finishing it. So I shot again."

"To stop him from suffering, Wayne?" I asked him.

Wayne nodded. "Yeah."

Wayne's gruesome work wasn't over. Maggie and Alex demanded his help in wrapping up the body in plastic and putting it in the trunk of Lucio's car. Finally, Wayne was told he could go. What happened to Bates' body?

Wayne shook his head. "Those two know. I wasn't part of that."

We took a quick break to get the stenographer ready to take Wayne's statement, and we found Jerry. I smiled at him.

"Wayne copped out," I told him, as Bill stood next to me.

Jerry clapped his hands together and he threw an arm around each of our shoulders. With one hand, he held his thumb and forefinger about two inches apart. "I'm gonna buy you guys a steak *this thick!*" He said with a relieved grin.

Things were progressing well in Greg's interview with Alex Lucio, too. "Ziggy's got Lucio wrapped around his finger," Jerry told us. "He's coming clean too."

If Alex Lucio thought *he* was good at talking, he had met his match. Greg was in his element that day, so much that I heard Lucio calling Greg's name from inside the interview room, some six hours after they started talking.

"Greg? Greg? Where did you go?" I heard Lucio call out.

I opened the interview room door and introduced myself. "He'll be back," I assured him. "He just went to take a leak I think."

"Ok, please," Lucio said, "He left me alone. I have to talk to him."

That's an investigator's dream scenario: a subject not only confessing but begging to tell you more. This hardly ever happens—unless you have Greg Smith on your squad. Greg squeezed every drop he could from Lucio. They had been in that interview room a good fourteen hours when they finally came out and walked into the stenos' office to do the sworn statement. He corroborated Wayne's story and put a few nails in Maggie's coffin too. After our unsuccessful attempt to find her that morning, she got wind of the indictment and fled.

Alex and Waye sealed Maggie's fate, but Alex wasn't done doing himself in: he agreed to take us out and show us where Howard Bates' body was buried. The irony of it was not lost on us when Alex took Greg and Jerry out to a swampy forest just a few miles west of our headquarters building on NW 25 Street. Howard Bates had been resting in the mud, damned near under our noses. The area now known as Doral hadn't grown up quite yet, and the area was still dotted with cow pastures and melaleuca-filled hammocks like the one Alex and Maggie had chosen to bury Bates' body. Swatting mosquitos, the three of them picked their way through bushes and puddles until Lucio pointed to the spot.

Imagine the surprise of the County personnel at Miami-Dade Water and Sewer when we told them we needed their help draining a swamp. They brought out a giant water vacuum truck and sucked up nearly a thousand gallons of water. Crime Scene joined Jerry in the messy detail, sifting and digging until a length of something wrapped in fabric peeked out of the black, sloshy earth. It bore a brand name, stamped into the material: Bolden Products. Inside the remains were partially broken up, and the fourteen months of decomposition, rain, and subterranean animal activity had done a fair amount of work. Still, all of Howard Bates' bones were recovered. The rear of Bates' skull was shattered.

A trial on a different case caused me to miss the dig; I would have loved to have taken part in getting the buried treasure after all the work we had done together. There are few feelings in life of closing a difficult case, and this one stands out as one of the toughest and longest investigations any of us had ever taken part in. The satisfaction was immense. It wasn't over, however. We still had Maggie out there somewhere, and we still had to get a win in court.

We got Maggie's face all over the news media and she was finally spotted living in a condo in Miami. We learned later that she had tried to run away to Colombia but she was too high maintenance for the lifestyle there. Maggie tried to convince us that Alex and Wayne had done everything themselves. This made no sense. What would bring Wayne Merced into the mix to do something this drastic? Only his undying love and devotion for Maggie.

Alex and Wayne both avoided the death penalty with guilty pleas and 40-year prison sentences, along with their requirement to testify against Maggie Carr. The first trial ended with a hung jury. We felt bad that Sheila Bates and her three terrific kids had to endure this all again, but they were troopers and steeled themselves for another try. The second trial got the conviction we were looking for. All told, it was four long years from the day we put Maggie in handcuffs to the time we heard the judge sentence her to life in prison.

That day, Judge Leslie Rothenberg surprised everyone by having Jerry, Greg, John, and me stand up in the courtroom. She explained to the jury just how hard we had worked to bring this case to closure, and we were given a thunderous ovation. I have never seen anything like that happen in a courtroom before or since.

Greg and I shared a couple of drinks with Howard's sons, Matt and Joe, at the hotel bar where they were staying on Miami Beach during the trial.

"We're forever grateful to you blokes," said Matt, raising his glass to us.

I figured being called a "bloke" was a favorable thing. I'll take that, from the victim's son, even over the applause in the courtroom.

Homicide work was all about team effort, and Cold Case was no different. Every lead that came in that was compelling enough for us to pull the case and review it, was discussed as a group. We all had input, and depending on what was going on at the time, we would typically pair up to work things. Like rotation homicide, there were usually several cases being worked at a time, and it was no different while we were involved in big efforts like Bates.

One of our responsibilities was to be Homicide's ambassador when detectives came in from other agencies to find witnesses or run down leads. We would do our best to be their guides, take them around, and of course accompany them to a suitable watering hole at days' end. So, when Austin, Texas PD Homicide called us to tell us about a murder fugitive that was coming to Miami on a cruise ship, we were pretty sure we would be helping them out and entertaining them.

"He's on his honeymoon cruise," the Austin detective told us. "We found out he was on board when they ran everyone for warrants because the ship was leaving U.S. waters. The ship is at sea now, and the next stop is Miami. Would you guys meet the ship and make the arrest?"

Of course, we would be glad to, we told him. When would they be flying in to do the interview?

"We won't be coming. We were hoping y'all could do the interview for us."

This was unheard of. I told John LeClaire about the phone call, and he was just as perplexed. You never handed off your subject to another agency to interview. To begin with, a murder investigation is something you *live* on a daily basis. You invest a lot of work, energy, time, and connection with family members. Calling the feeling "possessiveness" wouldn't be far off. If you are about to do something as momentous as arresting your subject, *you* want to be a part of that, especially with an opportunity to get a confession.

John and I could not imagine giving that opportunity to someone else. Besides, how could detectives from another agency know the areas, the streets, the situation as well as you? How in the hell could we interview a murder subject in a case that happened in Austin, Texas, a place neither I nor John had ever been?

"We're going to FedEx you the case file," the Austin investigator went on, "so you can study it and get familiar with everything and everyone."

As astonished as we were, John and I shrugged and decided we were up for the challenge. This was going to be new territory for us for sure. True to their word, a large case file arrived at our office via FedEx three days later with some notes from the investigator, wishing us luck. John and I studied it backwards and forwards. We got familiar with the people, read the witness statements, even looked at maps of Austin so we had a general understanding of the layout of where things happened and where people lived. The victim was shot while three of four friends were out target shooting. As it turned out, there was a love triangle situation, and the victim was pre-designated as one of the targets. We continued this crash course up to the night before the ship's arrival.

John and I met disembarking passengers at the cruise terminal, armed with a Miranda waiver form and a photo of our wanted subject. We had been in touch with the ship's bursar and security people beforehand, so they knew what was happening. To say the new bride was "surprised" when we stopped and handcuffed her new honey would be quite the understatement.

At the Homicide office he waived his right to counsel, and John and I started in on the interview. A couple of hours later we had a full confession. Our colleagues in Austin were thrilled, to say the least. We were pretty happy about it too, even though it didn't count on our books. The success we had in the interview room confirmed the concept most investigators know: getting confessions is mostly an art form. The facts and circumstances of the case itself are important, but not as crucial as being able to connect with the subject.

Four months later, I was contacted by the Texas prosecutor for trial. They flew me out to Austin (on my birthday, no less) and told me to wait at my hotel room for someone to call and come pick me up to testify. An hour passed, then two, then three. I dozed, watched TV, read, and watched TV some more. Then I got a phone call. It was the prosecutor.

"Thanks very much, Detective, but the case pled out. We're going to get you a taxi back to the airport." And just like that, I was on a plane home. From the moment we got the case, to the day the jury said "guilty", I never even met the other detectives, not to mention missing the post-trial beer and Texas barbecue I had been looking forward to.

One of Cold Case's biggest closures occurred in 1993, while we were in the middle of Bates investigation. Someone called the Crimestoppers anonymous tip line and put the caller in touch with us. I was the first one to speak with the caller, and he said, "I can solve the Abraham murder for you guys." He was either full of shit, or we were going to get really busy very soon. The high-profile Abraham case had been unsolved for eight years.

Everyone who grew up in Miami remembers the name Anthony Abraham. His car dealership dominated the busy corner of Southwest 8th Street and 42nd Avenue and was one of the biggest dealerships in Florida. No one could turn on a TV or a radio in the 60's and 70's and not hear an advertisement for "Anthony Abraham Chevrolet." A philanthropist and highly respected member of Miami's Lebanese-American community, Abraham and his wife Genevieve donated generously to causes and community needs of all kinds. All five of the couple's children were adopted. Abraham and Genevieve Abraham personified the title "pillars of the community."

The Abrahams closest friends were Sam and Bea Joseph, an elderly couple of Lebanese descent. Sam and Bea had a daughter with a deadly illness and Anthony and Genevieve financed the medical treatments for the girl. The Josephs lived in a modest apartment building they owned near 67th Avenue, about a five-minute drive from Abraham Chevrolet. Sam, a retired builder in his seventies, was also the building's manager.

On December 4th, 1984, friends of the Abrahams became concerned when Genevieve Abraham didn't show at a restaurant for a dinner date. Anthony was out of town on a business trip and couldn't be reached. The couple remembered that she was going to stop at the Joseph's first, so they went there. To their horror, the couple found Genevieve, Sam, and Bea dead in the living room. They had all been shot.

The murders shocked the city. Who would kill three seemingly innocent and harmless elderly people? Genevieve Abraham was found seated in a chair when she was shot in the head. Sam and Bea were found on the floor. At that time, Dave Rivers headed up a rotational squad and the lead was Billy Venturi. Their squad, along with anyone else who was available for leads, worked the case tirelessly amidst an uproar of news media sensation and speculation: was Anthony Abraham involved in some Middle Eastern underworld scheme? Miami was flooded with cocaine murders at the time. Could it be that this highly respected man and his family were the targets of some ruthless cartel hitman? Every theory one could imagine was being splashed all over newspapers and TV broadcasts. Through it all, a grief-stricken Anthony Abraham conducted himself with dignity and cooperated with our people fully. He was as clueless as to the motivation of the murders as everyone else. Venturi's lead list eventually got shorter and shorter—he had exhausted everything and looked under every rock. The case went cold.

The phone call I took in March of 1992 from a guy who called himself "Ralph", was the kind you covered the mouthpiece and waved everyone on the squad over while you took notes. Ralph wanted to meet us in a public place.

"Don't come looking like detectives, ok?" was Ralph's request. He told us how he would be dressed, and what kind of ball cap he would be wearing so we could identify him. We arranged to meet Ralph at a Denny's restaurant the next day. We all dressed down, jeans and t-shirts, polos. To make sure we weren't getting set up in some way, Jerry and I planned to sit with Ralph while Greg would sit by himself a couple of tables away, acting as a lone patron and keeping an eye on us and whomever else might show up.

Within ten minutes of the conversation, Ralph had us hanging on every word. His sister's brother-in-law did the murder. His name was Luis Rodriguez. Luis and another guy, Manuel "Tony" Rodriguez, were together at the crime scene. Tony, Ralph explained, was like a surrogate older brother to Luis. Ralph knew all this from his conversations with Luis, who confided in him a year or so after the murders. The three elderly people, he said, were killed in a robbery. Manny, he said, would have been the mastermind.

"He's a cold motherfucker," Ralph told us.

"I have to ask you something," I told Ralph. "Something that you will be asked again, probably several times over. For sure, a prosecutor will want to know. And if your information pans out, a jury will want to know too."

Ralph nodded, "Ok…"

"Why are you coming forward with this *now*? Why eight years later?"

Ralph's response was like something out of an episode of Twilight Zone.

"I was in a terrible car accident," he started. "I was almost killed—I was in a coma for two weeks. After I came out of it, I started to question why I was given a chance to live. That's when I realized, that with this second chance to live, it must be so that I can tell the truth about this case."

That was easy enough to research, and the accident and coma all turned out to be true. Accepting the spiritual aspect of his explanation was up to the individual.

Ralph was short on some details about names, places, and times, but that was reasonable enough—the guy had been in a coma. He met with us several more times, one of them with me at a Burger King on Bird Road, just east of the Palmetto Expressway. As we sat there talking, he looked out the window.

"Life can be pretty ironic, right?" he said, nodding to the billboard on the opposite side of the street. It blared, "Abraham Chevrolet".

With the Howard Bates investigation in full swing, it took us a while to start piecing things together. In Miami, "Rodriguez" is the equivalent of "Smith" or "Jones" in terms of commonality, and we had to make sure we had the right ones. By August 1993 we had a good handle on everyone and where they were. Manuel "Tony" Rodriguez was sitting in prison in central Florida serving time on a host of felonies. Luis was a family man, living in suburban Orlando with his wife and young daughter.

By this time, Sgt. David Rivers had been re-assigned from our Cold Case squad as Homicide's Admin Sergeant, and Sgt. Al Singleton took over as our supervisor. Al was a former Marine and Viet Nam Veteran who was skinnier than I was, and I've always been on the slim side. His wiry frame got him the nickname "Blade." Al was astute, direct, and practical. Though he would joke and laugh with any of us, he was all about the business at hand. He didn't tolerate ineptitude or slovenly work. He was even tempered, and never did anything to extreme.

"Everything in moderation," he said once, when we were all talking about drinking.

I loved working for Blade because you always knew where he was coming from. There was never any hidden agenda—what you saw was what you got. We put together a large list of leads we had to accomplish for our trip to Orlando, but the most critical part was finding Luis Rodriguez and getting him to talk to us. A confession from Luis was our main goal. We knew little about the guy, except that Ralph had characterized him as the follower, and Tony (Manuel) as the leader. Getting Luis to cooperate would throw open the doors to solving everything.

The county rented us an SUV and on August 7th, 1993, Blade, Greg, Jerry and I headed up the turnpike to Orlando. The most recent address we had for Luis was a small three-bedroom home in a middle-class neighborhood near some older industrial park areas. It was the kind of area you would find boat repair places, Wendy's restaurants, and cheap hotels.

To our surprise—and delight—Luis appeared at the door within moments of us knocking. He was a medium built guy with a small moustache. In the background we could hear a toddler running around the living room. His eyes went to each one of us, standing there in our ties.

"Luis," Greg said, "We're from Miami-Dade Police. We're homicide investigators. We'd like to have a little of your time."

He nodded, then said the words that took our breath away: "I knew you guys would show up one day." We could all but smell the end zone.

Jerry and Greg arranged with the Orange County Sheriff's Office for us to get an interview room. They went there with

Luis—who went without the slightest resistance—while Blade and I ran down a couple of other leads. After a few hours, Jerry beeped us.

"Come and get us," he said, trying to hide the excitement in his voice. "Luis gave us a full confession."

Jerry hired a local steno and got Luis' detailed confession in a sworn statement. Luis stayed locked up at Orange County Jail. We would go pick him up in the morning and head home, where we would book him into the Dade County Jail. On the ride to the Embassy Suites in Orlando, Jerry and Greg filled us in on everything.

Tony contacted Luis and told him where they could get some quick cash. Tony, it turned out, lived in the same building Sam and Bea Joseph owned. He had seen Sam collecting rent and most people paid him in cash. Tony had seen Sam walking around "with fat rolls of cash," Luis remembered. The day of the murder had been rent collection day, and Tony recruited Luis to go with him. They found the door to the Joseph's apartment slightly ajar and pushed their way in. Tony had a gun and corralled the three elderly people into the living room. He demanded that Sam get him all the money. He got frustrated that Sam wasn't moving fast enough, and shot him, then Bea. At that point, Tony tossed the handgun to Luis, who was standing guard over Genevieve Abraham. The last thing Genevieve Abraham saw in her life was Luis Rodriguez pointing a gun at her head.

There was no Lebanese business feud, or any other complex motive behind the killings, as so many people had speculated. Genevieve Abraham was simply in the wrong place at the wrong time.

You have a choice in police work; you can sit and try to analyze why someone would so mindlessly and viciously snuff out the lives of three completely innocent people who posed no threat at all to them. You can simply accept the fact that there are monsters in our midst. These are not the funny-looking monsters you were afraid of hiding under your bed as a kid, but *real* monsters, cloaked in the veil of human skin, monsters so inexplicably heartless and brutal that they will kill anyone, children, the helpless...anyone, just because it satisfies them or brings them financial gain. That was the way we—homicide investigators—-saw our world. Trying to make sense of it any other way was fruitless. Trying to delve into and somehow fix a person's childhood and upbringing was not our domain.

What we *did* do was celebrate our victories, even though we weren't completely done. There was the unknown still ahead—possible plea agreements or trials. But right now, all we knew was that we closed a huge case that was for nine years collecting dust. It was what our squad was all about—what our *job* was all about.

We changed clothes at the Embassy Suites and ended up at some nearby place with the words "bar and grill" in its name and clinked our beers together. It was a toast to the victims, and to old man Abraham, who would be more than thrilled when he heard the news back in Miami.

Whenever Ziggy and I would take long driving trips, we played "name that tune" to kill the time. Whoever was in the passenger seat put the car radio on "scan" and when either one of us recognized a song, we would pause it there, and challenge the other player. You only had to name the artist to get a point. Greg and I were always closely matched—he was five years my senior, so he got me pretty regularly on early to mid-60's songs, and I was better on the music a decade later. Sometimes I would win, sometimes he would, but it was always close. After about an hour or so at the bar, recounting the day's remarkable achievements, Blade approached me. He was enjoying being a part of the revelry and had clearly strayed from his philosophy of "everything in moderation."

"I hear," Al said, standing in front of me with a very buzzed countenance, "that you're quite the champion at 'Name that Tune.'"

I grinned. "Well, I'm ok...Ziggy's pretty good too. I guess he told you about our contests."

Blade nodded and reached over and grabbed a napkin from a stack on the bar. "Well," he said with a smirk, "I *challenge* you." He swung the napkin across my face, back and forth in an old-world slapping challenge.

I damned near spit out a mouthful of beer and was laughing too hard to respond; it was so completely out of character for him. Seeing him that tipsy and offering up the comical challenge was too much. I managed to croak out, "I accept!" It was decided that the contest would begin on our four-hour ride back to Miami the next day, providing Luis waived extradition to our County. It would end once we pulled into the Headquarters building.

The Blade hadn't been so drunk that he didn't remember his hilarious challenge. Luis waived extradition and we picked him up at the Orange County Jail. Luckily Luis was a compliant, even pleasant passenger. Being in a car for four hours with someone you've just arrested for murder has the potential to be uncomfortable, if not a downright annoyance. We told Luis the rules. We were going to keep the leg brace on him. He wouldn't be able to run. We would cuff him in the front, so that when we stopped for lunch, he could eat a sandwich without any problem.

"I'm not going to be any trouble," he said quietly. He looked relieved, even though it was a near certainty that he would be going to prison for the rest of his life.

Once we hit the turnpike, the contest was on, with Blade and me in the front seat and Jerry and Greg sitting on either side of Luis in the middle seat. It went back and forth, Blade getting a point, then me, and when I glanced back at the middle seat, Luis was smiling, enjoying the whole thing. At one point, we weren't sure of the score, but Luis had been keeping track.

"Ram is up by one point," Luis said. "It's 21-20."

"Ok, Luis," Jerry said, "you wanna be the scorekeeper?"

"Yeah," he said with a smile, "I'll keep score."

I suppose that beats looking out the window at the central Florida landscape and contemplating what life will be like away from your wife and little child. When we got back to Miami, I think I was ahead by a point or two, and Blade conceded. Luis kept score the whole time.

In every criminal case, one of the things a defense attorney does is explore the circumstances of the arrest and the treatment of the defendant while in police custody. If there is abuse or coercion, that can be enough to put that one kernel of doubt in a judge's mind during a motion to suppress a confession. Luis apparently told his defense counsel about the ride back from Orange County. At my deposition, his attorney asked,

"Detective, is it true that my client participated in a contest you all had amongst each other to correctly name songs on the radio?"

"Yes, that's true."

"And my client actually kept score of this game, correct?"

"Yes, that's right."

Luis' attorney wanted to establish that his client acted like a person confident in their own innocence. It was all moot—Luis' confession stood up to all Constitutional challenges, and he plead guilty. He agreed to testify against Tony and received a life sentence for each of the murders. Tony went to trial and was convicted on every count charged—Armed Burglary, Armed Robbery, and three counts of First-Degree Murder. During the sentencing phase, the jury voted 12-0 for a sentence of death on each conviction.

I know what it feels like to have my own cases go to trial and hear the jury say "guilty." It's a sweet feeling—the clock has ticked down to zero, and you finally *won*. Neither the murder of Howard Bates or the murders of Sam Joseph, Bea Joseph, and Genevieve Abraham were my cases. Every member of our squad, however, had put our backs into those investigations. We had spent countless hours away from our kids and our wives, time we couldn't get back. The closures of those cases, the relief and gratitude we saw on the faces of the Bates family members, on the face of Anthony Abraham, cannot be described. Experiencing that was the essence of our job. So they weren't "my" cases, but they damned well were *ours*.

Over the twenty-seven years I spent wearing the badge, I lost count of how many times people asked me, "why did you go into law enforcement?" I never could give them a clear answer. I had an inkling of why, but I could never explain it well. Now, though, I can point to cases like that, to my squad members, and to the faces of those family members, and I can say, "that's why."

EPILOGUE

The gathering at Hialeah Race Track on Sept. 13, 2007 was relaxed and fun. I was with a group of Realtors. I *was* a Realtor. I had to keep reminding myself that. Less than a year before, I had "pulled the pin" and stepped out of the Miami-Dade Police headquarters building as a civilian.

I was still getting used to the real estate office atmosphere. Everyone was so polite to each other. Cursing—while not completely outlawed—seemed to be frowned upon, because it was rarely heard unless you were having a private conversation with someone you had gotten to know. In my police life, I was used to coming in and people saying things like, "Hey asshole, when are you gonna close that case you've been milking for the last fucking month?" and shooting back with a similar expletive-filled remark. It was how we showed love for each other.

Today's outing at the racetrack was an office-sponsored "getaway" of sorts for anyone in the Coldwell Banker office who wanted to come. It was to forget the "stress" of everyday real estate work and unwind a bit. A choir practice, of sorts. It was nice. There were about twelve of us at the track, having margaritas and joking around. Some of us were placing a few bets and there was a long bank of closed-circuit TVs displaying readouts of the next race, the odds, the results of the last race, and so on. A couple of other monitors had the afternoon local channel news stations on.

That's when I saw it: a Miami-Dade Police Officer had been shot and killed. Three other officers were wounded. The officers had been pursuing a subject who had fled after a traffic stop; the guy ran into a house and started shooting at them.

Everything around me melted away and I watched the TV screen intently, trying to hear every word the news anchor was saying. The Realtors who I had been cavorting with, the horse races, the margaritas, it all just went out of focus. The TV anchor's words and the unfolding story had completely commandeered my attention. I found myself slowly pacing. Everyone else was oblivious to the news. I think one or two of my colleagues pointed at the screen and said something like, "Oh, isn't this horrible?" but I'm not sure because I had tuned them out. I was suddenly in "work" mode, and it wasn't preparing a marketing plan for a client's house. I became imbued with homicide detective energy; I was supposed to be out there, with those detectives, on the street. I was supposed to have my clipboard in hand, interviewing witnesses, attending the team briefing, getting leads assigned to me. One of my brothers was dead, and we—that is my former "we"—had to get to *work*. I was disoriented. I looked around at the rest of the group—they were smiling, laughing, drinking, betting. And there I was—after nine months of assimilating, learning how to be a Realtor, doing my best to blend into this new culture—suddenly feeling like a total stranger. I wanted to have my badge, tie, and gun again, and go help my team.

Officer Jose Somohano's killer was eventually corralled in an apartment complex in Broward County later that day. He opened fire again on our SRT officers and they returned fire, killing him. The 37-year-old Somohano left behind a wife and two children. I ended up leaving the racetrack early. I couldn't enjoy the day anymore.

I remained in real estate, and, unlike a lot of retired police officers, I remained in Miami. There was nothing pulling me anywhere else, and besides, real estate was suiting me. Miami—the sibling that had shared all the joys and sorrows with me—was now my partner in selling homes. Vivian and I divorced, but well before we knew that was going to happen did, we adopted a baby girl from Russia. I had a young daughter now, and my two sons were both out of the house. I wasn't leaving South Florida.

People talk about finding out "who" you are. There are books and self-help programs for this question, and I remember them being all the rage back in the early 80s. I think the more useful revelation is to discover *how* you are; that is, how you choose to *be*. Happiness, balance, and positivity are all choices, not happenstance. "Who" you are is the ongoing result of "how" you choose to be. At 27, I might have said, "I'm a homicide cop." At 66, I'm a teacher and a writer, but none of those things matter compared to how I choose to maintain my spirit. I believe we are a product of our life's choices, too. My nearly three decades of police work shaped and developed an important skillset: emotional resilience. The sailor who braves and endures a violent, stormy sea and arrives safely at port is still a sailor and doesn't remain terrified. He's grateful for his existence. He's also a better sailor.

The emotional resilience I mentioned is something that no one can train for. It follows no schedule or protocol that can be written down or hammered into policy. It is a deeply personal journey that develops only on the schedule of each individual's spiritual clock. In our job, we had to endure "the slow parade of tears" (to quote from Jackson Browne's poignant song, *Doctor, My Eyes*), and indeed, learn "how not to cry." The rest of Browne's song resonates in such intimate terms as to be familial. We are immersed in human events so traumatic that one can argue we are not "built" to survive them. Some of us, sadly, do not. But all of us carry with us the images and memories that have rained down upon us so heavily, without warning and without a manual explaining how to remedy the consequences. We are, in our own way "battle" veterans.

This is not to detract in any way the suffering of people with PTSD and other disorders caused by their upbringing, traumatic events, or chemical imbalances. I feel for those people. I was never in military combat. I never saw my friends blown up by a roadside bomb, but in my own abbreviated way, the things I dealt with in police work affected me. When I heard and read about the horrific murders of schoolchildren at Sandy Hook Elementary School, then at Marjory Stoneman Douglas High, and all the other places children have died so needlessly, I grieved for those little kids, their parents, and the survivors. But there was also a special place of understanding in my heart for the detectives and crime scene technicians who had to work that scene, count every projectile, document and photograph every wound on each body, and do it all without breaking down. I *know* that those images follow them around for their entire lives. I know that they cannot ever come close to forgetting what they did, what they saw. There are images you want to forget, but there are others that have shaped so much of your own personal history that you can never forget them.

During the trial of Michael Griffin, who shot and killed Joseph Martin, I saw little Joseph, Jr. all of eight years old, dressed up in a suit, bravely accompanying his mom to the suppression hearing and the trial itself. I felt for this boy so deeply that it kept me up at night. I went and talked to one of our counselors about it. I told him I don't cry at night, I just...stay up. It's like a thorn, sitting there, keeping me up with its nagging pain. I told him I felt like I had accumulated a lot of them.

"One day," the therapist told me, "you will retire. One by one, those thorns will come out. They might bleed a little bit when they do. You might be watching a movie and find yourself suddenly crying, and not knowing why. It might be that a thorn—maybe this one—is popping out."

They say you can't get the police officer "out of your blood." That, to some extent, is true. Every time I see a police officer, I immediately slow down a little to see if he or she is ok. I would, if I saw them in trouble, stop and do what I could to help. It's part of what you take with you when you leave, like the table centerpiece fancy banquet they tell you can take home. The food, drink and dancing of this banquet was over, and this was the centerpiece I took. But that keepsake doesn't define me—it reminds me of what I did, not who I am today. I have, like anyone who has spent as much time in police work as I have, "learned how not to cry." With each passing day and year, however, with each episode of *This is Us* I watch with my wife, tears come a little easier, and it is a comfort. Being able to cry is a reminder that you haven't lost your humanity.

Seventeen years after retirement, I'm not sure how many of those "thorns" are left, but I'm not worried about one or two of them popping out whenever they might. The people and cases I was so deeply involved in have succumbed to the unforgiving vagaries of time: Whitey Bulger was finally captured, and since has been killed in prison. Wayne Merced and Alex Lucio are out, and so are a few others I arrested for murder. Maggie Carr is still in prison. Friends have retired. Close friends—brothers like my great partner Greg Smith, our squad mate Jay Vas, and FDLE Agent Ed Royal—have passed away. Francis Wilcox, Jack Wilcox's widow, who called me every May 1st, failed to call on May 1st, 2023. I talked to her daughter, Jackie, and found out that she died peacefully at home.

Other great friends, like my old riding partner Bill Schwartz, who killed invisible bugs with me one night, remain, and we still reminisce with each other. Michael Headberg, who was shot and left to die after his family was slaughtered, is a thriving author who exchanges emails with me now. New people have emerged in my life, and I have found love—life-changing love—with my wife Mandira and her wonderful children.

The universe never stops challenging you, however. Just when you think you have a comfortable place, the unexpected jolts you out of your comfort zone and into a different reality. On April 26th, 2020, my 16-year-old daughter Linnea—the one I adopted from Russia—lost control of the car she was driving and struck a tree. She died on the scene. For the first time in my life, I was on the other side of a surreal scene that I will never forget: I stood in my in my ex-wife's driveway after being told there was no hospital to go to. As if in slow motion, I watched the Traffic Homicide investigator get out of his car and walk toward me with news I already knew in my heart. I had done this very thing more times than I could remember, and now the roles were reversed. I couldn't help at that moment wonder, "what words will he use?"

He showed us a picture of a tattoo she had on her shoulder and we knew.

"She didn't make it," he said.

It took days of pain and disorientation to understand that I had a new life skill to learn—grief. This was not the same grief of losing a parent. No, this grief impales you and never pulls out. I've learned that the death of your child is not something you "get over," rather it is something that it is added permanently to your backpack on life's hike; something you learn to carry with you. For all time.

The universe brings joy as well. My oldest son, Erik is married and has two beautiful children, so grandfathering is my latest added dimension. My son Greg is doing what he loves: teaching music. My stepchildren, whom I love as my own, are all living fruitful lives as they pursue their own educations and careers. With these beautiful lives—including the one who could only stay for sixteen years—I am rich beyond description.

I am still living with my sole sibling, Miami. Everywhere I go I have reminders of what Miami and I did together. There isn't a neighborhood in this county I can drive in without seeing a house, a building, or a field that doesn't remind me of a homicide, a chase, or an arrest I made. Or, of where my daughter played—and died.

That little house in South Miami I grew up in is still there, prettily decorated and looked after by none other than two teachers. There is still the ficus tree in front of that house I used to climb, and a fence in the back I used to hop to go into the alley and to the U-Totem to buy my football cards.

I don't think Jackson Browne had any background or family members in law enforcement. How and for whom he wrote those words, I have no idea. The first time I read them, though, I felt as though he was sitting in front of me—that he had written them about my life. No doctor cured my eyes—they still get blurry from time to time—but I somehow managed to see, even after keeping them open for so long.

One day I'll leave Miami. My wife and I will likely explore life somewhere else. I want to be in the Georgia mountains, sitting on my deck and looking out over an expanse of rolling green. Maybe we'll be there, or India, the Carolinas. Regardless of where I end up, my colorful brother, my crazy sister—Miami—will always be in my heart. The memories, all of them—harrowing, ironic, ecstatic, and astonishing—will be too. Regardless of how the place grows, and what it decides to become, I will remember the amazing experiences we had and the people we spent my days and nights with; the victims, the families, the attorneys, the street people, my friends, the officers and investigators, and above all, my parents, my children, my family. Because of them, south Florida will be the place I'll always treasure.

It will always be the place I wore the badge, the tie, and the gun.

****

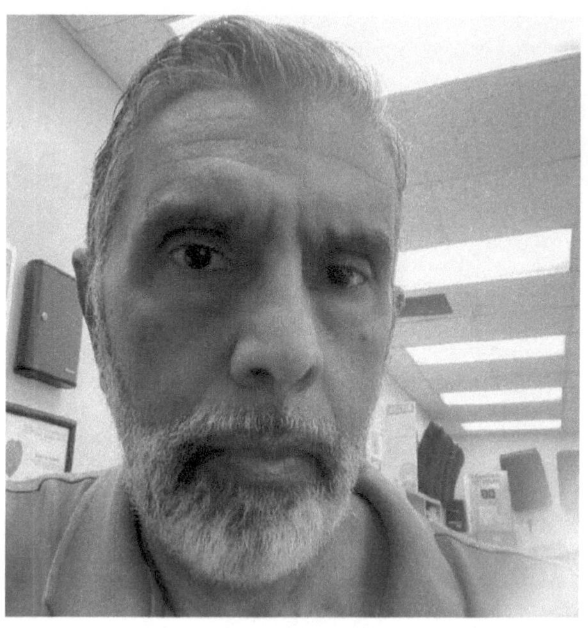

About the Author

Ramesh Nyberg was born in India in 1958 and arrived in the U.S. on New Year's Day, 1959 on a freighter. Since then he has lived in Miami, and became a police officer in 1979. He spent five years as a uniformed police officer during Miami's historic crime wave of the early 1980's. In 1985 became a homicide investigator in the Miami-Dade Police Department's elite Homicide Bureau, where he spent the rest of his career before retiring in 2006.He has six children and teaches Criminal Justice classes at a Miami magnet high school. Ramesh is working on a novel, and says he will continue to write fiction.

Read more at www.rameshnybergauthor.com.